LEARNING
FROM
DATA

The book website `AMLbook.com` contains supporting material for instructors and readers.

LEARNING FROM DATA
A SHORT COURSE

Yaser S. Abu-Mostafa
California Institute of Technology

Malik Magdon-Ismail
Rensselaer Polytechnic Institute

Hsuan-Tien Lin
National Taiwan University

AMLbook.com

Yaser S. Abu-Mostafa
Departments of Electrical Engineering
and Computer Science
California Institute of Technology
Pasadena, CA 91125, USA
yaser@caltech.edu

Malik Magdon-Ismail
Department of Computer Science

Rensselaer Polytechnic Institute
Troy, NY 12180, USA
magdon@cs.rpi.edu

Hsuan-Tien Lin
Department of Computer Science
and Information Engineering
National Taiwan University
Taipei, 106, Taiwan
htlin@csie.ntu.edu.tw

ISBN 10:1-60049-006-9
ISBN 13:978-1-60049-006-4

To our teachers, and to our students

Preface

This book is designed for a short course on machine learning. It is a short course, not a hurried course. From over a decade of teaching this material, we have distilled what we believe to be the core topics that every student of the subject should know. We chose the title 'learning from data' that faithfully describes what the subject is about, and made it a point to cover the topics in a story-like fashion. Our hope is that the reader can learn all the fundamentals of the subject by reading the book cover to cover.

Learning from data has distinct theoretical and practical tracks. If you read two books that focus on one track or the other, you may feel that you are reading about two different subjects altogether. In this book, we balance the theoretical and the practical, the mathematical and the heuristic. Our criterion for inclusion is relevance. Theory that establishes the conceptual framework for learning is included, and so are heuristics that impact the performance of real learning systems. Strengths and weaknesses of the different parts are spelled out. Our philosophy is to say it like it is: what we know, what we don't know, and what we partially know.

The book can be taught in exactly the order it is presented. The notable exception may be Chapter 2, which is the most theoretical chapter of the book. The theory of generalization that this chapter covers is central to learning from data, and we made an effort to make it accessible to a wide readership. However, instructors who are more interested in the practical side may skim over it, or delay it until after the practical methods of Chapter 3 are taught.

You will notice that we included exercises (in gray boxes) throughout the text. The main purpose of these exercises is to engage the reader and enhance understanding of a particular topic being covered. Our reason for separating the exercises out is that they are not crucial to the logical flow. Nevertheless, they contain useful information, and we strongly encourage you to read them, even if you don't do them to completion. Instructors may find some of the exercises appropriate as 'easy' homework problems, and we also provide additional problems of varying difficulty in the Problems section at the end of each chapter.

To help instructors with preparing their lectures based on the book, we provide supporting material on the book's website (`AMLbook.com`). There is also a forum that covers additional topics in learning from data. We will discuss these further in the Epilogue of this book.

Acknowledgment (in alphabetical order for each group): We would like to express our gratitude to the alumni of our Learning Systems Group at Caltech who gave us detailed expert feedback: Zehra Cataltepe, Ling Li, Amrit Pratap, and Joseph Sill. We thank the many students and colleagues who gave us useful feedback during the development of this book, especially Chun-Wei Liu. The Caltech Library staff, especially Kristin Buxton and David McCaslin, have given us excellent advice and help in our self-publishing effort. We also thank Lucinda Acosta for her help throughout the writing of this book.

Last, but not least, we would like to thank our families for their encouragement, their support, and most of all their patience as they endured the time demands that writing a book has imposed on us.

Yaser S. Abu-Mostafa, *Pasadena, California.*

Malik Magdon-Ismail, *Troy, New York.*

Hsuan-Tien Lin, *Taipei, Taiwan.*

March, 2012.

Contents

A complete table of the notation used in this book is included on page 193, right before the index of terms. We suggest referring to it as needed.

Chapter 1

The Learning Problem

If you show a picture to a three-year-old and ask if there is a tree in it, you will likely get the correct answer. If you ask a thirty-year-old what the definition of a tree is, you will likely get an inconclusive answer. We didn't learn what a tree is by studying the mathematical definition of trees. We learned it by looking at trees. In other words, we learned from 'data'.

Learning from data is used in situations where we don't have an analytic solution, but we do have data that we can use to construct an empirical solution. This premise covers a lot of territory, and indeed learning from data is one of the most widely used techniques in science, engineering, and economics, among other fields.

In this chapter, we present examples of learning from data and formalize the learning problem. We also discuss the main concepts associated with learning, and the different paradigms of learning that have been developed.

1.1   Problem Setup

What do financial forecasting, medical diagnosis, computer vision, and search engines have in common? They all have successfully utilized learning from data. The repertoire of such applications is quite impressive. Let us open the discussion with a real-life application to see how learning from data works.

Consider the problem of predicting how a movie viewer would rate the various movies out there. This is an important problem if you are a company that rents out movies, since you want to recommend to different viewers the movies they will like. Good recommender systems are so important to business that the movie rental company Netflix offered a prize of one million dollars to anyone who could improve their recommendations by a mere 10%.

The main difficulty in this problem is that the criteria that viewers use to rate movies are quite complex. Trying to model those explicitly is no easy task, so it may not be possible to come up with an analytic solution. However, we

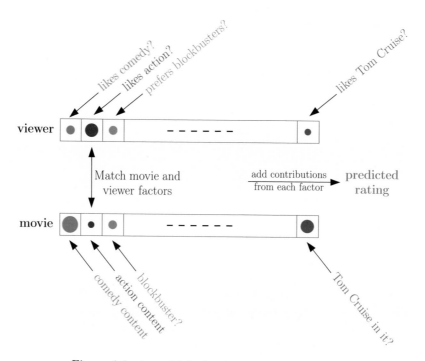

Figure 1.1: A model for how a viewer rates a movie

know that the historical rating data reveal a lot about how people rate movies, so we may be able to construct a good empirical solution. There is a great deal of data available to movie rental companies, since they often ask their viewers to rate the movies that they have already seen.

Figure 1.1 illustrates a specific approach that was widely used in the million-dollar competition. Here is how it works. You describe a movie as a long array of different factors, e.g., how much comedy is in it, how complicated is the plot, how handsome is the lead actor, etc. Now, you describe each viewer with corresponding factors; how much do they like comedy, do they prefer simple or complicated plots, how important are the looks of the lead actor, and so on. How this viewer will rate that movie is now estimated based on the match/mismatch of these factors. For example, if the movie is pure comedy and the viewer hates comedies, the chances are he won't like it. If you take dozens of these factors describing many facets of a movie's content and a viewer's taste, the conclusion based on matching all the factors will be a good predictor of how the viewer will rate the movie.

The power of learning from data is that this entire process can be automated, without any need for analyzing movie content or viewer taste. To do so, the learning algorithm 'reverse-engineers' these factors based solely on previous ratings. It starts with random factors, then tunes these factors to make them more and more aligned with how viewers have rated movies before, until they are ultimately able to *predict* how viewers rate movies in general. The factors we end up with may not be as intuitive as 'comedy content', and in fact can be quite subtle or even incomprehensible. After all, the algorithm is only trying to find the best way to predict how a viewer would rate a movie, not necessarily explain to us how it is done. This algorithm was part of the winning solution in the million-dollar competition.

1.1.1   Components of Learning

The movie rating application captures the essence of learning from data, and so do many other applications from vastly different fields. In order to abstract the common core of the learning problem, we will pick one application and use it as a metaphor for the different components of the problem. Let us take credit approval as our metaphor.

Suppose that a bank receives thousands of credit card applications every day, and it wants to automate the process of evaluating them. Just as in the case of movie ratings, the bank knows of no magical formula that can pinpoint when credit should be approved, but it has a lot of data. This calls for learning from data, so the bank uses historical records of previous customers to figure out a good formula for credit approval.

Each customer record has personal information related to credit, such as annual salary, years in residence, outstanding loans, etc. The record also keeps track of whether approving credit for that customer was a good idea, i.e., did the bank make money on that customer. This data guides the construction of a successful formula for credit approval that can be used on future applicants.

Let us give names and symbols to the main components of this learning problem. There is the input $\mathbf{x}$ (customer information that is used to make a credit decision), the unknown target function $f \colon \mathcal{X} \to \mathcal{Y}$ (ideal formula for credit approval), where $\mathcal{X}$ is the input space (set of all possible inputs $\mathbf{x}$), and $\mathcal{Y}$ is the output space (set of all possible outputs, in this case just a yes/no decision). There is a data set $\mathcal{D}$ of input-output examples $(\mathbf{x}_1, y_1), \cdots, (\mathbf{x}_N, y_N)$, where $y_n = f(\mathbf{x}_n)$ for $n = 1, ..., N$ (inputs corresponding to previous customers and the correct credit decision for them in hindsight). The examples are often referred to as data points. Finally, there is the learning algorithm that uses the data set $\mathcal{D}$ to pick a formula $g \colon \mathcal{X} \to \mathcal{Y}$ that approximates f. The algorithm chooses g from a set of candidate formulas under consideration, which we call the hypothesis set $\mathcal{H}$. For instance, $\mathcal{H}$ could be the set of all linear formulas from which the algorithm would choose the best linear fit to the data, as we will introduce later in this section.

When a new customer applies for credit, the bank will base its decision on g (the hypothesis that the learning algorithm produced), not on f (the ideal target function which remains unknown). The decision will be good only to the extent that g faithfully replicates f. To achieve that, the algorithm

3

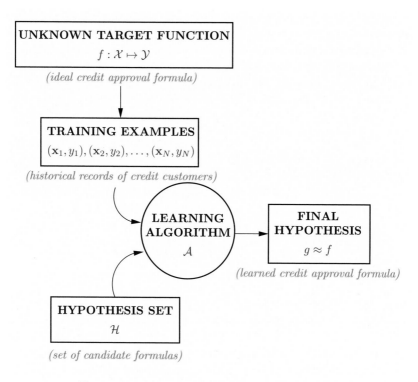

Figure 1.2: Basic setup of the learning problem

chooses g that best matches f on the *training* examples of previous customers, with the hope that it will continue to match f on new customers. Whether or not this hope is justified remains to be seen. Figure 1.2 illustrates the components of the learning problem.

Exercise 1.1

Express each of the following tasks in the framework of learning from data by specifying the input space $\mathcal{X}$, output space $\mathcal{Y}$, target function $f: \mathcal{X} \to \mathcal{Y}$, and the specifics of the data set that we will learn from.

(a) Medical diagnosis: A patient walks in with a medical history and some symptoms, and you want to identify the problem.

(b) Handwritten digit recognition (for example postal zip code recognition for mail sorting).

(c) Determining if an email is spam or not.

(d) Predicting how an electric load varies with price, temperature, and day of the week.

(e) A problem of interest to you for which there is no analytic solution, but you have data from which to construct an empirical solution.

We will use the setup in Figure 1.2 as our definition of the learning problem. Later on, we will consider a number of refinements and variations to this basic setup as needed. However, the essence of the problem will remain the same. There is a target to be learned. It is unknown to us. We have a set of examples generated by the target. The learning algorithm uses these examples to look for a hypothesis that approximates the target.

1.1.2 A Simple Learning Model

Let us consider the different components of Figure 1.2. Given a specific learning problem, the target function and training examples are dictated by the problem. However, the learning algorithm and hypothesis set are not. These are solution tools that we get to choose. The hypothesis set and learning algorithm are referred to informally as the *learning model*.

Here is a simple model. Let $\mathcal{X} = \mathbb{R}^d$ be the input space, where $\mathbb{R}^d$ is the d-dimensional Euclidean space, and let $\mathcal{Y} = \{+1, -1\}$ be the output space, denoting a binary (yes/no) decision. In our credit example, different coordinates of the input vector $\mathbf{x} \in \mathbb{R}^d$ correspond to salary, years in residence, outstanding debt, and the other data fields in a credit application. The binary output y corresponds to approving or denying credit. We specify the hypothesis set $\mathcal{H}$ through a functional form that all the hypotheses $h \in \mathcal{H}$ share. The functional form $h(\mathbf{x})$ that we choose here gives different weights to the different coordinates of $\mathbf{x}$, reflecting their relative importance in the credit decision. The weighted coordinates are then combined to form a 'credit score' and the result is compared to a threshold value. If the applicant passes the threshold, credit is approved; if not, credit is denied:

$$\text{Approve credit if} \quad \sum_{i=1}^{d} w_i x_i > \text{threshold},$$

$$\text{Deny credit if} \quad \sum_{i=1}^{d} w_i x_i < \text{threshold}.$$

This formula can be written more compactly as

$$h(\mathbf{x}) = \text{sign}\left(\left(\sum_{i=1}^{d} w_i x_i\right) + b\right), \tag{1.1}$$

where $x_1, \cdots, x_d$ are the components of the vector $\mathbf{x}$; $h(\mathbf{x}) = +1$ means 'approve credit' and $h(\mathbf{x}) = -1$ means 'deny credit'; $\text{sign}(s) = +1$ if $s > 0$ and $\text{sign}(s) = -1$ if $s < 0$.[1] The weights are $w_1, \cdots, w_d$, and the threshold is determined by the bias term b since in Equation (1.1), credit is approved if $\sum_{i=1}^{d} w_i x_i > -b$.

This model of $\mathcal{H}$ is called the *perceptron*, a name that it got in the context of artificial intelligence. The learning algorithm will search $\mathcal{H}$ by looking for

---

[1] The value of $\text{sign}(s)$ when $s = 0$ is a simple technicality that we ignore for the moment.

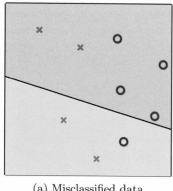 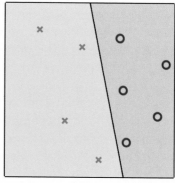

(a) Misclassified data   (b) Perfectly classified data

Figure 1.3: Perceptron classification of linearly separable data in a two-dimensional input space (a) Some training examples will be misclassified (blue points in red region and vice versa) for certain values of the weight parameters which define the separating line. (b) A final hypothesis that classifies all training examples correctly. (o is $+1$ and $\times$ is -1.)

weights and bias that perform well on the data set. Some of the weights $w_1, \cdots, w_d$ may end up being negative, corresponding to an adverse effect on credit approval. For instance, the weight of the 'outstanding debt' field should come out negative since more debt is not good for credit. The bias value b may end up being large or small, reflecting how lenient or stringent the bank should be in extending credit. The optimal choices of weights and bias define the final hypothesis $g \in \mathcal{H}$ that the algorithm produces.

Exercise 1.2

Suppose that we use a perceptron to detect spam messages. Let's say that each email message is represented by the frequency of occurrence of keywords, and the output is $+1$ if the message is considered spam.

(a) Can you think of some keywords that will end up with a large positive weight in the perceptron?

(b) How about keywords that will get a negative weight?

(c) What parameter in the perceptron directly affects how many border-line messages end up being classified as spam?

Figure 1.3 illustrates what a perceptron does in a two-dimensional case ($d = 2$). The plane is split by a line into two regions, the $+1$ decision region and the -1 decision region. Different values for the parameters w_1, w_2, b correspond to different lines $w_1 x_1 + w_2 x_2 + b = 0$. If the data set is *linearly separable*, there will be a choice for these parameters that classifies all the training examples correctly.

To simplify the notation of the perceptron formula, we will treat the bias b as a weight $w_0 = b$ and merge it with the other weights into one vector $\mathbf{w} = [w_0, w_1, \cdots, w_d]^{\mathrm{T}}$, where ^{T} denotes the transpose of a vector, so $\mathbf{w}$ is a column vector. We also treat $\mathbf{x}$ as a column vector and modify it to become $\mathbf{x} = [x_0, x_1, \cdots, x_d]^{\mathrm{T}}$, where the added coordinate x_0 is fixed at $x_0 = 1$. Formally speaking, the input space is now

$$\mathcal{X} = \{1\} \times \mathbb{R}^d = \{[x_0, x_1, \cdots, x_d]^{\mathrm{T}} \mid x_0 = 1, x_1 \in \mathbb{R}, \cdots, x_d \in \mathbb{R}\}.$$

With this convention, $\mathbf{w}^{\mathrm{T}}\mathbf{x} = \sum_{i=0}^{d} w_i x_i$, and so Equation (1.1) can be rewritten in vector form as

$$h(\mathbf{x}) = \text{sign}(\mathbf{w}^{\mathrm{T}}\mathbf{x}). \tag{1.2}$$

We now introduce the *perceptron learning algorithm* (PLA). The algorithm will determine what $\mathbf{w}$ should be, based on the data. Let us assume that the data set is linearly separable, which means that there is a vector $\mathbf{w}$ that makes (1.2) achieve the correct decision $h(\mathbf{x}_n) = y_n$ on all the training examples, as shown in Figure 1.3.

Our learning algorithm will find this $\mathbf{w}$ using a simple iterative method. Here is how it works. At iteration t, where $t = 0, 1, 2, \ldots$, there is a current value of the weight vector, call it $\mathbf{w}(t)$. The algorithm picks an example from $(\mathbf{x}_1, y_1) \cdots (\mathbf{x}_N, y_N)$ that is currently misclassified, call it $(\mathbf{x}(t), y(t))$, and uses it to update $\mathbf{w}(t)$. Since the example is misclassified, we have $y(t) \neq \text{sign}(\mathbf{w}^{\mathrm{T}}(t)\mathbf{x}(t))$. The update rule is

$$\mathbf{w}(t+1) = \mathbf{w}(t) + y(t)\mathbf{x}(t). \tag{1.3}$$

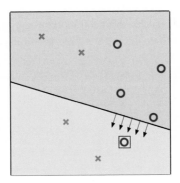

This rule moves the boundary in the direction of classifying $\mathbf{x}(t)$ correctly, as depicted in the figure above. The algorithm continues with further iterations until there are no longer misclassified examples in the data set.

Exercise 1.3

The weight update rule in (1.3) has the nice interpretation that it moves in the direction of classifying $\mathbf{x}(t)$ correctly.

(a) Show that $y(t)\mathbf{w}^{\mathsf{T}}(t)\mathbf{x}(t) < 0$. *[Hint: $\mathbf{x}(t)$ is misclassified by $\mathbf{w}(t)$.]*

(b) Show that $y(t)\mathbf{w}^{\mathsf{T}}(t+1)\mathbf{x}(t) > y(t)\mathbf{w}^{\mathsf{T}}(t)\mathbf{x}(t)$. *[Hint: Use (1.3).]*

(c) As far as classifying $\mathbf{x}(t)$ is concerned, argue that the move from $\mathbf{w}(t)$ to $\mathbf{w}(t+1)$ is a move 'in the right direction'.

Although the update rule in (1.3) considers only one training example at a time and may 'mess up' the classification of the other examples that are not involved in the current iteration, it turns out that the algorithm is guaranteed to arrive at the right solution in the end. The proof is the subject of Problem 1.3. The result holds regardless of which example we choose from among the misclassified examples in $(\mathbf{x}_1, y_1) \cdots (\mathbf{x}_N, y_N)$ at each iteration, and regardless of how we initialize the weight vector to start the algorithm. For simplicity, we can pick one of the misclassified examples at random (or cycle through the examples and always choose the first misclassified one), and we can initialize $\mathbf{w}(0)$ to the zero vector.

Within the infinite space of all weight vectors, the perceptron algorithm manages to find a weight vector that works, using a simple iterative process. This illustrates how a learning algorithm can effectively search an infinite hypothesis set using a finite number of simple steps. This feature is characteristic of many techniques that are used in learning, some of which are far more sophisticated than the perceptron learning algorithm.

Exercise 1.4

Let us create our own target function f and data set $\mathcal{D}$ and see how the perceptron learning algorithm works. Take $d = 2$ so you can visualize the problem, and choose a random line in the plane as your target function, where one side of the line maps to $+1$ and the other maps to -1. Choose the inputs $\mathbf{x}_n$ of the data set as random points in the plane, and evaluate the target function on each $\mathbf{x}_n$ to get the corresponding output y_n.

Now, generate a data set of size 20. Try the perceptron learning algorithm on your data set and see how long it takes to converge and how well the final hypothesis g matches your target f. You can find other ways to play with this experiment in Problem 1.4.

The perceptron learning algorithm succeeds in achieving its goal; finding a hypothesis that classifies all the points in the data set $\mathcal{D} = \{(\mathbf{x}_1, y_1) \cdots (\mathbf{x}_N, y_N)\}$ correctly. Does this mean that this hypothesis will also be successful in classifying new data points that are not in $\mathcal{D}$? This turns out to be the key question in the theory of learning, a question that will be thoroughly examined in this book.

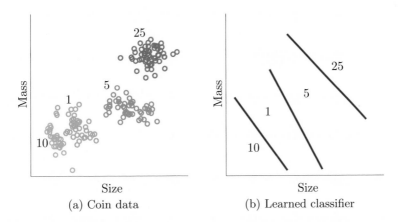

Figure 1.4: The learning approach to coin classification (a) Training data of pennies, nickels, dimes, and quarters (1, 5, 10, and 25 cents) are represented in a size-mass space where they fall into clusters. (b) A classification rule is learned from the data set by separating the four clusters. A new coin will be classified according to the region in the size-mass plane that it falls into.

1.1.3 Learning versus Design

So far, we have discussed what learning is. Now, we discuss what it is not. The goal is to distinguish between learning and a related approach that is used for similar problems. While learning is based on data, this other approach does not use data. It is a 'design' approach based on specifications, and is often discussed alongside the learning approach in pattern recognition literature.

Consider the problem of recognizing coins of different denominations, which is relevant to vending machines, for example. We want the machine to recognize quarters, dimes, nickels and pennies. We will contrast the 'learning from data' approach and the 'design from specifications' approach for this problem. We assume that each coin will be represented by its size and mass, a two-dimensional input.

In the learning approach, we are given a sample of coins from each of the four denominations and we use these coins as our data set. We treat the size and mass as the input vector, and the denomination as the output. Figure 1.4(a) shows what the data set may look like in the input space. There is some variation of size and mass within each class, but by and large coins of the same denomination cluster together. The learning algorithm searches for a hypothesis that classifies the data set well. If we want to classify a new coin, the machine measures its size and mass, and then classifies it according to the learned hypothesis in Figure 1.4(b).

In the design approach, we call the United States Mint and ask them about the specifications of different coins. We also ask them about the number

9

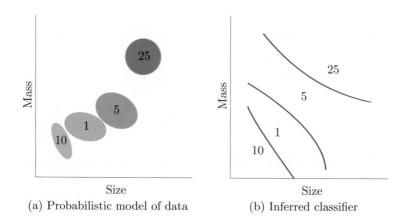

(a) Probabilistic model of data   (b) Inferred classifier

Figure 1.5: The design approach to coin classification (a) A probabilistic model for the size, mass, and denomination of coins is derived from known specifications. The figure shows the high probability region for each denomination (1, 5, 10, and 25 cents) according to the model. (b) A classification rule is derived analytically to minimize the probability of error in classifying a coin based on size and mass. The resulting regions for each denomination are shown.

of coins of each denomination in circulation, in order to get an estimate of the relative frequency of each coin. Finally, we make a physical model of the variations in size and mass due to exposure to the elements and due to errors in measurement. We put all of this information together and compute the full joint probability distribution of size, mass, and coin denomination (Figure 1.5(a)). Once we have that joint distribution, we can construct the optimal decision rule to classify coins based on size and mass (Figure 1.5(b)). The rule chooses the denomination that has the highest probability for a given size and mass, thus achieving the smallest possible probability of error.[2]

The main difference between the learning approach and the design approach is the role that data plays. In the design approach, the problem is well specified and one can analytically derive f without the need to see any data. In the learning approach, the problem is much less specified, and one needs data to pin down what f is.

Both approaches may be viable in some applications, but only the learning approach is possible in many applications where the target function is unknown. We are not trying to compare the utility or the performance of the two approaches. We are just making the point that the design approach is distinct from learning. This book is about learning.

---

[2]This is called Bayes optimal decision theory. Some learning models are based on the same theory by estimating the probability from data.

Exercise 1.5

Which of the following problems are more suited for the learning approach and which are more suited for the design approach?

(a) Determining the age at which a particular medical test should be performed

(b) Classifying numbers into primes and non-primes

(c) Detecting potential fraud in credit card charges

(d) Determining the time it would take a falling object to hit the ground

(e) Determining the optimal cycle for traffic lights in a busy intersection

1.2 Types of Learning

The basic premise of learning from data is the use of a set of observations to uncover an underlying process. It is a very broad premise, and difficult to fit into a single framework. As a result, different learning paradigms have arisen to deal with different situations and different assumptions. In this section, we introduce some of these paradigms.

The learning paradigm that we have discussed so far is called *supervised* learning. It is the most studied and most utilized type of learning, but it is not the only one. Some variations of supervised learning are simple enough to be accommodated within the same framework. Other variations are more profound and lead to new concepts and techniques that take on lives of their own. The most important variations have to do with the nature of the data set.

1.2.1 Supervised Learning

When the training data contains explicit examples of what the correct output should be for given inputs, then we are within the supervised learning setting that we have covered so far. Consider the hand-written digit recognition problem (task (b) of Exercise 1.1). A reasonable data set for this problem is a collection of images of hand-written digits, and for each image, what the digit actually is. We thus have a set of examples of the form (image , digit). The learning is supervised in the sense that some 'supervisor' has taken the trouble to look at each input, in this case an image, and determine the correct output, in this case one of the ten categories $\{0, 1, 2, 3, 4, 5, 6, 7, 8, 9\}$.

While we are on the subject of variations, there is more than one way that a data set can be presented to the learning process. Data sets are typically created and presented to us in their entirety at the outset of the learning process. For instance, historical records of customers in the credit-card application, and previous movie ratings of customers in the movie rating application, are already there for us to use. This protocol of a 'ready' data set is the most

11

common in practice, and it is what we will focus on in this book. However, it is worth noting that two variations of this protocol have attracted a significant body of work.

One is *active learning*, where the data set is acquired through queries that we make. Thus, we get to choose a point **x** in the input space, and the supervisor reports to us the target value for **x**. As you can see, this opens the possibility for strategic choice of the point **x** to maximize its information value, similar to asking a strategic question in a game of 20 questions.

Another variation is called *online learning*, where the data set is given to the algorithm one example at a time. This happens when we have streaming data that the algorithm has to process 'on the run'. For instance, when the movie recommendation system discussed in Section 1.1 is deployed, online learning can process new ratings from current users and movies. Online learning is also useful when we have limitations on computing and storage that preclude us from processing the whole data as a batch. We should note that online learning can be used in different paradigms of learning, not just in supervised learning.

1.2.2 Reinforcement Learning

When the training data does not explicitly contain the correct output for each input, we are no longer in a supervised learning setting. Consider a toddler learning not to touch a hot cup of tea. The experience of such a toddler would typically comprise a set of occasions when the toddler confronted a hot cup of tea and was faced with the decision of touching it or not touching it. Presumably, every time she touched it, the result was a high level of pain, and every time she didn't touch it, a much lower level of pain resulted (that of an unsatisfied curiosity). Eventually, the toddler learns that she is better off not touching the hot cup.

The training examples did not spell out what the toddler should have done, but they instead graded different actions that she has taken. Nevertheless, she uses the examples to reinforce the better actions, eventually learning what she should do in similar situations. This characterizes *reinforcement* learning, where the training example does not contain the target output, but instead contains some possible output together with a measure of how good that output is. In contrast to supervised learning where the training examples were of the form (input , correct output), the examples in reinforcement learning are of the form

(input , some output , grade for this output).

Importantly, the example does not say how good other outputs would have been for this particular input.

Reinforcement learning is especially useful for learning how to play a game. Imagine a situation in backgammon where you have a choice between different actions and you want to identify the best action. It is not a trivial task to ascertain what the best action is at a given stage of the game, so we cannot

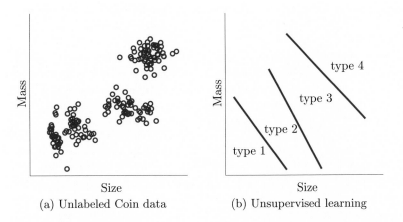

(a) Unlabeled Coin data   (b) Unsupervised learning

Figure 1.6: Unsupervised learning of coin classification (a) The same data set of coins in Figure 1.4(a) is again represented in the size-mass space, but without being labeled. They still fall into clusters. (b) An unsupervised classification rule treats the four clusters as different types. The rule may be somewhat ambiguous, as type 1 and type 2 could be viewed as one cluster

easily create supervised learning examples. If you use reinforcement learning instead, all you need to do is to take some action and report how well things went, and you have a training example. The reinforcement learning algorithm is left with the task of sorting out the information coming from different examples to find the best line of play.

1.2.3 Unsupervised Learning

In the unsupervised setting, the training data does not contain any output information at all. We are just given input examples $\mathbf{x}_1, \cdots, \mathbf{x}_N$. You may wonder how we could possibly learn anything from mere inputs. Consider the coin classification problem that we discussed earlier in Figure 1.4. Suppose that we didn't know the denomination of any of the coins in the data set. This *unlabeled data* is shown in Figure 1.6(a). We still get similar clusters, but they are now unlabeled so all points have the same 'color'. The decision regions in unsupervised learning may be identical to those in supervised learning, but without the labels (Figure 1.6(b)). However, the correct clustering is less obvious now, and even the number of clusters may be ambiguous.

Nonetheless, this example shows that we can learn *something* from the inputs by themselves. Unsupervised learning can be viewed as the task of spontaneously finding patterns and structure in input data. For instance, if our task is to categorize a set of books into topics, and we only use general properties of the various books, we can identify books that have similar properties and put them together in one category, without naming that category.

Unsupervised learning can also be viewed as a way to create a higher-level representation of the data. Imagine that you don't speak a word of Spanish, but your company will relocate you to Spain next month. They will arrange for Spanish lessons once you are there, but you would like to prepare yourself a bit before you go. All you have access to is a Spanish radio station. For a full month, you continuously bombard yourself with Spanish; this is an unsupervised learning experience since you don't know the meaning of the words. However, you gradually develop a better representation of the language in your brain by becoming more tuned to its common sounds and structures. When you arrive in Spain, you will be in a better position to start your Spanish lessons. Indeed, unsupervised learning can be a precursor to supervised learning. In other cases, it is a stand-alone technique.

Exercise 1.6

For each of the following tasks, identify which type of learning is involved (supervised, reinforcement, or unsupervised) and the training data to be used. If a task can fit more than one type, explain how and describe the training data for each type.

  (a) Recommending a book to a user in an online bookstore

  (b) Playing tic-tac-toe

  (c) Categorizing movies into different types

  (d) Learning to play music

  (e) Credit limit: Deciding the maximum allowed debt for each bank customer

---

Our main focus in this book will be supervised learning, which is the most popular form of learning from data.

1.2.4 Other Views of Learning

The study of learning has evolved somewhat independently in a number of fields that started historically at different times and in different domains, and these fields have developed different emphases and even different jargons. As a result, learning from data is a diverse subject with many aliases in the scientific literature. The main field dedicated to the subject is called *machine learning*, a name that distinguishes it from human learning. We briefly mention two other important fields that approach learning from data in their own ways.

Statistics shares the basic premise of learning from data, namely the use of a set of observations to uncover an underlying process. In this case, the process is a probability distribution and the observations are samples from that distribution. Because statistics is a mathematical field, emphasis is given to situations where most of the questions can be answered with rigorous proofs. As a result, statistics focuses on somewhat idealized models and analyzes them in great detail. This is the main difference between the statistical approach

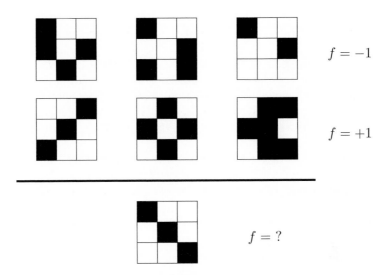

Figure 1.7: A visual learning problem. The first two rows show the training examples (each input $\mathbf{x}$ is a 9-bit vector represented visually as a 3×3 black-and-white array). The inputs in the first row have $f(\mathbf{x}) = -1$, and the inputs in the second row have $f(\mathbf{x}) = +1$. Your task is to learn from this data set what f is, then apply f to the test input at the bottom. Do you get -1 or $+1$?

to learning and how we approach the subject here. We make less restrictive assumptions and deal with more general models than in statistics. Therefore, we end up with weaker results that are nonetheless broadly applicable.

Data mining is a practical field that focuses on finding patterns, correlations, or anomalies in large relational databases. For example, we could be looking at medical records of patients and trying to detect a cause-effect relationship between a particular drug and long-term effects. We could also be looking at credit card spending patterns and trying to detect potential fraud. Technically, data mining is the same as learning from data, with more emphasis on data analysis than on prediction. Because databases are usually huge, computational issues are often critical in data mining. Recommender systems, which were illustrated in Section 1.1 with the movie rating example, are also considered part of data mining.

1.3 Is Learning Feasible?

The target function f is the object of learning. The most important assertion about the target function is that it is *unknown*. We really mean unknown.

This raises a natural question. How could a limited data set reveal enough information to pin down the entire target function? Figure 1.7 illustrates this difficulty. A simple learning task with 6 training examples of a ±1 target function is shown. Try to learn what the function is then apply it to the test input given. Do you get −1 or +1? Now, show the problem to your friends and see if they get the same answer.

The chances are the answers were not unanimous, and for good reason. There is simply more than one function that fits the 6 training examples, and some of these functions have a value of −1 on the test point and others have a value of +1. For instance, if the true f is +1 when the pattern is symmetric, the value for the test point would be +1. If the true f is +1 when the top left square of the pattern is white, the value for the test point would be −1. Both functions agree with all the examples in the data set, so there isn't enough information to tell us which would be the correct answer.

This does not bode well for the feasibility of learning. To make matters worse, we will now see that the difficulty we experienced in this simple problem is the rule, not the exception.

1.3.1 Outside the Data Set

When we get the training data $\mathcal{D}$, e.g., the first two rows of Figure 1.7, we know the value of f on all the points in $\mathcal{D}$. This doesn't mean that we have learned f, since it doesn't guarantee that we know anything about f outside of $\mathcal{D}$. We know what we have already seen, but that's not learning. That's memorizing.

Does the data set $\mathcal{D}$ tell us anything outside of $\mathcal{D}$ that we didn't know before? If the answer is yes, then we have learned *something*. If the answer is no, we can conclude that learning is not feasible.

Since we maintain that f is an unknown function, we can prove that f remains unknown outside of $\mathcal{D}$. Instead of going through a formal proof for the general case, we will illustrate the idea in a concrete case. Consider a Boolean target function over a three-dimensional input space $\mathcal{X} = \{0, 1\}^3$. We are given a data set $\mathcal{D}$ of five examples represented in the table below. We denote the binary output by ○/● for visual clarity,

$\mathbf{x}_n$	y_n
0 0 0	○
0 0 1	●
0 1 0	●
0 1 1	○
1 0 0	●

where $y_n = f(\mathbf{x}_n)$ for $n = 1, 2, 3, 4, 5$. The advantage of this simple Boolean case is that we can enumerate the entire input space (since there are only $2^3 = 8$ distinct input vectors), and we can enumerate the set of all possible target functions (since f is a Boolean function on 3 Boolean inputs, and there are only $2^{2^3} = 256$ distinct Boolean functions on 3 Boolean inputs).

Let us look at the problem of learning f. Since f is unknown except inside $\mathcal{D}$, any function that agrees with $\mathcal{D}$ could conceivably be f. The table below shows all such functions $f_1, \cdots, f_8$. It also shows the data set $\mathcal{D}$ (in blue) and what the final hypothesis g may look like.

$\mathbf{x}$	y	g	f_1	f_2	f_3	f_4	f_5	f_6	f_7	f_8
0 0 0	○	○	○	○	○	○	○	○	○	○
0 0 1	●	●	●	●	●	●	●	●	●	●
0 1 0	●	●	●	●	●	●	●	●	●	●
0 1 1	○	○	○	○	○	○	○	○	○	○
1 0 0	●	●	●	●	●	●	●	●	●	●
1 0 1		?	○	○	○	○	●	●	●	●
1 1 0		?	○	○	●	●	○	○	●	●
1 1 1		?	○	●	○	●	○	●	○	●

The final hypothesis g is chosen based on the five examples in $\mathcal{D}$. The table shows the case where g is chosen to match f on these examples.

If we remain true to the notion of unknown target, we cannot exclude any of $f_1, \cdots, f_8$ from being the true f. Now, we have a dilemma. The whole purpose of learning f is to be able to predict the value of f on points that we haven't seen before. The quality of the learning will be determined by how close our prediction is to the true value. Regardless of what g predicts on the three points we haven't seen before (those outside of $\mathcal{D}$, denoted by red question marks), it can agree or disagree with the target, depending on which of $f_1, \cdots, f_8$ turns out to be the true target. It is easy to verify that any 3 bits that replace the red question marks are as good as any other 3 bits.

Exercise 1.7

For each of the following learning scenarios in the above problem, evaluate the performance of g on the three points in $\mathcal{X}$ outside $\mathcal{D}$. To measure the performance, compute how many of the 8 possible target functions agree with g on all three points, on two of them, on one of them, and on none of them.

(a) $\mathcal{H}$ has only two hypotheses, one that always returns '●' and one that always returns '○'. The learning algorithm picks the hypothesis that matches the data set the most.

(b) The same $\mathcal{H}$, but the learning algorithm now picks the hypothesis that matches the data set the *least*.

(c) $\mathcal{H} = \{\text{XOR}\}$ (only one hypothesis which is always picked), where XOR is defined by $\text{XOR}(\mathbf{x}) = \bullet$ if the number of 1's in $\mathbf{x}$ is odd and $\text{XOR}(\mathbf{x}) = \circ$ if the number is even.

(d) $\mathcal{H}$ contains all possible hypotheses (all Boolean functions on three variables), and the learning algorithm picks the hypothesis that agrees with all training examples, but otherwise disagrees the most with the XOR.

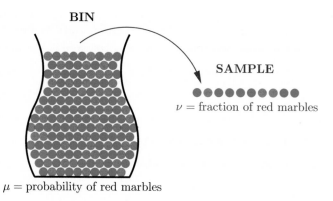

Figure 1.8: A random sample is picked from a bin of red and green marbles. The probability μ of red marbles in the bin is unknown. What does the fraction ν of red marbles in the sample tell us about μ?

It doesn't matter what the algorithm does or what hypothesis set $\mathcal{H}$ is used. Whether $\mathcal{H}$ has a hypothesis that perfectly agrees with $\mathcal{D}$ (as depicted in the table) or not, and whether the learning algorithm picks that hypothesis or picks another one that disagrees with $\mathcal{D}$ (different green bits), it makes no difference whatsoever as far as the performance outside of $\mathcal{D}$ is concerned. Yet the performance outside $\mathcal{D}$ is all that matters in learning!

This dilemma is not restricted to Boolean functions, but extends to the general learning problem. As long as f is an unknown function, knowing $\mathcal{D}$ cannot exclude any pattern of values for f outside of $\mathcal{D}$. Therefore, the predictions of g outside of $\mathcal{D}$ are meaningless.

Does this mean that learning from data is doomed? If so, this will be a very short book ☺. Fortunately, learning is alive and well, and we will see why. We won't have to change our basic assumption to do that. The target function will continue to be unknown, and we still mean *unknown*.

1.3.2 Probability to the Rescue

We will show that we can indeed infer something outside $\mathcal{D}$ using only $\mathcal{D}$, but in a probabilistic way. What we infer may not be much compared to learning a full target function, but it will establish the principle that we can reach outside $\mathcal{D}$. Once we establish that, we will take it to the general learning problem and pin down what we can and cannot learn.

Let's take the simplest case of picking a sample, and see when we can say something about the objects outside the sample. Consider a bin that contains red and green marbles, possibly infinitely many. The proportion of red and green marbles in the bin is such that if we pick a marble at random, the probability that it will be red is μ and the probability that it will be green is $1 - \mu$. We assume that the value of μ is unknown to us.

We pick a random sample of N independent marbles (with replacement) from this bin, and observe the fraction ν of red marbles within the sample (Figure 1.8). What does the value of ν tell us about the value of μ?

One answer is that regardless of the colors of the N marbles that we picked, we still don't know the color of any marble that we didn't pick. We can get mostly green marbles in the sample while the bin has mostly red marbles. Although this is certainly *possible*, it is by no means *probable*.

Exercise 1.8

If $\mu = 0.9$, what is the probability that a sample of 10 marbles will have $\nu \leq 0.1$? *[Hints: 1. Use binomial distribution. 2. The answer is a very small number.]*

The situation is similar to taking a poll. A random sample from a population tends to agree with the views of the population at large. The probability distribution of the random variable ν in terms of the parameter μ is well understood, and when the sample size is big, ν tends to be close to μ.

To quantify the relationship between ν and μ, we use a simple bound called the *Hoeffding Inequality*. It states that for any sample size N,

$$\mathbb{P}\left[|\nu - \mu| > \epsilon\right] \leq 2e^{-2\epsilon^2 N} \qquad \text{for any } \epsilon > 0. \qquad (1.4)$$

Here, $\mathbb{P}[\cdot]$ denotes the probability of an event, in this case with respect to the random sample we pick, and ϵ is any positive value we choose. Putting Inequality (1.4) in words, it says that as the sample size N grows, it becomes exponentially unlikely that ν will deviate from μ by more than our 'tolerance' ϵ.

The only quantity that is random in (1.4) is ν which depends on the random sample. By contrast, μ is not random. It is just a constant, albeit unknown to us. There is a subtle point here. The utility of (1.4) is to infer the value of μ using the value of ν, although it is μ that affects ν, not vice versa. However, since the effect is that ν tends to be close to μ, we infer that μ 'tends' to be close to ν.

Although $\mathbb{P}\left[|\nu - \mu| > \epsilon\right]$ depends on μ, as μ appears in the argument and also affects the distribution of ν, we are able to bound the probability by $2e^{-2\epsilon^2 N}$ which does not depend on μ. Notice that only the size N of the sample affects the bound, not the size of the bin. The bin can be large or small, finite or infinite, and we still get the same bound when we use the same sample size.

Exercise 1.9

If $\mu = 0.9$, use the Hoeffding Inequality to bound the probability that a sample of 10 marbles will have $\nu \leq 0.1$ and compare the answer to the previous exercise.

If we choose ϵ to be very small in order to make ν a good approximation of μ, we need a larger sample size N to make the RHS of Inequality (1.4) small. We

19

can then assert that it is likely that ν will indeed be a good approximation of μ. Although this assertion does not give us the exact value of μ, and doesn't even guarantee that the approximate value holds, knowing that we are within $\pm\epsilon$ of μ most of the time is a significant improvement over not knowing anything at all.

The fact that the sample was randomly selected from the bin is the reason we are able to make any kind of statement about μ being close to ν. If the sample was not randomly selected but picked in a particular way, we would lose the benefit of the probabilistic analysis and we would again be in the dark outside of the sample.

How does the bin model relate to the learning problem? It seems that the unknown here was just the value of μ while the unknown in learning is an entire function $f : \mathcal{X} \rightarrow \mathcal{Y}$. The two situations can be connected. Take any single hypothesis $h \in \mathcal{H}$ and compare it to f on each point $\mathbf{x} \in \mathcal{X}$. If $h(\mathbf{x}) = f(\mathbf{x})$, color the point $\mathbf{x}$ green. If $h(\mathbf{x}) \neq f(\mathbf{x})$, color the point $\mathbf{x}$ red. The color that each point gets is not known to us, since f is unknown. However, if we pick $\mathbf{x}$ at random according to some probability distribution P over the input space $\mathcal{X}$, we know that $\mathbf{x}$ will be red with some probability, call it μ, and green with probability $1 - \mu$. Regardless of the value of μ, the space $\mathcal{X}$ now behaves like the bin in Figure 1.8.

The training examples play the role of a sample from the bin. If the inputs $\mathbf{x}_1, \cdots, \mathbf{x}_N$ in $\mathcal{D}$ are picked independently according to P, we will get a random sample of red $(h(\mathbf{x}_n) \neq f(\mathbf{x}_n))$ and green $(h(\mathbf{x}_n) = f(\mathbf{x}_n))$ points. Each point will be red with probability μ and green with probability $1 - \mu$. The color of each point will be known to us since both $h(\mathbf{x}_n)$ and $f(\mathbf{x}_n)$ are known for $n = 1, \cdots, N$ (the function h is our hypothesis so we can evaluate it on any point, and $f(\mathbf{x}_n) = y_n$ is given to us for all points in the data set $\mathcal{D}$). The learning problem is now reduced to a bin problem, under the assumption that the inputs in $\mathcal{D}$ are picked independently according to some distribution P on $\mathcal{X}$. Any P will translate to some μ in the equivalent bin. Since μ is allowed to be unknown, P can be unknown to us as well. Figure 1.9 adds this probabilistic component to the basic learning setup depicted in Figure 1.2.

With this equivalence, the Hoeffding Inequality can be applied to the learning problem, allowing us to make a prediction outside of $\mathcal{D}$. Using ν to predict μ tells us something about f, although it doesn't tell us what f is. What μ tells us is the error rate h makes in approximating f. If ν happens to be close to zero, we can predict that h will approximate f well over the entire input space. If not, we are out of luck.

Unfortunately, we have no control over ν in our current situation, since ν is based on a particular hypothesis h. In real learning, we explore an entire hypothesis set $\mathcal{H}$, looking for some $h \in \mathcal{H}$ that has a small error rate. If we have only one hypothesis to begin with, we are not really learning, but rather 'verifying' whether that particular hypothesis is good or bad. Let us see if we can extend the bin equivalence to the case where we have multiple hypotheses in order to capture real learning.

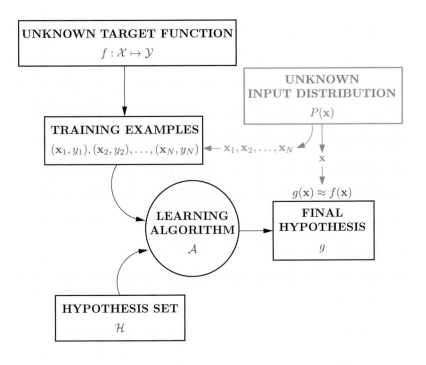

Figure 1.9: Probability added to the basic learning setup

To do that, we start by introducing more descriptive names for the different components that we will use. The error rate within the sample, which corresponds to ν in the bin model, will be called the *in-sample error*,

$$
\begin{aligned}
E_{\text{in}}(h) \;\; &= \;\; (\text{fraction of } \mathcal{D} \text{ where } f \text{ and } h \text{ disagree}) \\
&= \;\; \frac{1}{N} \sum_{n=1}^{N} [\![h(\mathbf{x}_n) \neq f(\mathbf{x}_n)]\!]\,,
\end{aligned}
$$

where $[\![\text{statement}]\!] = 1$ if the statement is true, and $= 0$ if the statement is false. We have made explicit the dependency of E_{in} on the particular h that we are considering. In the same way, we define the *out-of-sample error*

$$
E_{\text{out}}(h) = \mathbb{P}\left[h(\mathbf{x}) \neq f(\mathbf{x})\right],
$$

which corresponds to μ in the bin model. The probability is based on the distribution P over $\mathcal{X}$ which is used to sample the data points $\mathbf{x}$.

21

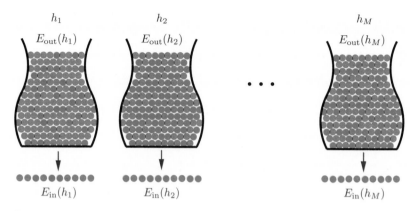

Figure 1.10: Multiple bins depict the learning problem with M hypotheses

Substituting the new notation E_{in} for ν and E_{out} for μ, the Hoeffding Inequality (1.4) can be rewritten as

$$\mathbb{P}\left[|E_{\text{in}}(h) - E_{\text{out}}(h)| > \epsilon\right] \le 2e^{-2\epsilon^2 N} \qquad \text{for any } \epsilon > 0, \qquad (1.5)$$

where N is the number of training examples. The in-sample error E_{in}, just like ν, is a random variable that depends on the sample. The out-of-sample error E_{out}, just like μ, is unknown but not random.

Let us consider an entire hypothesis set $\mathcal{H}$ instead of just one hypothesis h, and assume for the moment that $\mathcal{H}$ has a finite number of hypotheses

$$\mathcal{H} = \{h_1, h_2, \cdots, h_M\}.$$

We can construct a bin equivalent in this case by having M bins as shown in Figure 1.10. Each bin still represents the input space $\mathcal{X}$, with the red marbles in the mth bin corresponding to the points $\mathbf{x} \in \mathcal{X}$ where $h_m(\mathbf{x}) \ne f(\mathbf{x})$. The probability of red marbles in the mth bin is $E_{\text{out}}(h_m)$ and the fraction of red marbles in the mth sample is $E_{\text{in}}(h_m)$, for $m = 1, \cdots, M$. Although the Hoeffding Inequality (1.5) still applies to each bin individually, the situation becomes more complicated when we consider all the bins simultaneously. Why is that? The inequality stated that

$$\mathbb{P}\left[|E_{\text{in}}(h) - E_{\text{out}}(h)| > \epsilon\right] \le 2e^{-2\epsilon^2 N} \qquad \text{for any } \epsilon > 0,$$

where the hypothesis h is *fixed* before you generate the data set, and the probability is with respect to random data sets $\mathcal{D}$; we emphasize that the assumption "h is fixed *before* you generate the data set" is critical to the validity of this bound. If you are allowed to change h after you generate the data set, the assumptions that are needed to prove the Hoeffding Inequality no longer hold. With multiple hypotheses in $\mathcal{H}$, the learning algorithm picks the final hypothesis g based on $\mathcal{D}$, i.e. *after* generating the data set. The statement we would like to make is not

$$\text{``}\mathbb{P}[|E_{\text{in}}(h_m) - E_{\text{out}}(h_m)| > \epsilon] \text{ is small''}$$

(for any particular, fixed $h_m \in \mathcal{H}$), but rather

$$\text{``}\mathbb{P}[|E_{\text{in}}(g) - E_{\text{out}}(g)| > \epsilon] \text{ is small'' for the final hypothesis } g.$$

The hypothesis g is *not fixed* ahead of time before generating the data, because which hypothesis is selected to be g depends on the data. So, we cannot just plug in g for h in the Hoeffding inequality. The next exercise considers a simple coin experiment that further illustrates the difference between a fixed h and the final hypothesis g selected by the learning algorithm.

Exercise 1.10

Here is an experiment that illustrates the difference between a single bin and multiple bins. Run a computer simulation for flipping $1,000$ fair coins. Flip each coin independently 10 times. Let's focus on 3 coins as follows: c_1 is the first coin flipped; c_{rand} is a coin you choose at random; c_{min} is the coin that had the minimum frequency of heads (pick the earlier one in case of a tie). Let ν_1, ν_{rand} and ν_{min} be the fraction of heads you obtain for the respective three coins.

(a) What is μ for the three coins selected?

(b) Repeat this entire experiment a large number of times (e.g., $100,000$ runs of the entire experiment) to get several instances of ν_1, ν_{rand} and ν_{min} and plot the histograms of the distributions of ν_1, ν_{rand} and ν_{min}. Notice that which coins end up being c_{rand} and c_{min} may differ from one run to another.

(c) Using (b), plot estimates for $\mathbb{P}[|\nu - \mu| > \epsilon]$ as a function of ϵ, together with the Hoeffding bound $2e^{-2\epsilon^2 N}$ (on the same graph).

(d) Which coins obey the Hoeffding bound, and which ones do not? Explain why.

(e) Relate part (d) to the multiple bins in Figure 1.10.

The way to get around this is to try to bound $\mathbb{P}[|E_{\text{in}}(g) - E_{\text{out}}(g)| > \epsilon]$ in a way that does not depend on which g the learning algorithm picks. There is a simple but crude way of doing that. Since g has to be one of the h_m's regardless of the algorithm and the sample, it is always true that

$$\text{``}|E_{\text{in}}(g) - E_{\text{out}}(g)| > \epsilon\text{''} \implies \quad \text{``} \quad |E_{\text{in}}(h_1) - E_{\text{out}}(h_1)| > \epsilon$$
$$\textbf{or } |E_{\text{in}}(h_2) - E_{\text{out}}(h_2)| > \epsilon$$
$$\cdots$$
$$\textbf{or } |E_{\text{in}}(h_M) - E_{\text{out}}(h_M)| > \epsilon \text{''}.$$

where $\mathcal{B}_1 \implies \mathcal{B}_2$ means that event $\mathcal{B}_1$ implies event $\mathcal{B}_2$. Although the events on the RHS cover a lot more than the LHS, the RHS has the property we want; the hypotheses h_m are fixed. We now apply two basic rules in probability;

$$\text{if } \mathcal{B}_1 \implies \mathcal{B}_2, \text{ then } \mathbb{P}[\mathcal{B}_1] \leq \mathbb{P}[\mathcal{B}_2],$$

and, if $\mathcal{B}_1, \mathcal{B}_2, \cdots, \mathcal{B}_M$ are any events, then

$$\mathbb{P}[\mathcal{B}_1 \text{ or } \mathcal{B}_2 \text{ or } \cdots \text{ or } \mathcal{B}_M] \leq \mathbb{P}[\mathcal{B}_1] + \mathbb{P}[\mathcal{B}_2] + \cdots + \mathbb{P}[\mathcal{B}_M].$$

The second rule is known as the *union bound*. Putting the two rules together, we get

$$
\begin{aligned}
\mathbb{P}[\, |E_{\text{in}}(g) - E_{\text{out}}(g)| > \epsilon \,] \quad \leq \quad & \mathbb{P}[\quad |E_{\text{in}}(h_1) - E_{\text{out}}(h_1)| > \epsilon \\
& \textbf{or } |E_{\text{in}}(h_2) - E_{\text{out}}(h_2)| > \epsilon \\
& \quad \cdots \\
& \textbf{or } |E_{\text{in}}(h_M) - E_{\text{out}}(h_M)| > \epsilon \,] \\
\leq \quad & \sum_{m=1}^{M} \mathbb{P}[|E_{\text{in}}(h_m) - E_{\text{out}}(h_m)| > \epsilon].
\end{aligned}
$$

Applying the Hoeffding Inequality (1.5) to the M terms one at a time, we can bound each term in the sum by $2e^{-2\epsilon^2 N}$. Substituting, we get

$$\mathbb{P}[|E_{\text{in}}(g) - E_{\text{out}}(g)| > \epsilon] \leq 2Me^{-2\epsilon^2 N}. \tag{1.6}$$

Mathematically, this is a 'uniform' version of (1.5). We are trying to simultaneously approximate all $E_{\text{out}}(h_m)$'s by the corresponding $E_{\text{in}}(h_m)$'s. This allows the learning algorithm to choose any hypothesis based on E_{in} and expect that the corresponding E_{out} will uniformly follow suit, regardless of which hypothesis is chosen.

The downside for uniform estimates is that the probability bound $2Me^{-2\epsilon^2 N}$ is a factor of M looser than the bound for a single hypothesis, and will only be meaningful if M is finite. We will improve on that in Chapter 2.

1.3.3 Feasibility of Learning

We have introduced two apparently conflicting arguments about the feasibility of learning. One argument says that we cannot learn anything outside of $\mathcal{D}$, and the other says that we can. We would like to reconcile these two arguments and pinpoint the sense in which learning is feasible:

1. Let us reconcile the two arguments. The question of whether $\mathcal{D}$ tells us anything outside of $\mathcal{D}$ that we didn't know before has two different answers. If we insist on a deterministic answer, which means that $\mathcal{D}$ tells us something certain about f outside of $\mathcal{D}$, then the answer is no. If we accept a probabilistic answer, which means that $\mathcal{D}$ tells us something likely about f outside of $\mathcal{D}$, then the answer is yes.

Exercise 1.11

We are given a data set $\mathcal{D}$ of 25 training examples from an unknown target function $f: \mathcal{X} \to \mathcal{Y}$, where $\mathcal{X} = \mathbb{R}$ and $\mathcal{Y} = \{-1, +1\}$. To learn f, we use a simple hypothesis set $\mathcal{H} = \{h_1, h_2\}$ where h_1 is the constant $+1$ function and h_2 is the constant -1.

We consider two learning algorithms, S (smart) and C (crazy). S chooses the hypothesis that agrees the most with $\mathcal{D}$ and C chooses the other hypothesis deliberately. Let us see how these algorithms perform out of sample from the deterministic and probabilistic points of view. Assume in the probabilistic view that there is a probability distribution on $\mathcal{X}$, and let $\mathbb{P}[f(\mathbf{x}) = +1] = p$.

(a) Can S produce a hypothesis that is *guaranteed* to perform better than random on any point outside $\mathcal{D}$?

(b) Assume for the rest of the exercise that all the examples in $\mathcal{D}$ have $y_n = +1$. Is it *possible* that the hypothesis that C produces turns out to be better than the hypothesis that S produces?

(c) If $p = 0.9$, what is the probability that S will produce a better hypothesis than C?

(d) Is there any value of p for which it is more likely than not that C will produce a better hypothesis than S?

By adopting the probabilistic view, we get a positive answer to the feasibility question without paying too much of a price. The only assumption we make in the probabilistic framework is that the examples in $\mathcal{D}$ are generated independently. We don't insist on using any particular probability distribution, or even on knowing what distribution is used. However, whatever distribution we use for generating the examples, we must also use when we evaluate how well g approximates f (Figure 1.9). That's what makes the Hoeffding Inequality applicable. Of course this ideal situation may not always happen in practice, and some variations of it have been explored in the literature.

2. Let us pin down what we mean by the feasibility of learning. Learning produces a hypothesis g to approximate the unknown target function f. If learning is successful, then g should approximate f well, which means $E_{\text{out}}(g) \approx 0$. However, this is not what we get from the probabilistic analysis. What we get instead is $E_{\text{out}}(g) \approx E_{\text{in}}(g)$. We still have to make $E_{\text{in}}(g) \approx 0$ in order to conclude that $E_{\text{out}}(g) \approx 0$.

We cannot guarantee that we will find a hypothesis that achieves $E_{\text{in}}(g) \approx 0$, but at least we will know if we find it. Remember that $E_{\text{out}}(g)$ is an unknown quantity, since f is unknown, but $E_{\text{in}}(g)$ is a quantity that we can evaluate. We have thus traded the condition $E_{\text{out}}(g) \approx 0$, one that we cannot ascertain, for the condition $E_{\text{in}}(g) \approx 0$, which we can ascertain. What enabled this is the Hoeffding Inequality (1.6):

$$\mathbb{P}[|E_{\text{in}}(g) - E_{\text{out}}(g)| > \epsilon] \leq 2Me^{-2\epsilon^2 N}$$

that assures us that $E_{\text{out}}(g) \approx E_{\text{in}}(g)$ so we can use E_{in} as a proxy for E_{out}.

Exercise 1.12

A friend comes to you with a learning problem. She says the target function f is *completely* unknown, but she has $4,000$ data points. She is willing to pay you to solve her problem and produce for her a g which approximates f. What is the best that you can promise her among the following:

(a) After learning you will provide her with a g that you will guarantee approximates f well out of sample.

(b) After learning you will provide her with a g, and with high probability the g which you produce will approximate f well out of sample.

(c) One of two things will happen.

   (i) You will produce a hypothesis g;

   (ii) You will declare that you failed.

If you do return a hypothesis g, then with high probability the g which you produce will approximate f well out of sample.

One should note that there are cases where we won't insist that $E_{\text{in}}(g) \approx 0$. Financial forecasting is an example where market unpredictability makes it impossible to get a forecast that has anywhere near zero error. All we hope for is a forecast that gets it right more often than not. If we get that, our bets will win in the long run. This means that a hypothesis that has $E_{\text{in}}(g)$ somewhat below 0.5 will work, provided of course that $E_{\text{out}}(g)$ is close enough to $E_{\text{in}}(g)$.

The feasibility of learning is thus split into two questions:

---

1. Can we make sure that $E_{\text{out}}(g)$ is close enough to $E_{\text{in}}(g)$?

2. Can we make $E_{\text{in}}(g)$ small enough?

The Hoeffding Inequality (1.6) addresses the first question only. The second question is answered after we run the learning algorithm on the actual data and see how small we can get E_{in} to be.

Breaking down the feasibility of learning into these two questions provides further insight into the role that different components of the learning problem play. One such insight has to do with the 'complexity' of these components.

The complexity of $\mathcal{H}$. If the number of hypotheses M goes up, we run more risk that $E_{\text{in}}(g)$ will be a poor estimator of $E_{\text{out}}(g)$ according to Inequality (1.6). M can be thought of as a measure of the 'complexity' of the hypothesis set $\mathcal{H}$ that we use. If we want an affirmative answer to the first question, we need to keep the complexity of $\mathcal{H}$ in check. However, if we want an affirmative answer to the second question, we stand a better chance if $\mathcal{H}$ is more complex, since g has to come from $\mathcal{H}$. So, a more complex $\mathcal{H}$ gives us more flexibility in finding some g that fits the data well, leading to small $E_{\mathrm{in}}(g)$. This tradeoff in the complexity of $\mathcal{H}$ is a major theme in learning theory that we will study in detail in Chapter 2.

The complexity of f. Intuitively, a complex target function f should be harder to learn than a simple f. Let us examine if this can be inferred from the two questions above. A close look at Inequality (1.6) reveals that the complexity of f does not affect how well $E_{\mathrm{in}}(g)$ approximates $E_{\mathrm{out}}(g)$. If we fix the hypothesis set and the number of training examples, the inequality provides the same bound whether we are trying to learn a simple f (for instance a constant function) or a complex f (for instance a highly nonlinear function). However, this doesn't mean that we can learn complex functions as easily as we learn simple functions. Remember that (1.6) affects the first question only. If the target function is complex, the second question comes into play since the data from a complex f are harder to fit than the data from a simple f. This means that we will get a worse value for $E_{\mathrm{in}}(g)$ when f is complex. We might try to get around that by making our hypothesis set more complex so that we can fit the data better and get a lower $E_{\mathrm{in}}(g)$, but then E_{out} won't be as close to E_{in} per (1.6). Either way we look at it, a complex f is harder to learn as we expected. In the extreme case, if f is too complex, we may not be able to learn it at all.

Fortunately, most target functions in real life are not too complex; we can learn them from a reasonable $\mathcal{D}$ using a reasonable $\mathcal{H}$. This is obviously a practical observation, not a mathematical statement. Even when we cannot learn a particular f, we will at least be able to tell that we can't. As long as we make sure that the complexity of $\mathcal{H}$ gives us a good Hoeffding bound, our success or failure in learning f can be determined by our success or failure in fitting the training data.

1.4 Error and Noise

We close this chapter by revisiting two notions in the learning problem in order to bring them closer to the real world. The first notion is what approximation means when we say that our hypothesis approximates the target function well. The second notion is about the nature of the target function. In many situations, there is noise that makes the output of f not uniquely determined by the input. What are the ramifications of having such a 'noisy' target on the learning problem?

1.4.1 Error Measures

Learning is not expected to replicate the target function perfectly. The final hypothesis g is only an approximation of f. To quantify how well g approximates f, we need to define an error measure[3] that quantifies how far we are from the target.

The choice of an error measure affects the outcome of the learning process. Different error measures may lead to different choices of the final hypothesis, even if the target and the data are the same, since the value of a particular error measure may be small while the value of another error measure in the same situation is large. Therefore, which error measure we use has consequences for what we learn. What are the criteria for choosing one error measure over another? We address this question here.

First, let's formalize this notion a bit. An error measure quantifies how well each hypothesis h in the model approximates the target function f,

$$\text{Error} \;=\; E(h, f).$$

While $E(h, f)$ is based on the entirety of h and f, it is almost universally defined based on the errors on individual input points $\mathbf{x}$. If we define a pointwise error measure $e(h(\mathbf{x}), f(\mathbf{x}))$, the overall error will be the average value of this pointwise error. So far, we have been working with the classification error $e(h(\mathbf{x}), f(\mathbf{x})) = [\![h(\mathbf{x}) \neq f(\mathbf{x})]\!]$.

In an ideal world, $E(h, f)$ should be user-specified. The same learning task in different contexts may warrant the use of different error measures. One may view $E(h, f)$ as the 'cost' of using h when you should use f. This cost depends on what h is used for, and cannot be dictated just by our learning techniques. Here is a case in point.

Example 1.1 (Fingerprint verification). Consider the problem of verifying that a fingerprint belongs to a particular person. What is the appropriate error measure?

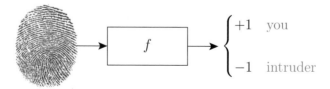

The target function takes as input a fingerprint, and returns $+1$ if it belongs to the right person, and -1 if it belongs to an intruder.

---

[3]This measure is also called an error *function* in the literature, and sometimes the error is referred to as *cost*, *objective*, or *risk*.

There are two types of error that our hypothesis h can make here. If the correct person is rejected ($h = -1$ but $f = +1$), it is called false reject, and if an incorrect person is accepted ($h = +1$ but $f = -1$), it is called false accept.

		f	
		$+1$	-1
h	$+1$	no error	false accept
	-1	false reject	no error

How should the error measure be defined in this problem? If the right person is accepted or an intruder is rejected, the error is clearly zero. We need to specify the error values for a false accept and for a false reject. The right values depend on the application.

Consider two potential clients of this fingerprint system. One is a supermarket who will use it at the checkout counter to verify that you are a member of a discount program. The other is the CIA who will use it at the entrance to a secure facility to verify that you are authorized to enter that facility.

For the supermarket, a false reject is costly because if a customer gets wrongly rejected, she may be discouraged from patronizing the supermarket in the future. All future revenue from this annoyed customer is lost. On the other hand, the cost of a false accept is minor. You just gave away a discount to someone who didn't deserve it, and that person left their fingerprint in your system – they must be bold indeed.

For the CIA, a false accept is a disaster. An unauthorized person will gain access to a highly sensitive facility. This should be reflected in a much higher cost for the false accept. False rejects, on the other hand, can be tolerated since authorized persons are employees (rather than customers as with the supermarket). The inconvenience of retrying when rejected is just part of the job, and they must deal with it.

The costs of the different types of errors can be tabulated in a matrix. For our examples, the matrices might look like:

		f	
		$+1$	-1
h	$+1$	0	1
	-1	10	0

		f	
		$+1$	-1
h	$+1$	0	1000
	-1	1	0

Supermarket   CIA

These matrices should be used to weight the different types of errors when we compute the total error. When the learning algorithm minimizes a cost-weighted error measure, it automatically takes into consideration the utility of the hypothesis that it will produce. In the supermarket and CIA scenarios, this could lead to two completely different final hypotheses. □

The moral of this example is that the choice of the error measure depends on how the system is going to be used, rather than on any inherent criterion

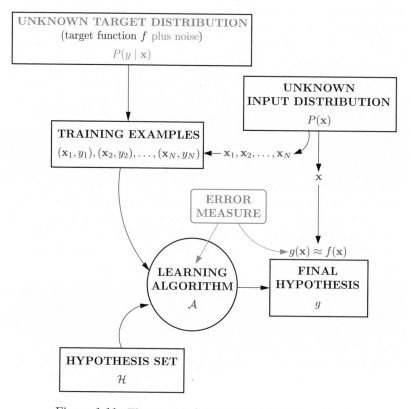

Figure 1.11: The general (supervised) learning problem

that we can independently determine during the learning process. However, this ideal choice may not be possible in practice for two reasons. One is that the user may not provide an error specification, which is not uncommon. The other is that the weighted cost may be a difficult objective function for optimizers to work with. Therefore, we often look for other ways to define the error measure, sometimes with purely practical or analytic considerations in mind. We have already seen an example of this with the simple binary error used in this chapter, and we will see other error measures in later chapters.

1.4.2 Noisy Targets

In many practical applications, the data we learn from are not generated by a deterministic target function. Instead, they are generated in a noisy way such that the output is not uniquely determined by the input. For instance, in the credit-card example we presented in Section 1.1, two customers may have identical salaries, outstanding loans, etc., but end up with different credit behavior. Therefore, the credit 'function' is not really a deterministic function, but a noisy one.

This situation can be readily modeled within the same framework that we have. Instead of $y = f(\mathbf{x})$, we can take the output y to be a random variable that is affected by, rather than determined by, the input $\mathbf{x}$. Formally, we have a target *distribution* $P(y \mid \mathbf{x})$ instead of a target function $y = f(\mathbf{x})$. A data point $(\mathbf{x}, y)$ is now generated by the joint distribution $P(\mathbf{x}, y) = P(\mathbf{x})P(y \mid \mathbf{x})$.

One can think of a noisy target as a deterministic target plus added noise. If y is real-valued for example, one can take the expected value of y given $\mathbf{x}$ to be the deterministic $f(\mathbf{x})$, and consider $y - f(\mathbf{x})$ as pure noise that is added to f.

This view suggests that a deterministic target function can be considered a special case of a noisy target, just with zero noise. Indeed, we can formally express any function f as a distribution $P(y \mid \mathbf{x})$ by choosing $P(y \mid \mathbf{x})$ to be zero for all y except $y = f(\mathbf{x})$. Therefore, there is no loss of generality if we consider the target to be a distribution rather than a function. Figure 1.11 modifies the previous Figures 1.2 and 1.9 to illustrate the general learning problem, covering both deterministic and noisy targets.

Exercise 1.13

Consider the bin model for a hypothesis h that makes an error with probability μ in approximating a deterministic target function f (both h and f are binary functions). If we use the same h to approximate a noisy version of f given by

$$P(y \mid \mathbf{x}) = \begin{cases} \lambda & y = f(\mathbf{x}), \\ 1 - \lambda & y \neq f(\mathbf{x}). \end{cases}$$

(a) What is the probability of error that h makes in approximating y?

(b) At what value of λ will the performance of h be independent of μ?
   [Hint: The noisy target will look completely random.]

There is a difference between the role of $P(y \mid \mathbf{x})$ and the role of $P(\mathbf{x})$ in the learning problem. While both distributions model probabilistic aspects of $\mathbf{x}$ and y, the target distribution $P(y \mid \mathbf{x})$ is what we are trying to learn, while the input distribution $P(\mathbf{x})$ only quantifies the relative importance of the point $\mathbf{x}$ in gauging how well we have learned.

Our entire analysis of the feasibility of learning applies to noisy target functions as well. Intuitively, this is because the Hoeffding Inequality (1.6) applies to an arbitrary, unknown target function. Assume we randomly picked all the y's according to the distribution $P(y \mid \mathbf{x})$ over the entire input space $\mathcal{X}$. This realization of $P(y \mid \mathbf{x})$ is effectively a target function. Therefore, the inequality will be valid no matter which particular random realization the 'target function' happens to be.

This does not mean that learning a noisy target is as easy as learning a deterministic one. Remember the two questions of learning? With the same learning model, E_{out} may be as close to E_{in} in the noisy case as it is in the deterministic case, but E_{in} itself will likely be worse in the noisy case since it is hard to fit the noise.

In Chapter 2, where we prove a stronger version of (1.6), we will assume the target to be a probability distribution $P(y \mid \mathbf{x})$, thus covering the general case.

1.5 Problems

Problem 1.1 We have 2 opaque bags, each containing 2 balls. One bag has 2 black balls and the other has a black and a white ball. You pick a bag at random and then pick one of the balls in that bag at random. When you look at the ball it is black. You now pick the second ball from that same bag. What is the probability that this ball is also black? *[Hint: Use Bayes' Theorem:* $\mathbb{P}[A \text{ and } B] = \mathbb{P}[A \mid B]\,\mathbb{P}[B] = \mathbb{P}[B \mid A]\,\mathbb{P}[A].]$

Problem 1.2 Consider the perceptron in two dimensions: $h(\mathbf{x}) = \text{sign}(\mathbf{w}^\mathsf{T}\mathbf{x})$ where $\mathbf{w} = [w_0, w_1, w_2]^\mathsf{T}$ and $\mathbf{x} = [1, x_1, x_2]^\mathsf{T}$. Technically, $\mathbf{x}$ has three coordinates, but we call this perceptron two-dimensional because the first coordinate is fixed at 1.

(a) Show that the regions on the plane where $h(\mathbf{x}) = +1$ and $h(\mathbf{x}) = -1$ are separated by a line. If we express this line by the equation $x_2 = ax_1 + b$, what are the slope a and intercept b in terms of w_0, w_1, w_2?

(b) Draw a picture for the cases $\mathbf{w} = [1, 2, 3]^\mathsf{T}$ and $\mathbf{w} = -[1, 2, 3]^\mathsf{T}$.

In more than two dimensions, the $+1$ and -1 regions are separated by a *hyperplane*, the generalization of a line.

Problem 1.3 Prove that the PLA eventually converges to a linear separator for separable data. The following steps will guide you through the proof. Let $\mathbf{w}^*$ be an optimal set of weights (one which separates the data). The essential idea in this proof is to show that the PLA weights $\mathbf{w}(t)$ get "more aligned" with $\mathbf{w}^*$ with every iteration. For simplicity, assume that $\mathbf{w}(0) = \mathbf{0}$.

(a) Let $\rho = \min_{1 \le n \le N} y_n(\mathbf{w}^{*\mathsf{T}}\mathbf{x}_n)$. Show that $\rho > 0$.

(b) Show that $\mathbf{w}^\mathsf{T}(t)\mathbf{w}^* \ge \mathbf{w}^\mathsf{T}(t{-}1)\mathbf{w}^*{+}\rho$, and conclude that $\mathbf{w}^\mathsf{T}(t)\mathbf{w}^* \ge t\rho$. *[Hint: Use induction.]*

(c) Show that $\|\mathbf{w}(t)\|^2 \le \|\mathbf{w}(t-1)\|^2 + \|\mathbf{x}(t-1)\|^2$.

   [Hint: $y(t-1) \cdot (\mathbf{w}^\mathsf{T}(t-1)\mathbf{x}(t-1)) \le 0$ because $\mathbf{x}(t-1)$ was misclassified by $\mathbf{w}(t-1)$.]

(d) Show by induction that $\|\mathbf{w}(t)\|^2 \le tR^2$, where $R = \max_{1 \le n \le N} \|\mathbf{x}_n\|$.

(continued on next page)

33

(e) Using (b) and (d), show that

$$\frac{\mathbf{w}^{\mathrm{T}}(t)}{\|\mathbf{w}(t)\|}\mathbf{w}^* \geq \sqrt{t} \cdot \frac{\rho}{R},$$

and hence prove that

$$t \leq \frac{R^2\|\mathbf{w}^*\|^2}{\rho^2}.$$

$\left[\textit{Hint: } \frac{\mathbf{w}^{\mathrm{T}}(t)\mathbf{w}^*}{\|\mathbf{w}(t)\|\,\|\mathbf{w}^*\|} \leq 1. \textit{ Why?}\right]$

In practice, PLA converges more quickly than the bound $\frac{R^2\|\mathbf{w}^*\|^2}{\rho^2}$ suggests. Nevertheless, because we do not know ρ in advance, we can't determine the number of iterations to convergence, which does pose a problem if the data is non-separable.

Problem 1.4   In Exercise 1.4, we use an artificial data set to study the perceptron learning algorithm. This problem leads you to explore the algorithm further with data sets of different sizes and dimensions.

(a) Generate a linearly separable data set of size 20 as indicated in Exercise 1.4. Plot the examples $\{(\mathbf{x}_n, y_n)\}$ as well as the target function f on a plane. Be sure to mark the examples from different classes differently, and add labels to the axes of the plot.

(b) Run the perceptron learning algorithm on the data set above. Report the number of updates that the algorithm takes before converging. Plot the examples $\{(\mathbf{x}_n, y_n)\}$, the target function f, and the final hypothesis g in the same figure. Comment on whether f is close to g.

(c) Repeat everything in (b) with another randomly generated data set of size 20. Compare your results with (b).

(d) Repeat everything in (b) with another randomly generated data set of size 100. Compare your results with (b).

(e) Repeat everything in (b) with another randomly generated data set of size $1,000$. Compare your results with (b).

(f) Modify the algorithm such that it takes $\mathbf{x}_n \in \mathbb{R}^{10}$ instead of $\mathbb{R}^2$. Randomly generate a linearly separable data set of size $1,000$ with $\mathbf{x}_n \in \mathbb{R}^{10}$ and feed the data set to the algorithm. How many updates does the algorithm take to converge?

(g) Repeat the algorithm on the same data set as (f) for 100 experiments. In the iterations of each experiment, pick $\mathbf{x}(t)$ randomly instead of deterministically. Plot a histogram for the number of updates that the algorithm takes to converge.

(h) Summarize your conclusions with respect to accuracy and running time as a function of N and d.

Problem 1.5   The perceptron learning algorithm works like this: In each iteration t, pick a random $(\mathbf{x}(t), y(t))$ and compute the 'signal' $s(t) = \mathbf{w}^{\mathsf{T}}(t)\mathbf{x}(t)$. If $y(t) \cdot s(t) \le 0$, update $\mathbf{w}$ by

$$\mathbf{w}(t+1) \longleftarrow \mathbf{w}(t) + y(t) \cdot \mathbf{x}(t) \ ;$$

One may argue that this algorithm does not take the 'closeness' between $s(t)$ and $y(t)$ into consideration. Let's look at another perceptron learning algorithm: In each iteration, pick a random $(\mathbf{x}(t), y(t))$ and compute $s(t)$. If $y(t) \cdot s(t) \le 1$, update $\mathbf{w}$ by

$$\mathbf{w}(t+1) \longleftarrow \mathbf{w}(t) + \eta \cdot (y(t) - s(t)) \cdot \mathbf{x}(t) \ ,$$

where η is a constant. That is, if $s(t)$ agrees with $y(t)$ well (their product is > 1), the algorithm does nothing. On the other hand, if $s(t)$ is further from $y(t)$, the algorithm changes $\mathbf{w}(t)$ more. In this problem, you are asked to implement this algorithm and study its performance.

(a) Generate a training data set of size 100 similar to that used in Exercise 1.4. Generate a test data set of size $10,000$ from the same process. To get g, run the algorithm above with $\eta = 100$ on the training data set, until a maximum of $1,000$ updates has been reached. Plot the training data set, the target function f, and the final hypothesis g on the same figure. Report the error on the test set.

(b) Use the data set in (a) and redo everything with $\eta = 1$.

(c) Use the data set in (a) and redo everything with $\eta = 0.01$.

(d) Use the data set in (a) and redo everything with $\eta = 0.0001$.

(e) Compare the results that you get from (a) to (d).

The algorithm above is a variant of the so-called Adaline (*Adaptive Linear Neuron*) algorithm for perceptron learning.

Problem 1.6   Consider a sample of 10 marbles drawn independently from a bin that holds red and green marbles. The probability of a red marble is μ. For $\mu = 0.05$, $\mu = 0.5$, and $\mu = 0.8$, compute the probability of getting no red marbles ($\nu = 0$) in the following cases.

(a) We draw only one such sample. Compute the probability that $\nu = 0$.

(b) We draw $1,000$ independent samples. Compute the probability that (at least) one of the samples has $\nu = 0$.

(c) Repeat (b) for $1,000,000$ independent samples.

Problem 1.7   A sample of heads and tails is created by tossing a coin a number of times independently. Assume we have a number of coins that generate different samples independently. For a given coin, let the probability of heads (probability of error) be μ. The probability of obtaining k heads in N tosses of this coin is given by the binomial distribution:

$$P[k \mid N, \mu] = \binom{N}{k} \mu^k (1 - \mu)^{N-k}.$$

Remember that the training error ν is $\frac{k}{N}$.

(a) Assume the sample size (N) is 10. If all the coins have $\mu = 0.05$ compute the probability that at least one coin will have $\nu = 0$ for the case of 1 coin, $1,000$ coins, $1,000,000$ coins. Repeat for $\mu = 0.8$.

(b) For the case $N = 6$ and 2 coins with $\mu = 0.5$ for both coins, plot the probability

$$P[\max_i |\nu_i - \mu_i| > \epsilon]$$

for ϵ in the range $[0, 1]$ (the $\max$ is over coins). On the same plot show the bound that would be obtained using the Hoeffding Inequality . Remember that for a single coin, the Hoeffding bound is

$$P[|\nu - \mu| > \epsilon] \leq 2e^{-2N\epsilon^2}.$$

[Hint: Use $P[A$ or $B] = P[A] + P[B] - P[A$ and $B] = P[A] + P[B] - P[A]P[B]$, where the last equality follows by independence, to evaluate $P[\max \ldots]$]

Problem 1.8   The Hoeffding Inequality is one form of the *law of large numbers*. One of the simplest forms of that law is the *Chebyshev Inequality*, which you will prove here.

(a) If t is a non-negative random variable, prove that for any $\alpha > 0$, $P[t \geq \alpha] \leq \mathbb{E}(t)/\alpha$.

(b) If u is any random variable with mean μ and variance σ^2, prove that for any $\alpha > 0$, $P[(u - \mu)^2 \geq \alpha] \leq \frac{\sigma^2}{\alpha}$. *[Hint: Use (a)]*

(c) If $u_1, \cdots, u_N$ are iid random variables, each with mean μ and variance σ^2, and $u = \frac{1}{N} \sum_{n=1}^{N} u_n$, prove that for any $\alpha > 0$,

$$P[(u - \mu)^2 \geq \alpha] \leq \frac{\sigma^2}{N\alpha}.$$

Notice that the RHS of this Chebyshev Inequality goes down linearly in N, while the counterpart in Hoeffding's Inequality goes down exponentially. In Problem 1.9, we develop an exponential bound using a similar approach.

36

Problem 1.9   In this problem, we derive a form of the law of large numbers that has an exponential bound, called the *Chernoff bound*. We focus on the simple case of flipping a fair coin, and use an approach similar to Problem 1.8.

(a) Let t be a (finite) random variable, α be a positive constant, and s be a positive parameter. If $T(s) = \mathbb{E}_t(e^{st})$, prove that

$$\mathbb{P}[t \geq \alpha] \leq e^{-s\alpha} T(s) .$$

[Hint: e^{st} is monotonically increasing in t.]

(b) Let $u_1, \cdots, u_N$ be iid random variables, and let $u = \frac{1}{N} \sum_{n=1}^{N} u_n$. If $U(s) = \mathbb{E}_{u_n}(e^{su_n})$ (for any n), prove that

$$\mathbb{P}[u \geq \alpha] \leq \left(e^{-s\alpha} U(s) \right)^N .$$

(c) Suppose $\mathbb{P}[u_n = 0] = \mathbb{P}[u_n = 1] = \frac{1}{2}$ (fair coin). Evaluate $U(s)$ as a function of s, and minimize $e^{-s\alpha}U(s)$ with respect to s for fixed α, $0 < \alpha < 1$.

(d) Conclude in (c) that, for $0 < \epsilon < \frac{1}{2}$,

$$\mathbb{P}[u \geq \mathbb{E}(u) + \epsilon] \leq 2^{-\beta N} ,$$

where $\beta = 1 + (\frac{1}{2} + \epsilon) \log_2 (\frac{1}{2} + \epsilon) + (\frac{1}{2} - \epsilon) \log_2 (\frac{1}{2} - \epsilon)$ and $\mathbb{E}(u) = \frac{1}{2}$. Show that $\beta > 0$, hence the bound is exponentially decreasing in N.

Problem 1.10   Assume that $\mathcal{X} = \{\mathbf{x}_1, \mathbf{x}_2, \ldots, \mathbf{x}_N, \mathbf{x}_{N+1}, \ldots, \mathbf{x}_{N+M}\}$ and $\mathcal{Y} = \{-1, +1\}$ with an unknown target function $f: \mathcal{X} \to \mathcal{Y}$. The training data set $\mathcal{D}$ is $(\mathbf{x}_1, y_1), \cdots, (\mathbf{x}_N, y_N)$. Define the *off-training-set error* of a hypothesis h with respect to f by

$$E_{\text{off}}(h, f) = \frac{1}{M} \sum_{m=1}^{M} [\![h(\mathbf{x}_{N+m}) \neq f(\mathbf{x}_{N+m})]\!] .$$

(a) Say $f(\mathbf{x}) = +1$ for all $\mathbf{x}$ and

$$h(\mathbf{x}) = \begin{cases} +1, & \text{for } \mathbf{x} = \mathbf{x}_k \text{ and } k \text{ is odd and } 1 \leq k \leq M + N \\ -1, & \text{otherwise} \end{cases} .$$

What is $E_{\text{off}}(h, f)$?

(b) We say that a target function f can 'generate' $\mathcal{D}$ in a noiseless setting if $y_n = f(\mathbf{x}_n)$ for all $(\mathbf{x}_n, y_n) \in \mathcal{D}$. For a fixed $\mathcal{D}$ of size N, how many possible $f: \mathcal{X} \to \mathcal{Y}$ can generate $\mathcal{D}$ in a noiseless setting?

(c) For a given hypothesis h and an integer k between 0 and M, how many of those f in (b) satisfy $E_{\text{off}}(h, f) = \frac{k}{M}$?

(d) For a given hypothesis h, if all those f that generate $\mathcal{D}$ in a noiseless setting are equally likely in probability, what is the expected off-training-set error $\mathbb{E}_f[E_{\text{off}}(h, f)]$?

(continued on next page)

(e) A deterministic algorithm A is defined as a procedure that takes $\mathcal{D}$ as an input, and outputs a hypothesis $h = A(\mathcal{D})$. Argue that for any two deterministic algorithms A_1 and A_2,

$$\mathbb{E}_f\big[E_{\text{off}}(A_1(\mathcal{D}), f)\big] = \mathbb{E}_f\big[E_{\text{off}}(A_2(\mathcal{D}), f)\big].$$

You have now proved that in a noiseless setting, for a fixed $\mathcal{D}$, if all possible f are equally likely, any two deterministic algorithms are equivalent in terms of the expected off-training-set error. Similar results can be proved for more general settings.

Problem 1.11   The matrix which tabulates the cost of various errors for the CIA and Supermarket applications in Example 1.1 is called a *risk* or *loss matrix*.

For the two risk matrices in Example 1.1, explicitly write down the in-sample error E_{in} that one should minimize to obtain g. This in-sample error should weight the different types of errors based on the risk matrix. *[Hint: Consider $y_n = +1$ and $y_n = -1$ separately.]*

Problem 1.12   This problem investigates how changing the error measure can change the result of the learning process. You have N data points $y_1 \leq \cdots \leq y_N$ and wish to estimate a 'representative' value.

(a) If your algorithm is to find the hypothesis h that minimizes the in-sample sum of squared deviations,

$$E_{\text{in}}(h) = \sum_{n=1}^{N}(h - y_n)^2,$$

then show that your estimate will be the in-sample mean,

$$h_{\text{mean}} = \frac{1}{N}\sum_{n=1}^{N} y_n.$$

(b) If your algorithm is to find the hypothesis h that minimizes the in-sample sum of absolute deviations,

$$E_{\text{in}}(h) = \sum_{n=1}^{N}|h - y_n|,$$

then show that your estimate will be the in-sample median h_{med}, which is any value for which half the data points are at most h_{med} and half the data points are at least h_{med}.

(c) Suppose y_N is perturbed to $y_N + \epsilon$, where $\epsilon \to \infty$. So, the single data point y_N becomes an outlier. What happens to your two estimators h_{mean} and h_{med}?

Chapter 2

Training versus Testing

Before the final exam, a professor may hand out some practice problems and solutions to the class. Although these problems are not the exact ones that will appear on the exam, studying them will help you do better. They are the 'training set' in your learning.

If the professor's goal is to help you do better in the exam, why not give out the exam problems themselves? Well, nice try ☺. Doing well in the exam is not the goal in and of itself. The goal is for you to learn the course material. The exam is merely a way to gauge how well you have learned the material. If the exam problems are known ahead of time, your performance on them will no longer accurately gauge how well you have learned.

The same distinction between training and testing happens in learning from data. In this chapter, we will develop a mathematical theory that characterizes this distinction. We will also discuss the conceptual and practical implications of the contrast between training and testing.

2.1 Theory of Generalization

The out-of-sample error E_{out} measures how well our training on $\mathcal{D}$ has *generalized* to data that we have not seen before. E_{out} is based on the performance over the entire input space $\mathcal{X}$. Intuitively, if we want to estimate the value of E_{out} using a sample of data points, these points must be 'fresh' test points that have not been used for training, similar to the questions on the final exam that have not been used for practice.

The in-sample error E_{in}, by contrast, is based on data points that have been used for training. It expressly measures training performance, similar to your performance on the practice problems that you got before the final exam. Such performance has the benefit of looking at the solutions and adjusting accordingly, and may not reflect the ultimate performance in a real test. We began the analysis of in-sample error in Chapter 1, and we will extend this analysis to the general case in this chapter. We will also make the contrast between a training set and a test set more precise.

A word of warning: this chapter is the heaviest in this book in terms of mathematical abstraction. To make it easier on the not-so-mathematically inclined, we will tell you which part you can safely skip without 'losing the plot'. The mathematical results provide fundamental insights into learning from data, and we will interpret these results in practical terms.

Generalization error. We have already discussed how the value of E_{in} does not always generalize to a similar value of E_{out}. Generalization is a key issue in learning. One can define the *generalization error* as the discrepancy between E_{in} and E_{out}.[1] The Hoeffding Inequality (1.6) provides a way to characterize the generalization error with a probabilistic bound,

$$\mathbb{P}\left[|E_{\text{in}}(g) - E_{\text{out}}(g)| > \epsilon\right] \le 2Me^{-2\epsilon^2 N},$$

for any $\epsilon > 0$. This can be rephrased as follows. Pick a tolerance level δ, for example $\delta = 0.05$, and assert with probability at least $1 - \delta$ that

$$E_{\text{out}}(g) \le E_{\text{in}}(g) + \sqrt{\frac{1}{2N} \ln \frac{2M}{\delta}}. \tag{2.1}$$

We refer to the type of inequality in (2.1) as a *generalization bound* because it bounds E_{out} in terms of E_{in}. To see that the Hoeffding Inequality implies this generalization bound, we rewrite (1.6) as follows: with probability at least $1 - 2Me^{-2N\epsilon^2}$, $|E_{\text{out}} - E_{\text{in}}| \le \epsilon$, which implies $E_{\text{out}} \le E_{\text{in}} + \epsilon$. We may now identify $\delta = 2Me^{-2N\epsilon^2}$, from which $\epsilon = \sqrt{\frac{1}{2N} \ln \frac{2M}{\delta}}$, and (2.1) follows.

Notice that the other side of $|E_{\text{out}} - E_{\text{in}}| \le \epsilon$ also holds, that is, $E_{\text{out}} \ge E_{\text{in}} - \epsilon$ for all $h \in \mathcal{H}$. This is important for learning, but in a more subtle way. Not only do we want to know that the hypothesis g that we choose (say the one with the best training error) will continue to do well out of sample (i.e., $E_{\text{out}} \le E_{\text{in}} + \epsilon$), but we also want to be sure that we did the best we could with our $\mathcal{H}$ (no other hypothesis $h \in \mathcal{H}$ has $E_{\text{out}}(h)$ significantly better than $E_{\text{out}}(g)$). The $E_{\text{out}}(h) \ge E_{\text{in}}(h) - \epsilon$ direction of the bound assures us that we couldn't do much better because every hypothesis with a higher E_{in} than the g we have chosen will have a comparably higher E_{out}.

The error bound $\sqrt{\frac{1}{2N} \ln \frac{2M}{\delta}}$ in (2.1), or 'error bar' if you will, depends on M, the size of the hypothesis set $\mathcal{H}$. If $\mathcal{H}$ is an infinite set, the bound goes to infinity and becomes meaningless. Unfortunately, almost all interesting learning models have infinite $\mathcal{H}$, including the simple perceptron which we discussed in Chapter 1.

In order to study generalization in such models, we need to derive a counterpart to (2.1) that deals with infinite $\mathcal{H}$. We would like to replace M with

---

[1] Sometimes 'generalization error' is used as another name for E_{out}, but not in this book.

something finite, so that the bound is meaningful. To do this, we notice that the way we got the M factor in the first place was by taking the disjunction of events:

$$\text{``}|E_{\text{in}}(h_1) - E_{\text{out}}(h_1)| > \epsilon\text{''} \quad \textbf{or}$$
$$\text{``}|E_{\text{in}}(h_2) - E_{\text{out}}(h_2)| > \epsilon\text{''} \quad \textbf{or}$$
$$\vdots$$
$$\text{``}|E_{\text{in}}(h_M) - E_{\text{out}}(h_M)| > \epsilon\text{''} \ , \tag{2.2}$$

which is guaranteed to include the event "$|E_{\text{in}}(g) - E_{\text{out}}(g)| > \epsilon$" since g is always one of the hypotheses in $\mathcal{H}$. We then over-estimated the probability using the union bound. Let $\mathcal{B}_m$ be the ($\mathcal{B}$ad) event that "$|E_{\text{in}}(h_m) - E_{\text{out}}(h_m)| > \epsilon$". Then,

$$\mathbb{P}[\mathcal{B}_1 \ \textbf{or} \ \mathcal{B}_2 \ \textbf{or} \ \cdots \ \textbf{or} \ \mathcal{B}_M] \leq \mathbb{P}[\mathcal{B}_1] + \mathbb{P}[\mathcal{B}_2] + \cdots + \mathbb{P}[\mathcal{B}_M].$$

If the events $\mathcal{B}_1, \mathcal{B}_2, \cdots, \mathcal{B}_M$ are strongly overlapping, the union bound becomes particularly loose as illustrated in the figure to the right for an example with 3 hypotheses; the areas of different events correspond to their probabilities. The union bound says that the total area covered by $\mathcal{B}_1$, $\mathcal{B}_2$, or $\mathcal{B}_3$ is smaller than the sum of the individual areas, which is true but is a gross overestimate when the areas overlap heavily as in this example. The events "$|E_{\text{in}}(h_m) - E_{\text{out}}(h_m)| > \epsilon$"; $m = 1, \cdots, M$, are often strongly overlapping. If h_1 is very similar to h_2 for instance,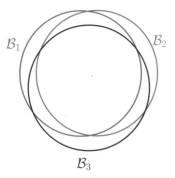
the two events "$|E_{\text{in}}(h_1) - E_{\text{out}}(h_1)| > \epsilon$" and "$|E_{\text{in}}(h_2) - E_{\text{out}}(h_2)| > \epsilon$" are likely to coincide for most data sets. In a typical learning model, many hypotheses are indeed very similar. If you take the perceptron model for instance, as you slowly vary the weight vector $\mathbf{w}$, you get infinitely many hypotheses that differ from each other only infinitesimally.

The mathematical theory of generalization hinges on this observation. Once we properly account for the overlaps of the different hypotheses, we will be able to replace the number of hypotheses M in (2.1) by an effective number which is finite even when M is infinite, and establish a more useful condition under which E_{out} is close to E_{in}.

2.1.1 Effective Number of Hypotheses

We now introduce the *growth function*, the quantity that will formalize the effective number of hypotheses. The growth function is what will replace M

in the generalization bound (2.1). It is a combinatorial quantity that captures how different the hypotheses in $\mathcal{H}$ are, and hence how much overlap the different events in (2.2) have.

We will start by defining the growth function and studying its basic properties. Next, we will show how we can bound the value of the growth function. Finally, we will show that we can replace M in the generalization bound with the growth function. These three steps will yield the generalization bound that we need, which applies to infinite $\mathcal{H}$. We will focus on binary target functions for the purpose of this analysis, so each $h \in \mathcal{H}$ maps $\mathcal{X}$ to $\{-1, +1\}$.

The definition of the growth function is based on the number of different hypotheses that $\mathcal{H}$ can implement, but only over a finite sample of points rather than over the entire input space $\mathcal{X}$. If $h \in \mathcal{H}$ is applied to a finite sample $\mathbf{x}_1, \cdots, \mathbf{x}_N \in \mathcal{X}$, we get an N-tuple $h(\mathbf{x}_1), \cdots, h(\mathbf{x}_N)$ of ± 1's. Such an N-tuple is called a *dichotomy* since it splits $\mathbf{x}_1, \cdots, \mathbf{x}_N$ into two groups: those points for which h is -1 and those for which h is $+1$. Each $h \in \mathcal{H}$ generates a dichotomy on $\mathbf{x}_1, \cdots, \mathbf{x}_N$, but two different h's may generate the same dichotomy if they happen to give the same pattern of ± 1's on this particular sample.

Definition 2.1. *Let $\mathbf{x}_1, \cdots, \mathbf{x}_N \in \mathcal{X}$. The dichotomies generated by $\mathcal{H}$ on these points are defined by*

$$\mathcal{H}(\mathbf{x}_1, \cdots, \mathbf{x}_N) = \{ (h(\mathbf{x}_1), \cdots, h(\mathbf{x}_N)) \mid h \in \mathcal{H} \}. \qquad (2.3)$$

One can think of the dichotomies $\mathcal{H}(\mathbf{x}_1, \cdots, \mathbf{x}_N)$ as a set of hypotheses just like $\mathcal{H}$ is, except that the hypotheses are seen through the eyes of N points only. A larger $\mathcal{H}(\mathbf{x}_1, \cdots, \mathbf{x}_N)$ means $\mathcal{H}$ is more 'diverse' – generating more dichotomies on $\mathbf{x}_1, \cdots, \mathbf{x}_N$. The growth function is based on the number of dichotomies.

Definition 2.2. *The growth function is defined for a hypothesis set $\mathcal{H}$ by*

$$m_{\mathcal{H}}(N) = \max_{\mathbf{x}_1, \cdots, \mathbf{x}_N \in \mathcal{X}} |\mathcal{H}(\mathbf{x}_1, \cdots, \mathbf{x}_N)|,$$

where $|\cdot|$ denotes the cardinality (number of elements) of a set.

In words, $m_{\mathcal{H}}(N)$ is the maximum number of dichotomies that can be generated by $\mathcal{H}$ on any N points. To compute $m_{\mathcal{H}}(N)$, we consider all possible choices of N points $\mathbf{x}_1, \cdots, \mathbf{x}_N$ from $\mathcal{X}$ and pick the one that gives us the most dichotomies. Like M, $m_{\mathcal{H}}(N)$ is a measure of the number of hypotheses in $\mathcal{H}$, except that a hypothesis is now considered on N points instead of the entire $\mathcal{X}$. For any $\mathcal{H}$, since $\mathcal{H}(\mathbf{x}_1, \cdots, \mathbf{x}_N) \subseteq \{-1, +1\}^N$ (the set of all possible dichotomies on any N points), the value of $m_{\mathcal{H}}(N)$ is at most $|\{-1, +1\}^N|$, hence

$$m_{\mathcal{H}}(N) \leq 2^N.$$

If $\mathcal{H}$ is capable of generating all possible dichotomies on $\mathbf{x}_1, \cdots, \mathbf{x}_N$, then $\mathcal{H}(\mathbf{x}_1, \cdots, \mathbf{x}_N) = \{-1, +1\}^N$ and we say that $\mathcal{H}$ can *shatter* $\mathbf{x}_1, \cdots, \mathbf{x}_N$. This signifies that $\mathcal{H}$ is as diverse as can be on this particular sample.

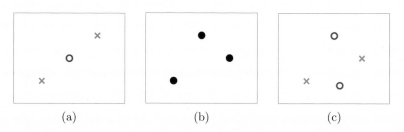

Figure 2.1: Illustration of the growth function for a two-dimensional perceptron. The dichotomy of red versus blue on the 3 colinear points in part (a) cannot be generated by a perceptron, but all 8 dichotomies on the 3 points in part (b) can. By contrast, the dichotomy of red versus blue on the 4 points in part (c) cannot be generated by a perceptron. At most 14 out of the possible 16 dichotomies on any 4 points can be generated.

Example 2.1. If $\mathcal{X}$ is a Euclidean plane and $\mathcal{H}$ is a two-dimensional perceptron, what are $m_{\mathcal{H}}(3)$ and $m_{\mathcal{H}}(4)$? Figure 2.1(a) shows a dichotomy on 3 points that the perceptron cannot generate, while Figure 2.1(b) shows another 3 points that the perceptron can shatter, generating all $2^3 = 8$ dichotomies. Because the definition of $m_{\mathcal{H}}(N)$ is based on the maximum number of dichotomies, $m_{\mathcal{H}}(3) = 8$ in spite of the case in Figure 2.1(a).

In the case of 4 points, Figure 2.1(c) shows a dichotomy that the perceptron cannot generate. One can verify that there are no 4 points that the perceptron can shatter. The most a perceptron can do on any 4 points is 14 dichotomies out of the possible 16, where the 2 missing dichotomies are as depicted in Figure 2.1(c) with blue and red corresponding to $-1, +1$ or to $+1, -1$. Hence, $m_{\mathcal{H}}(4) = 14$.   □

Let us now illustrate how to compute $m_{\mathcal{H}}(N)$ for some simple hypothesis sets. These examples will confirm the intuition that $m_{\mathcal{H}}(N)$ grows faster when the hypothesis set $\mathcal{H}$ becomes more complex. This is what we expect of a quantity that is meant to replace M in the generalization bound (2.1).

Example 2.2. Let us find a formula for $m_{\mathcal{H}}(N)$ in each of the following cases.

1. *Positive rays:* $\mathcal{H}$ consists of all hypotheses $h \colon \mathbb{R} \to \{-1, +1\}$ of the form $h(x) = \mathrm{sign}(x - a)$, i.e., the hypotheses are defined in a one-dimensional input space, and they return -1 to the left of some value a and $+1$ to the right of a.

To compute $m_{\mathcal{H}}(N)$, we notice that given N points, the line is split by the points into $N + 1$ regions. The dichotomy we get on the N points is decided by which region contains the value a. As we vary a, we will get $N + 1$ different dichotomies. Since this is the most we can get for any N points, the growth function is

$$m_{\mathcal{H}}(N) = N + 1.$$

Notice that if we picked N points where some of the points coincided (which is allowed), we will get less than $N + 1$ dichotomies. This does not affect the value of $m_{\mathcal{H}}(N)$ since it is defined based on the maximum number of dichotomies.

2. *Positive intervals*: $\mathcal{H}$ consists of all hypotheses in one dimension that return $+1$ within some interval and -1 otherwise. Each hypothesis is specified by the two end values of that interval.

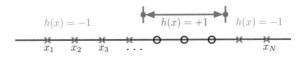

To compute $m_{\mathcal{H}}(N)$, we notice that given N points, the line is again split by the points into $N + 1$ regions. The dichotomy we get is decided by which two regions contain the end values of the interval, resulting in $\binom{N+1}{2}$ different dichotomies. If both end values fall in the same region, the resulting hypothesis is the constant -1 regardless of which region it is. Adding up these possibilities, we get

$$m_{\mathcal{H}}(N) = \binom{N + 1}{2} + 1 = \frac{1}{2}N^2 + \frac{1}{2}N + 1.$$

Notice that $m_{\mathcal{H}}(N)$ grows as the square of N, faster than the linear $m_{\mathcal{H}}(N)$ of the 'simpler' positive ray case.

3. *Convex sets*: $\mathcal{H}$ consists of all hypotheses in two dimensions $h\colon \mathbb{R}^2 \to \{-1, +1\}$ that are positive inside some convex set and negative elsewhere (a set is convex if the line segment connecting any two points in the set lies entirely within the set).

To compute $m_{\mathcal{H}}(N)$ in this case, we need to choose the N points carefully. Per the next figure, choose N points on the perimeter of a circle. Now consider any dichotomy on these points, assigning an arbitrary pattern of ± 1's to the N points. If you connect the $+1$ points with a polygon, the hypothesis made up of the closed interior of the polygon (which has to be convex since its vertices are on the perimeter of a circle) agrees with the dichotomy on all N points. For the dichotomies that have less than three $+1$ points, the convex set will be a line segment, a point, or an empty set.

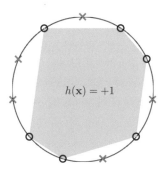

This means that any dichotomy on these N points can be realized using a convex hypothesis, so $\mathcal{H}$ manages to shatter these points and the growth function has the maximum possible value

$$m_\mathcal{H}(N) = 2^N.$$

Notice that if the N points were chosen at random in the plane rather than on the perimeter of a circle, many of the points would be 'internal' and we wouldn't be able to shatter all the points with convex hypotheses as we did for the perimeter points. However, this doesn't matter as far as $m_\mathcal{H}(N)$ is concerned, since it is defined based on the maximum (2^N in this case). □

It is not practical to try to compute $m_\mathcal{H}(N)$ for every hypothesis set we use. Fortunately, we don't have to. Since $m_\mathcal{H}(N)$ is meant to replace M in (2.1), we can use an upper bound on $m_\mathcal{H}(N)$ instead of the exact value, and the inequality in (2.1) will still hold. Getting a good bound on $m_\mathcal{H}(N)$ will prove much easier than computing $m_\mathcal{H}(N)$ itself, thanks to the notion of a *break point*.

Definition 2.3. *If no data set of size k can be shattered by $\mathcal{H}$, then k is said to be a break point for $\mathcal{H}$.*

If k is a break point, then $m_\mathcal{H}(k) < 2^k$. Example 2.1 shows that $k = 4$ is a break point for two-dimensional perceptrons. In general, it is easier to find a break point for $\mathcal{H}$ than to compute the full growth function for that $\mathcal{H}$.

> **Exercise 2.1**
>
> By inspection, find a break point k for each hypothesis set in Example 2.2 (if there is one). Verify that $m_\mathcal{H}(k) < 2^k$ using the formulas derived in that Example.

We now use the break point k to derive a bound on the growth function $m_\mathcal{H}(N)$ for all values of N. For example, the fact that no 4 points can be shattered by the two-dimensional perceptron puts a significant constraint on the number of dichotomies that can be realized by the perceptron on 5 or more points. We will exploit this idea to get a significant bound on $m_{\mathcal{H}}(N)$ in general.

2.1.2   Bounding the Growth Function

The most important fact about growth functions is that if the condition $m_{\mathcal{H}}(N) = 2^N$ breaks at any point, we can bound $m_{\mathcal{H}}(N)$ for all values of N by a simple polynomial based on this break point. The fact that the bound is polynomial is crucial. Absent a break point (as is the case in the convex hypothesis example), $m_{\mathcal{H}}(N) = 2^N$ for all N. If $m_{\mathcal{H}}(N)$ replaced M in Equation (2.1), the bound $\sqrt{\frac{1}{2N} \ln \frac{2M}{\delta}}$ on the generalization error would not go to zero regardless of how many training examples N we have. However, if $m_{\mathcal{H}}(N)$ can be bounded by a polynomial – any polynomial –, the generalization error will go to zero as $N \to \infty$. This means that we will generalize well given a sufficient number of examples.

> **Begin safe skip:** If you trust our math, you can skip the following part without compromising the logical sequence. A similar green box will tell you when to rejoin.

To prove the polynomial bound, we will introduce a combinatorial quantity that counts the maximum number of dichotomies given that there is a break point, without having to assume any particular form of $\mathcal{H}$. This bound will therefore apply to any $\mathcal{H}$.

Definition 2.4. $B(N, k)$ *is the maximum number of dichotomies on N points such that no subset of size k of the N points can be shattered by these dichotomies.*

The definition of $B(N, k)$ assumes a break point k, then tries to find the most dichotomies on N points without imposing any further restrictions. Since $B(N, k)$ is defined as a maximum, it will serve as an upper bound for any $m_{\mathcal{H}}(N)$ that has a break point k;

$$m_{\mathcal{H}}(N) \le B(N, k) \quad \text{if } k \text{ is a break point for } \mathcal{H}.$$

The notation B comes from 'Binomial' and the reason will become clear shortly. To evaluate $B(N, k)$, we start with the two boundary conditions $k = 1$ and $N = 1$.

$$
\begin{aligned}
B(N, 1) &= 1 \\
B(1, k) &= 2 \text{ for } k > 1 .
\end{aligned}
$$

$B(N, 1) = 1$ for all N since if no subset of size 1 can be shattered, then only one dichotomy can be allowed. A second different dichotomy must differ on at least one point and then that subset of size 1 would be shattered. $B(1, k) = 2$ for $k > 1$ since in this case there do not even exist subsets of size k; the constraint is vacuously true and we have 2 possible dichotomies ($+1$ and -1) on the one point.

We now assume $N \geq 2$ and $k \geq 2$ and try to develop a recursion. Consider the $B(N, k)$ dichotomies in definition 2.4, where no k points can be shattered. We list these dichotomies in the following table,

		# of rows	$\mathbf{x}_1$	$\mathbf{x}_2$	$\dots$	$\mathbf{x}_{N-1}$	$\mathbf{x}_N$
			$+1$	$+1$	$\dots$	$+1$	$+1$
			-1	$+1$	$\dots$	$+1$	-1
	S_1	α	$\vdots$	$\vdots$	$\vdots$	$\vdots$	$\vdots$
			$+1$	-1	$\dots$	-1	-1
			-1	$+1$	$\dots$	-1	$+1$
			$+1$	-1	$\dots$	$+1$	$+1$
			-1	-1	$\dots$	$+1$	$+1$
	S_2^+	β	$\vdots$	$\vdots$	$\vdots$	$\vdots$	$\vdots$
			$+1$	-1	$\dots$	$+1$	$+1$
S_2			-1	-1	$\dots$	-1	$+1$
			$+1$	-1	$\dots$	$+1$	-1
			-1	-1	$\dots$	$+1$	-1
	S_2^-	β	$\vdots$	$\vdots$	$\vdots$	$\vdots$	$\vdots$
			$+1$	-1	$\dots$	$+1$	-1
			-1	-1	$\dots$	-1	-1

where $\mathbf{x}_1, \cdots, \mathbf{x}_N$ in the table are labels for the N points of the dichotomy. We have chosen a convenient order in which to list the dichotomies, as follows. Consider the dichotomies on $\mathbf{x}_1, \cdots, \mathbf{x}_{N-1}$. Some dichotomies on these $N - 1$ points appear only once (with either $+1$ or -1 in the $\mathbf{x}_N$ column, but not both). We collect these dichotomies in the set S_1. The remaining dichotomies on the first $N - 1$ points appear twice, once with $+1$ and once with -1 in the $\mathbf{x}_N$ column. We collect these dichotomies in the set S_2 which can be divided into two equal parts, S_2^+ and S_2^- (with $+1$ and -1 in the $\mathbf{x}_N$ column, respectively). Let S_1 have α rows, and let S_2^+ and S_2^- have β rows each. Since the total number of rows in the table is $B(N, k)$ by construction, we have

$$B(N, k) = \alpha + 2\beta. \qquad (2.4)$$

The total number of different dichotomies on the first $N - 1$ points is given by $\alpha + \beta$; since S_2^+ and S_2^- are identical on these $N - 1$ points, their dichotomies are redundant. Since no subset of k of these first $N - 1$ points can be shattered (since no k-subset of all N points can be shattered), we deduce that

$$\alpha + \beta \le B(N-1, k) \tag{2.5}$$

by definition of B. Further, no subset of size $k-1$ of the first $N-1$ points can be shattered by the dichotomies in S_2^+. If there existed such a subset, then taking the corresponding set of dichotomies in S_2^- and adding $\mathbf{x}_N$ to the data points yields a subset of size k that is shattered, which we know cannot exist in this table by definition of $B(N, k)$. Therefore,

$$\beta \le B(N-1, k-1). \tag{2.6}$$

Substituting the two Inequalities (2.5) and (2.6) into (2.4), we get

$$B(N, k) \le B(N-1, k) + B(N-1, k-1). \tag{2.7}$$

We can use (2.7) to recursively compute a bound on $B(N, k)$, as shown in the following table.

		\multicolumn{6}{c}{k}
		1	2	3	4	5	6	...
	1	1	2	2	2	2	2	...
	2	1	3	4	4	4	4	...
	3	1	4	7	8	8	8	...
N	4	1	5	11	...	...	...	...
	5	1	6	:			
	6	1	7	:			
	:	:	:	:			

where the first row ($N = 1$) and the first column ($k = 1$) are the boundary conditions that we already calculated. We can also use the recursion to bound $B(N, k)$ analytically.

Lemma 2.3 (Sauer's Lemma).

$$B(N, k) \le \sum_{i=0}^{k-1} \binom{N}{i}$$

Proof. The statement is true whenever $k = 1$ or $N = 1$, by inspection. The proof is by induction on N. Assume the statement is true for all $N \le N_o$ and all k. We need to prove the statement for $N = N_o + 1$ and all k. Since the statement is already true when $k = 1$ (for all values of N) by the initial condition, we only need to worry about $k \ge 2$. By (2.7),

$$B(N_o + 1, k) \le B(N_o, k) + B(N_o, k - 1).$$

48

Applying the induction hypothesis to each term on the RHS, we get

$$
\begin{aligned}
B(N_o + 1, k) &\leq \sum_{i=0}^{k-1} \binom{N_o}{i} + \sum_{i=0}^{k-2} \binom{N_o}{i} \\
&= 1 + \sum_{i=1}^{k-1} \binom{N_o}{i} + \sum_{i=1}^{k-1} \binom{N_o}{i-1} \\
&= 1 + \sum_{i=1}^{k-1} \left[\binom{N_o}{i} + \binom{N_o}{i-1} \right] \\
&= 1 + \sum_{i=1}^{k-1} \binom{N_o + 1}{i} = \sum_{i=0}^{k-1} \binom{N_o + 1}{i},
\end{aligned}
$$

where the combinatorial identity $\binom{N_o+1}{i} = \binom{N_o}{i} + \binom{N_o}{i-1}$ has been used. This identity can be proved by noticing that to calculate the number of ways to pick i objects from $N_o + 1$ distinct objects, either the first object is included, in $\binom{N_o}{i-1}$ ways, or the first object is not included, in $\binom{N_o}{i}$ ways. We have thus proved the induction step, so the statement is true for all N and k.   ∎

It turns out that $B(N, k)$ in fact equals $\sum_{i=0}^{k-1} \binom{N}{i}$ (see Problem 2.4), but we only need the inequality of Lemma 2.3 to bound the growth function. For a given break point k, the bound $\sum_{i=0}^{k-1} \binom{N}{i}$ is polynomial in N, as each term in the sum is polynomial (of degree $i \leq k - 1$). Since $B(N, k)$ is an upper bound on any $m_{\mathcal{H}}(N)$ that has a break point k, we have proved

> **End safe skip:** Those who skipped are now rejoining us. The next theorem states that any growth function $m_{\mathcal{H}}(N)$ with a break point is bounded by a polynomial.

Theorem 2.4. If $m_{\mathcal{H}}(k) < 2^k$ for some value k, then

$$
m_{\mathcal{H}}(N) \leq \sum_{i=0}^{k-1} \binom{N}{i} \tag{2.8}
$$

for all N. The RHS is polynomial in N of degree $k - 1$.

The implication of Theorem 2.4 is that if $\mathcal{H}$ has a break point, we have what we want to ensure good generalization; a polynomial bound on $m_{\mathcal{H}}(N)$.

Exercise 2.2

(a) Verify the bound of Theorem 2.4 in the three cases of Example 2.2:

  (i) Positive rays: $\mathcal{H}$ consists of all hypotheses in one dimension of the form $h(x) = \text{sign}(x - a)$.

  (ii) Positive intervals: $\mathcal{H}$ consists of all hypotheses in one dimension that are positive within some interval and negative elsewhere.

  (iii) Convex sets: $\mathcal{H}$ consists of all hypotheses in two dimensions that are positive inside some convex set and negative elsewhere.

  (Note: you can use the break points you found in Exercise 2.1.)

(b) Does there exist a hypothesis set for which $m_{\mathcal{H}}(N) = N + 2^{\lfloor N/2 \rfloor}$ (where $\lfloor N/2 \rfloor$ is the largest integer $\leq N/2$)?

2.1.3 The VC Dimension

Theorem 2.4 bounds the entire growth function in terms of any break point. The smaller the break point, the better the bound. This leads us to the following definition of a single parameter that characterizes the growth function.

Definition 2.5. *The Vapnik-Chervonenkis dimension of a hypothesis set $\mathcal{H}$, denoted by $d_{\text{vc}}(\mathcal{H})$ or simply d_{vc}, is the largest value of N for which $m_{\mathcal{H}}(N) = 2^N$. If $m_{\mathcal{H}}(N) = 2^N$ for all N, then $d_{\text{vc}}(\mathcal{H}) = \infty$.*

If d_{vc} is the VC dimension of $\mathcal{H}$, then $k = d_{\text{vc}} + 1$ is a break point for $m_{\mathcal{H}}$ since $m_{\mathcal{H}}(N)$ cannot equal 2^N for any $N > d_{\text{vc}}$ by definition. It is easy to see that no smaller break point exists since $\mathcal{H}$ can shatter d_{vc} points, hence it can also shatter any subset of these points.

Exercise 2.3

Compute the VC dimension of $\mathcal{H}$ for the hypothesis sets in parts (i), (ii), (iii) of Exercise 2.2(a).

Since $k = d_{\text{vc}} + 1$ is a break point for $m_{\mathcal{H}}$, Theorem 2.4 can be rewritten in terms of the VC dimension:

$$m_{\mathcal{H}}(N) \leq \sum_{i=0}^{d_{\text{vc}}} \binom{N}{i}. \tag{2.9}$$

Therefore, the VC dimension is the order of the polynomial bound on $m_{\mathcal{H}}(N)$. It is also the best we can do using this line of reasoning, because no smaller break point than $k = d_{\text{vc}} + 1$ exists. The form of the polynomial bound can be further simplified to make the dependency on d_{vc} more salient. We state a useful form here, which can be proved by induction (Problem 2.5).

$$m_{\mathcal{H}}(N) \leq N^{d_{\text{vc}}} + 1. \tag{2.10}$$

Now that the growth function has been bounded in terms of the VC dimension, we have only one more step left in our analysis, which is to replace the number of hypotheses M in the generalization bound (2.1) with the growth function $m_{\mathcal{H}}(N)$. If we manage to do that, the VC dimension will play a pivotal role in the generalization question. If we were to directly replace M by $m_{\mathcal{H}}(N)$ in (2.1), we would get a bound of the form

$$E_{\text{out}} \overset{?}{\leq} E_{\text{in}} + \sqrt{\frac{1}{2N} \ln \frac{2m_{\mathcal{H}}(N)}{\delta}} \; .$$

Unless $d_{\text{vc}}(\mathcal{H}) = \infty$, we know that $m_{\mathcal{H}}(N)$ is bounded by a polynomial in N; thus, $\ln m_{\mathcal{H}}(N)$ grows logarithmically in N regardless of the order of the polynomial, and so it will be crushed by the $\frac{1}{N}$ factor. Therefore, for any fixed tolerance δ, the bound on E_{out} will be arbitrarily close to E_{in} for sufficiently large N.

Only if $d_{\text{vc}}(\mathcal{H}) = \infty$ will this argument fail, as the growth function in this case is exponential in N. For any finite value of d_{vc}, the error bar will converge to zero at a speed determined by d_{vc}, since d_{vc} is the order of the polynomial. The smaller d_{vc} is, the faster the convergence to zero.

It turns out that we cannot just replace M with $m_{\mathcal{H}}(N)$ in the generalization bound (2.1), but rather we need to make other adjustments as we will see shortly. However, the general idea above is correct, and d_{vc} will still play the role that we discussed here. One implication of this discussion is that there is a division of models into two classes. The 'good models' have finite d_{vc}, and for sufficiently large N, E_{in} will be close to E_{out}; for good models, the in-sample performance generalizes to out of sample. The 'bad models' have infinite d_{vc}. With a bad model, no matter how large the data set is, we cannot make generalization conclusions from E_{in} to E_{out} based on the VC analysis.[2]

Because of its significant role, it is worthwhile to try to gain some insight about the VC dimension before we proceed to the formalities of deriving the new generalization bound. One way to gain insight about d_{vc} is to try to compute it for learning models that we are familiar with. Perceptrons are one case where we can compute d_{vc} exactly. This is done in two steps. First, we show that d_{vc} is at least a certain value, then we show that it is at most the same value. There is a logical difference in arguing that d_{vc} is at least a certain value, as opposed to at most a certain value. This is because

$$d_{\text{vc}} \geq N \iff \text{ there } \textbf{exists } \mathcal{D} \text{ of size } N \text{ such that } \mathcal{H} \text{ shatters } \mathcal{D},$$

hence we have different conclusions in the following cases.

1. There is a set of N points that can be shattered by $\mathcal{H}$. In this case, we can conclude that $d_{\text{vc}} \geq N$.

---

[2]In some cases with infinite d_{vc}, such as the convex sets that we discussed, alternative analysis based on an 'average' growth function can establish good generalization behavior.

2. Any set of N points can be shattered by $\mathcal{H}$. In this case, we have more than enough information to conclude that $d_{\text{vc}} \geq N$.

3. There is a set of N points that cannot be shattered by $\mathcal{H}$. Based only on this information, we cannot conclude anything about the value of d_{vc}.

4. No set of N points can be shattered by $\mathcal{H}$. In this case, we can conclude that $d_{\text{vc}} < N$.

Exercise 2.4

Consider the input space $\mathcal{X} = \{1\} \times \mathbb{R}^d$ (including the constant coordinate $x_0 = 1$). Show that the VC dimension of the perceptron (with $d + 1$ parameters, counting w_0) is exactly $d + 1$ by showing that it is at least $d + 1$ and at most $d + 1$, as follows.

(a) To show that $d_{\text{vc}} \geq d + 1$, find $d + 1$ points in $\mathcal{X}$ that the perceptron can shatter. *[Hint: Construct a nonsingular $(d + 1) \times (d + 1)$ matrix whose rows represent the $d + 1$ points, then use the nonsingularity to argue that the perceptron can shatter these points.]*

(b) To show that $d_{\text{vc}} \leq d + 1$, show that no set of $d + 2$ points in $\mathcal{X}$ can be shattered by the perceptron. *[Hint: Represent each point in $\mathcal{X}$ as a vector of length $d + 1$, then use the fact that any $d + 2$ vectors of length $d + 1$ have to be linearly dependent. This means that some vector is a linear combination of all the other vectors. Now, if you choose the class of these other vectors carefully, then the classification of the dependent vector will be dictated. Conclude that there is some dichotomy that cannot be implemented, and therefore that for $N \geq d + 2$, $m_{\mathcal{H}}(N) < 2^N$.]*

The VC dimension of a d-dimensional perceptron[3] is indeed $d + 1$. This is consistent with Figure 2.1 for the case $d = 2$, which shows a VC dimension of 3. The perceptron case provides a nice intuition about the VC dimension, since $d + 1$ is also the number of parameters in this model. One can view the VC dimension as measuring the 'effective' number of parameters. The more parameters a model has, the more diverse its hypothesis set is, which is reflected in a larger value of the growth function $m_{\mathcal{H}}(N)$. In the case of perceptrons, the effective parameters correspond to explicit parameters in the model, namely $w_0, w_1, \cdots, w_d$. In other models, the effective parameters may be less obvious or implicit. The VC dimension measures these effective parameters or 'degrees of freedom' that enable the model to express a diverse set of hypotheses.

Diversity is not necessarily a good thing in the context of generalization. For example, the set of all possible hypotheses is as diverse as can be, so $m_{\mathcal{H}}(N) = 2^N$ for all N and $d_{\text{vc}}(\mathcal{H}) = \infty$. In this case, no generalization at all is to be expected, as the final version of the generalization bound will show.

---

[3] $\mathcal{X} = \{1\} \times \mathbb{R}^d$ is considered d-dimensional since the first coordinate $x_0 = 1$ is fixed.

2.1.4   The VC Generalization Bound

If we treated the growth function as an effective number of hypotheses, and replaced M in the generalization bound (2.1) with $m_{\mathcal{H}}(N)$, the resulting bound would be

$$E_{\text{out}}(g) \overset{?}{\leq} E_{\text{in}}(g) + \sqrt{\frac{1}{2N} \ln \frac{2m_{\mathcal{H}}(N)}{\delta}}. \tag{2.11}$$

It turns out that this is not exactly the form that will hold. The quantities in red need to be technically modified to make (2.11) true. The correct bound, which is called the VC generalization bound, is given in the following theorem; it holds for any binary target function f, any hypothesis set $\mathcal{H}$, any learning algorithm $\mathcal{A}$, and any input probability distribution P.

Theorem 2.5 (VC generalization bound). For any tolerance $\delta > 0$,

$$E_{\text{out}}(g) \leq E_{\text{in}}(g) + \sqrt{\frac{8}{N} \ln \frac{4m_{\mathcal{H}}(2N)}{\delta}} \tag{2.12}$$

with probability $\geq 1 - \delta$.

If you compare the blue items in (2.12) to their red counterparts in (2.11), you notice that all the blue items move the bound in the weaker direction. However, as long as the VC dimension is finite, the error bar still converges to zero (albeit at a slower rate), since $m_{\mathcal{H}}(2N)$ is also polynomial of order d_{vc} in N, just like $m_{\mathcal{H}}(N)$. This means that, with enough data, *each and every hypothesis* in an infinite $\mathcal{H}$ with a finite VC dimension will generalize well from E_{in} to E_{out}. The key is that the effective number of hypotheses, represented by the finite growth function, has replaced the actual number of hypotheses in the bound.

The VC generalization bound is the most important mathematical result in the theory of learning. It establishes the feasibility of learning with infinite hypothesis sets. Since the formal proof is somewhat lengthy and technical, we illustrate the main ideas in a sketch of the proof, and include the formal proof as an appendix. There are two parts to the proof; the justification that the growth function can replace the number of hypotheses in the first place, and the reason why we had to change the red items in (2.11) into the blue items in (2.12).

Sketch of the proof.   The data set $\mathcal{D}$ is the source of randomization in the original Hoeffding Inequality. Consider the space of all possible data sets. Let us think of this space as a 'canvas' (Figure 2.2(a)). Each $\mathcal{D}$ is a point on that canvas. The probability of a point is determined by which $\mathbf{x}_n$'s in $\mathcal{X}$ happen to be in that particular $\mathcal{D}$, and is calculated based on the distribution P over $\mathcal{X}$. Let's think of probabilities of different events as areas on that canvas, so the total area of the canvas is 1.

53

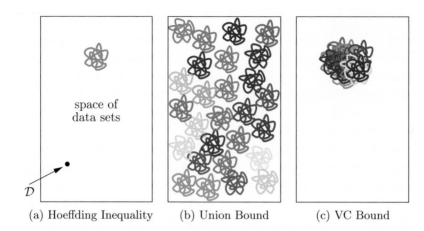

(a) Hoeffding Inequality   (b) Union Bound   (c) VC Bound

Figure 2.2: Illustration of the proof of the VC bound, where the 'canvas' represents the space of all data sets, with areas corresponding to probabilities. (a) For a given hypothesis, the colored points correspond to data sets where E_{in} does not generalize well to E_{out}. The Hoeffding Inequality guarantees a small colored area. (b) For several hypotheses, the union bound assumes no overlaps, so the total colored area is large. (c) The VC bound keeps track of overlaps, so it estimates the total area of bad generalization to be relatively small.

For a given hypothesis $h \in \mathcal{H}$, the event "$|E_{in}(h) - E_{out}(h)| > \epsilon$" consists of all points $\mathcal{D}$ for which the statement is true. For a particular h, let us paint all these 'bad' points using one color. What the basic Hoeffding Inequality tells us is that the colored area on the canvas will be small (Figure 2.2(a)).

Now, if we take another $h \in \mathcal{H}$, the event "$|E_{in}(h) - E_{out}(h)| > \epsilon$" may contain different points, since the event depends on h. Let us paint these points with a different color. The area covered by all the points we colored will be at most the sum of the two individual areas, which is the case only if the two areas have no points in common. This is the worst case that the union bound considers. If we keep throwing in a new colored area for each $h \in \mathcal{H}$, and never overlap with previous colors, the canvas will soon be mostly covered in color (Figure 2.2(b)). Even if each h contributed very little, the sheer number of hypotheses will eventually make the colored area cover the whole canvas. This was the problem with using the union bound in the Hoeffding Inequality (1.6), and not taking the overlaps of the colored areas into consideration.

The bulk of the VC proof deals with how to account for the overlaps. Here is the idea. If you were told that the hypotheses in $\mathcal{H}$ are such that each point on the canvas that is colored will be colored 100 times (because of 100 different h's), then the total colored area is now $1/100$ of what it would have been if the colored points had not overlapped at all. This is the essence of the VC bound as illustrated in (Figure 2.2(c)). The argument goes as follows.

Many hypotheses share the same dichotomy on a given $\mathcal{D}$, since there are finitely many dichotomies even with an infinite number of hypotheses. Any statement based on $\mathcal{D}$ alone will be simultaneously true or simultaneously false for all the hypotheses that look the same on that particular $\mathcal{D}$. What the growth function enables us to do is to account for this kind of hypothesis redundancy in a precise way, so we can get a factor similar to the '100' in the above example.

When $\mathcal{H}$ is infinite, the redundancy factor will also be infinite since the hypotheses will be divided among a finite number of dichotomies. Therefore, the reduction in the total colored area when we take the redundancy into consideration will be dramatic. If it happens that the number of dichotomies is only a polynomial, the reduction will be so dramatic as to bring the total probability down to a very small value. This is the essence of the proof of Theorem 2.5.

The reason $m_{\mathcal{H}}(2N)$ appears in the VC bound instead of $m_{\mathcal{H}}(N)$ is that the proof uses a sample of $2N$ points instead of N points. Why do we need $2N$ points? The event "$|E_{\text{in}}(h) - E_{\text{out}}(h)| > \epsilon$" depends not only on $\mathcal{D}$, but also on the entire $\mathcal{X}$ because $E_{\text{out}}(h)$ is based on $\mathcal{X}$. This breaks the main premise of grouping h's based on their behavior on $\mathcal{D}$, since aspects of each h outside of $\mathcal{D}$ affect the truth of "$|E_{\text{in}}(h) - E_{\text{out}}(h)| > \epsilon$." To remedy that, we consider the artificial event "$|E_{\text{in}}(h) - E'_{\text{in}}(h)| > \epsilon$" instead, where E_{in} and E'_{in} are based on two samples $\mathcal{D}$ and $\mathcal{D}'$ each of size N. This is where the $2N$ comes from. It accounts for the total size of the two samples $\mathcal{D}$ and $\mathcal{D}'$. Now, the truth of the statement "$|E_{\text{in}}(h) - E'_{\text{in}}(h)| > \epsilon$" depends exclusively on the total sample of size $2N$, and the above redundancy argument will hold.

Of course we have to justify why the two-sample condition "$|E_{\text{in}}(h) - E'_{\text{in}}(h)| > \epsilon$" can replace the original condition "$|E_{\text{in}}(h) - E_{\text{out}}(h)| > \epsilon$." In doing so, we end up having to shrink the ϵ's by a factor of 4, and also end up with a factor of 2 in the estimate of the overall probability. This accounts for the $\frac{8}{N}$ instead of $\frac{1}{2N}$ in the VC bound and for having 4 instead of 2 as the multiplicative factor of the growth function. When you put all this together, you get the formula in (2.12). $\square$

2.2 Interpreting the Generalization Bound

The VC generalization bound (2.12) is a universal result in the sense that it applies to all hypothesis sets, learning algorithms, input spaces, probability distributions, and binary target functions. It can be extended to other types of target functions as well. Given the generality of the result, one would suspect that the bound it provides may not be particularly tight in any given case, since the same bound has to cover a lot of different cases. Indeed, the bound is quite loose.

Exercise 2.5

Suppose we have a simple learning model whose growth function is $m_{\mathcal{H}}(N) = N + 1$, hence $d_{\mathrm{vc}} = 1$. Use the VC bound (2.12) to estimate the probability that E_{out} will be within 0.1 of E_{in} given 100 training examples. *[Hint: The estimate will be ridiculous.]*

Why is the VC bound so loose? The slack in the bound can be attributed to a number of technical factors. Among them,

1. The basic Hoeffding Inequality used in the proof already has a slack. The inequality gives the same bound whether E_{out} is close to 0.5 or close to zero. However, the variance of E_{in} is quite different in these two cases. Therefore, having one bound capture both cases will result in some slack.

2. Using $m_{\mathcal{H}}(N)$ to quantify the number of dichotomies on N points, regardless of which N points are in the data set, gives us a worst-case estimate. This does allow the bound to be independent of the probability distribution P over $\mathcal{X}$. However, we would get a more tuned bound if we considered specific $\mathbf{x}_1, \cdots, \mathbf{x}_N$ and used $|\mathcal{H}(\mathbf{x}_1, \cdots, \mathbf{x}_N)|$ or its expected value instead of the upper bound $m_{\mathcal{H}}(N)$. For instance, in the case of convex sets in two dimensions, which we examined in Example 2.2, if you pick N points at random in the plane, they will likely have far fewer dichotomies than 2^N, while $m_{\mathcal{H}}(N) = 2^N$.

3. Bounding $m_{\mathcal{H}}(N)$ by a simple polynomial of order d_{vc}, as given in (2.10), will contribute further slack to the VC bound.

Some effort could be put into tightening the VC bound, but many highly technical attempts in the literature have resulted in only diminishing returns. The reality is that the VC line of analysis leads to a very loose bound. Why did we bother to go through the analysis then? Two reasons. First, the VC analysis is what establishes the feasibility of learning for infinite hypothesis sets, the only kind we use in practice. Second, although the bound is loose, it tends to be equally loose for different learning models, and hence is useful for comparing the generalization performance of these models. This is an observation from practical experience, not a mathematical statement. In real applications, learning models with lower d_{vc} tend to generalize better than those with higher d_{vc}. Because of this observation, the VC analysis proves useful in practice, and some rules of thumb have emerged in terms of the VC dimension. For instance, requiring that N be at least $10 \times d_{\mathrm{vc}}$ to get decent generalization is a popular rule of thumb.

Thus, the VC bound can be used as a guideline for generalization, relatively if not absolutely. With this understanding, let us look at the different ways the bound is used in practice.

2.2.1 Sample Complexity

The sample complexity denotes how many training examples N are needed to achieve a certain generalization performance. The performance is specified by two parameters, ϵ and δ. The error tolerance ϵ determines the allowed generalization error, and the confidence parameter δ determines how often the error tolerance ϵ is violated. How fast N grows as ϵ and δ become smaller[4] indicates how much data is needed to get good generalization.

We can use the VC bound to estimate the sample complexity for a given learning model. Fix $\delta > 0$, and suppose we want the generalization error to be at most ϵ. From Equation (2.12), the generalization error is bounded by $\sqrt{\frac{8}{N} \ln \frac{4m_{\mathcal{H}}(2N)}{\delta}}$, and so it suffices to make $\sqrt{\frac{8}{N} \ln \frac{4m_{\mathcal{H}}(2N)}{\delta}} \leq \epsilon$. It follows that

$$N \geq \frac{8}{\epsilon^2} \ln \left(\frac{4m_{\mathcal{H}}(2N)}{\delta} \right)$$

suffices to obtain generalization error at most ϵ (with probability at least $1-\delta$). This gives an implicit bound for the sample complexity N, since N appears on both sides of the inequality. If we replace $m_{\mathcal{H}}(2N)$ in (2.12) by its polynomial upper bound in (2.10) which is based on the the VC dimension, we get a similar bound

$$N \geq \frac{8}{\epsilon^2} \ln \left(\frac{4((2N)^{d_{\text{vc}}} + 1)}{\delta} \right), \tag{2.13}$$

which is again implicit in N. We can obtain a numerical value for N using simple iterative methods.

Example 2.6. Suppose that we have a learning model with $d_{\text{vc}} = 3$ and would like the generalization error to be at most 0.1 with confidence 90% (so $\epsilon = 0.1$ and $\delta = 0.1$). How big a data set do we need? Using (2.13), we need

$$N \geq \frac{8}{0.1^2} \ln \left(\frac{4(2N)^3 + 4}{0.1} \right).$$

Trying an initial guess of $N = 1,000$ in the RHS, we get

$$N \geq \frac{8}{0.1^2} \ln \left(\frac{4(2 \times 1000)^3 + 4}{0.1} \right) \approx 21,193.$$

We then try the new value $N = 21,193$ in the RHS and continue this iterative process, rapidly converging to an estimate of $N \approx 30,000$. If d_{vc} were 4, a similar calculation will find that $N \approx 40,000$. For $d_{\text{vc}} = 5$, we get $N \approx 50,000$. You can see that the inequality suggests that the number of examples needed is approximately proportional to the VC dimension, as has been observed in practice. The constant of proportionality it suggests is 10,000, which is a *gross* overestimate; a more practical constant of proportionality is closer to 10. □

---

[4]The term 'complexity' comes from a similar metaphor in computational complexity.

2.2.2　Penalty for Model Complexity

Sample complexity fixes the performance parameters ϵ (generalization error) and δ (confidence parameter) and estimates how many examples N are needed. In most practical situations, however, we are given a fixed data set $\mathcal{D}$, so N is also fixed. In this case, the relevant question is what performance can we expect given this particular N. The bound in (2.12) answers this question: with probability at least $1 - \delta$,

$$E_{\text{out}}(g) \leq E_{\text{in}}(g) + \sqrt{\frac{8}{N} \ln \left(\frac{4m_{\mathcal{H}}(2N)}{\delta} \right)} .$$

If we use the polynomial bound based on d_{vc} instead of $m_{\mathcal{H}}(2N)$, we get another valid bound on the out-of-sample error,

$$E_{\text{out}}(g) \leq E_{\text{in}}(g) + \sqrt{\frac{8}{N} \ln \left(\frac{4((2N)^{d_{\text{vc}}} + 1)}{\delta} \right)} . \tag{2.14}$$

Example 2.7. Suppose that $N = 100$ and we have a 90% confidence requirement ($\delta = 0.1$). We could ask what error bar can we offer with this confidence, if $\mathcal{H}$ has $d_{\text{vc}} = 1$. Using (2.14), we have

$$E_{\text{out}}(g) \leq E_{\text{in}}(g) + \sqrt{\frac{8}{100} \ln \left(\frac{4(201)}{0.1} \right)} \approx E_{\text{in}}(g) + 0.848 \tag{2.15}$$

with confidence $\geq 90\%$. This is a pretty poor bound on E_{out}. Even if $E_{\text{in}} = 0$, E_{out} may still be close to 1. If $N = 1,000$, then we get $E_{\text{out}}(g) \leq E_{\text{in}}(g) + 0.301$, a somewhat more respectable bound. □

Let us look more closely at the two parts that make up the bound on E_{out} in (2.12). The first part is E_{in}, and the second part is a term that increases as the VC dimension of $\mathcal{H}$ increases.

$$E_{\text{out}}(g) \leq E_{\text{in}}(g) + \Omega(N, \mathcal{H}, \delta), \tag{2.16}$$

where

$$\begin{aligned}
\Omega(N, \mathcal{H}, \delta) &= \sqrt{\frac{8}{N} \ln \left(\frac{4m_{\mathcal{H}}(2N)}{\delta} \right)} \\
&\leq \sqrt{\frac{8}{N} \ln \left(\frac{4((2N)^{d_{\text{vc}}} + 1)}{\delta} \right)} .
\end{aligned}$$

One way to think of $\Omega(N, \mathcal{H}, \delta)$ is that it is a penalty for model complexity. It penalizes us by worsening the bound on E_{out} when we use a more complex $\mathcal{H}$ (larger d_{vc}). If someone manages to fit a simpler model with the same training

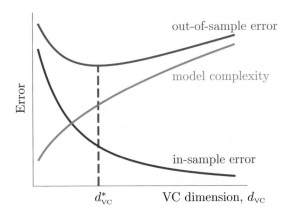

Figure 2.3: When we use a more complex learning model, one that has higher VC dimension d_{vc}, we are likely to fit the training data better resulting in a lower in-sample error, but we pay a higher penalty for model complexity. A combination of the two, which estimates the out-of-sample error, thus attains a minimum at some intermediate d_{vc}^*.

error, they will get a more favorable estimate for E_{out}. The penalty $\Omega(N, \mathcal{H}, \delta)$ gets worse if we insist on higher confidence (lower δ), and it gets better when we have more training examples, as we would expect.

Although $\Omega(N, \mathcal{H}, \delta)$ goes up when $\mathcal{H}$ has a higher VC dimension, E_{in} is likely to go down with a higher VC dimension as we have more choices within $\mathcal{H}$ to fit the data. Therefore, we have a tradeoff: more complex models help E_{in} and hurt $\Omega(N, \mathcal{H}, \delta)$. The optimal model is a compromise that minimizes a combination of the two terms, as illustrated informally in Figure 2.3.

2.2.3   The Test Set

As we have seen, the generalization bound gives us a loose estimate of the out-of-sample error E_{out} based on E_{in}. While the estimate can be useful as a guideline for the training process, it is next to useless if the goal is to get an accurate forecast of E_{out}. If you are developing a system for a customer, you need a more accurate estimate so that your customer knows how well the system is expected to perform.

An alternative approach that we alluded to in the beginning of this chapter is to estimate E_{out} by using a *test set*, a data set that was not involved in the training process. The final hypothesis g is evaluated on the test set, and the result is taken as an estimate of E_{out}. We would like to now take a closer look at this approach.

Let us call the error we get on the test set E_{test}. When we report E_{test} as our estimate of E_{out}, we are in fact asserting that E_{test} generalizes very well to E_{out}. After all, E_{test} is just a sample estimate like E_{in}. How do we know that E_{test} generalizes well? We can answer this question with authority now that we have developed the theory of generalization in concrete mathematical terms.

The effective number of hypotheses that matters in the generalization behavior of E_{test} is 1. There is only one hypothesis as far as the test set is concerned, and that's the final hypothesis g that the training phase produced. This hypothesis would not change if we used a different test set as it would if we used a different training set. Therefore, the simple Hoeffding Inequality is valid in the case of a test set. Had the choice of g been affected by the test set in any shape or form, it wouldn't be considered a *test* set any more and the simple Hoeffding Inequality would not apply.

Therefore, the generalization bound that applies to E_{test} is the simple Hoeffding Inequality with one hypothesis. This is a much tighter bound than the VC bound. For example, if you have $1,000$ data points in the test set, E_{test} will be within $\pm 5\%$ of E_{out} with probability $\geq 98\%$. The bigger the test set you use, the more accurate E_{test} will be as an estimate of E_{out}.

Exercise 2.6

A data set has 600 examples. To properly test the performance of the final hypothesis, you set aside a randomly selected subset of 200 examples which are never used in the training phase; these form a test set. You use a learning model with $1,000$ hypotheses and select the final hypothesis g based on the 400 training examples. We wish to estimate $E_{\text{out}}(g)$. We have access to two estimates: $E_{\text{in}}(g)$, the in-sample error on the 400 training examples; and, $E_{\text{test}}(g)$, the test error on the 200 test examples that were set aside.

(a) Using a 5% error tolerance ($\delta = 0.05$), which estimate has the higher 'error bar'?

(b) Is there any reason why you shouldn't reserve even more examples for testing?

Another aspect that distinguishes the test set from the training set is that the test set is not biased. Both sets are finite samples that are bound to have some variance due to sample size, but the test set doesn't have an optimistic or pessimistic bias in its estimate of E_{out}. The training set has an optimistic bias, since it was used to choose a hypothesis that looked good *on it*. The VC generalization bound implicitly takes that bias into consideration, and that's why it gives a huge error bar. The test set just has straight finite-sample variance, but no bias. When you report the value of E_{test} to your customer and they try your system on new data, they are as likely to be pleasantly surprised as unpleasantly surprised, though quite likely not to be surprised at all.

There is a price to be paid for having a test set. The test set does not affect the outcome of our learning process, which only uses the training set. The test set just tells us how well we did. Therefore, if we set aside some of the data points provided by the customer as a test set, we end up using fewer examples for training. Since the training set is used to select one of the hypotheses in $\mathcal{H}$, training examples are essential to finding a good hypothesis. If we take a big chunk of the data for testing and end up with too few examples for training, we may not get a good hypothesis from the training part even if we can reliably evaluate it in the testing part. We may end up reporting to the customer, with high confidence mind you, that the g we are delivering is terrible ☺. There is thus a tradeoff to setting aside test examples. We will address that tradeoff in more detail and learn some clever tricks to get around it in Chapter 4.

In some of the learning literature, E_{test} is used as synonymous with E_{out}. When we report experimental results in this book, we will often treat E_{test} based on a large test set as if it was E_{out} because of the closeness of the two quantities.

2.2.4 Other Target Types

Although the VC analysis was based on binary target functions, it can be extended to real-valued functions, as well as to other types of functions. The proofs in those cases are quite technical, and they do not add to the insight that the VC analysis of binary functions provides. Therefore, we will introduce an alternative approach that covers real-valued functions and provides new insights into generalization. The approach is based on bias-variance analysis, and will be discussed in the next section.

In order to deal with real-valued functions, we need to adapt the definitions of E_{in} and E_{out} that have so far been based on binary functions. We defined E_{in} and E_{out} in terms of binary error; either $h(\mathbf{x}) = f(\mathbf{x})$ or else $h(\mathbf{x}) \neq f(\mathbf{x})$. If f and h are real-valued, a more appropriate error measure would gauge how far $f(\mathbf{x})$ and $h(\mathbf{x})$ are from each other, rather than just whether their values are exactly the same.

An error measure that is commonly used in this case is the squared error $\mathrm{e}(h(\mathbf{x}), f(\mathbf{x})) = (h(\mathbf{x}) - f(\mathbf{x}))^2$. We can define in-sample and out-of-sample versions of this error measure. The out-of-sample error is based on the expected value of the error measure over the entire input space $\mathcal{X}$,

$$E_{\text{out}}(h) = \mathbb{E}\left[(h(\mathbf{x}) - f(\mathbf{x}))^2\right],$$

while the in-sample error is based on averaging the error measure over the data set,

$$E_{\text{in}}(h) = \frac{1}{N} \sum_{n=1}^{N} (h(\mathbf{x}_n) - f(\mathbf{x}_n))^2.$$

These definitions make E_{in} a sample estimate of E_{out} just as it was in the case of binary functions. In fact, the error measure used for binary functions can also be expressed as a squared error.

Exercise 2.7

For binary target functions, show that $\mathbb{P}[h(\mathbf{x}) \neq f(\mathbf{x})]$ can be written as an expected value of a mean-squared error measure in the following cases.

(a) The convention used for the binary function is 0 or 1.

(b) The convention used for the binary function is ± 1.

[Hint: The difference between (a) and (b) is just a scale.]

Just as the sample frequency of error converges to the overall probability of error per Hoeffding's Inequality, the sample average of squared error converges to the expected value of that error (assuming finite variance). This is a manifestation of what is referred to as the 'law of large numbers' and Hoeffding's Inequality is just one form of that law. The same issues of the data set size and the hypothesis set complexity come into play just as they did in the VC analysis.

2.3 Approximation-Generalization Tradeoff

The VC analysis showed us that the choice of $\mathcal{H}$ needs to strike a balance between approximating f on the training data and generalizing on new data. The ideal $\mathcal{H}$ is a singleton hypothesis set containing only the target function. Unfortunately, we are better off buying a lottery ticket than hoping to have this $\mathcal{H}$. Since we do not know the target function, we resort to a larger model hoping that it will contain a good hypothesis, and hoping that the data will pin down that hypothesis. When you select your hypothesis set, you should balance these two conflicting goals; to have some hypothesis in $\mathcal{H}$ that can approximate f, and to enable the data to zoom in on the right hypothesis.

The VC generalization bound is one way to look at this tradeoff. If $\mathcal{H}$ is too simple, we may fail to approximate f well and end up with a large in-sample error term. If $\mathcal{H}$ is too complex, we may fail to generalize well because of the large model complexity term. There is another way to look at the approximation-generalization tradeoff which we will present in this section. It is particularly suited for squared error measures, rather than the binary error used in the VC analysis. The new way provides a different angle; instead of bounding E_{out} by E_{in} plus a penalty term Ω, we will decompose E_{out} into two different error terms.

2.3.1 Bias and Variance

The bias-variance decomposition of out-of-sample error is based on squared error measures. The out-of-sample error is

$$E_{\text{out}}(g^{(\mathcal{D})}) = \mathbb{E}_{\mathbf{x}}\left[(g^{(\mathcal{D})}(\mathbf{x}) - f(\mathbf{x}))^2\right], \tag{2.17}$$

where $\mathbb{E}_\mathbf{x}$ denotes the expected value with respect to $\mathbf{x}$ (based on the probability distribution on the input space $\mathcal{X}$). We have made explicit the dependence of the final hypothesis g on the data $\mathcal{D}$, as this will play a key role in the current analysis. We can rid Equation (2.17) of the dependence on a particular data set by taking the expectation with respect to all data sets. We then get the expected out-of-sample error for our learning model, independent of any particular realization of the data set,

$$
\begin{aligned}
\mathbb{E}_\mathcal{D}\left[E_{\text{out}}(g^{(\mathcal{D})})\right] &= \mathbb{E}_\mathcal{D}\left[\mathbb{E}_\mathbf{x}[(g^{(\mathcal{D})}(\mathbf{x}) - f(\mathbf{x}))^2]\right] \\
&= \mathbb{E}_\mathbf{x}\left[\mathbb{E}_\mathcal{D}[(g^{(\mathcal{D})}(\mathbf{x}) - f(\mathbf{x}))^2]\right] \\
&= \mathbb{E}_\mathbf{x}\left[\mathbb{E}_\mathcal{D}[g^{(\mathcal{D})}(\mathbf{x})^2] - 2\,\mathbb{E}_\mathcal{D}\,[g^{(\mathcal{D})}(\mathbf{x})]f(\mathbf{x}) + f(\mathbf{x})^2\right].
\end{aligned}
$$

The term $\mathbb{E}_\mathcal{D}[g^{(\mathcal{D})}(\mathbf{x})]$ gives an 'average function', which we denote by $\bar{g}(\mathbf{x})$. One can interpret $\bar{g}(\mathbf{x})$ in the following operational way. Generate many data sets $\mathcal{D}_1, \ldots, \mathcal{D}_K$ and apply the learning algorithm to each data set to produce final hypotheses $g_1, \ldots, g_K$. We can then estimate the average function for any $\mathbf{x}$ by $\bar{g}(\mathbf{x}) \approx \frac{1}{K}\sum_{k=1}^{K} g_k(\mathbf{x})$. Essentially, we are viewing $g(\mathbf{x})$ as a random variable, with the randomness coming from the randomness in the data set; $\bar{g}(\mathbf{x})$ is the expected value of this random variable (for a particular $\mathbf{x}$), and $\bar{g}$ is a *function*, the average function, composed of these expected values. The function $\bar{g}$ is a little counterintuitive; for one thing, $\bar{g}$ need not be in the model's hypothesis set, even though it is the average of functions that are.

> **Exercise 2.8**
>
> (a) Show that if $\mathcal{H}$ is closed under linear combination (any linear combination of hypotheses in $\mathcal{H}$ is also a hypothesis in $\mathcal{H}$), then $\bar{g} \in \mathcal{H}$.
>
> (b) Give a model for which the average function $\bar{g}$ is not in the model's hypothesis set. [Hint: Use a very simple model.]
>
> (c) For binary classification, do you expect $\bar{g}$ to be a binary function?

We can now rewrite the expected out-of-sample error in terms of $\bar{g}$:

$$
\begin{aligned}
&\mathbb{E}_\mathcal{D}[E_{\text{out}}(g^{(\mathcal{D})})] \\
&= \mathbb{E}_\mathbf{x}\left[\mathbb{E}_\mathcal{D}[g^{(\mathcal{D})}(\mathbf{x})^2] - 2\bar{g}(\mathbf{x})f(\mathbf{x}) + f(\mathbf{x})^2\right], \\
&= \mathbb{E}_\mathbf{x}\Big[\underbrace{\mathbb{E}_\mathcal{D}[g^{(\mathcal{D})}(\mathbf{x})^2] - \bar{g}(\mathbf{x})^2}_{\mathbb{E}_\mathcal{D}\left[(g^{(\mathcal{D})}(\mathbf{x}) - \bar{g}(\mathbf{x}))^2\right]} + \underbrace{\bar{g}(\mathbf{x})^2 - 2\bar{g}(\mathbf{x})f(\mathbf{x}) + f(\mathbf{x})^2}_{(\bar{g}(\mathbf{x}) - f(\mathbf{x}))^2}\Big],
\end{aligned}
$$

where the last reduction follows since $\bar{g}(\mathbf{x})$ is constant with respect to $\mathcal{D}$. The term $(\bar{g}(\mathbf{x}) - f(\mathbf{x}))^2$ measures how much the average function that we would learn using different data sets $\mathcal{D}$ deviates from the target function that generated these data sets. This term is appropriately called the **bias**:

$$
\text{bias}(\mathbf{x}) = (\bar{g}(\mathbf{x}) - f(\mathbf{x}))^2,
$$

as it measures how much our learning model is biased away from the target function.[5] This is because $\bar{g}$ has the benefit of learning from an unlimited number of data sets, so it is only limited in its ability to approximate f by the limitation in the learning model itself. The term $\mathbb{E}_{\mathcal{D}}\left[(g^{(\mathcal{D})}(\mathbf{x}) - \bar{g}(\mathbf{x}))^2\right]$ is the variance of the random variable $g^{(\mathcal{D})}(\mathbf{x})$,

$$\text{var}(\mathbf{x}) = \mathbb{E}_{\mathcal{D}}[(g^{(\mathcal{D})}(\mathbf{x}) - \bar{g}(\mathbf{x}))^2],$$

which measures the variation in the final hypothesis, depending on the data set. We thus arrive at the bias-variance decomposition of out-of-sample error,

$$\begin{aligned}
\mathbb{E}_{\mathcal{D}}[E_{\text{out}}(g^{(\mathcal{D})})] &= \mathbb{E}_{\mathbf{x}}[\text{bias}(\mathbf{x}) + \text{var}(\mathbf{x})] \\
&= \text{bias} + \text{var},
\end{aligned}$$

where $\text{bias} = \mathbb{E}_{\mathbf{x}}[\text{bias}(\mathbf{x})]$ and $\text{var} = \mathbb{E}_{\mathbf{x}}[\text{var}(\mathbf{x})]$. Our derivation assumed that the data was noiseless. A similar derivation with noise in the data would lead to an additional noise term in the out-of-sample error (Problem 2.22). The noise term is unavoidable no matter what we do, so the terms we are interested in are really the bias and var.

The approximation-generalization tradeoff is captured in the bias-variance decomposition. To illustrate, let's consider two extreme cases: a very small model (with one hypothesis) and a very large one with all hypotheses.

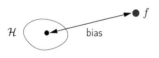   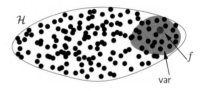

Very small model. Since there is only one hypothesis, both the average function $\bar{g}$ and the final hypothesis $g^{(\mathcal{D})}$ will be the same, for any data set. Thus, var $= 0$. The bias will depend solely on how well this single hypothesis approximates the target f, and unless we are extremely lucky, we expect a large bias.

Very large model. The target function is in $\mathcal{H}$. Different data sets will lead to different hypotheses that agree with f on the data set, and are spread around f in the red region. Thus, bias ≈ 0 because $\bar{g}$ is likely to be close to f. The var is large (heuristically represented by the size of the red region in the figure).

One can also view the variance as a measure of 'instability' in the learning model. Instability manifests in wild reactions to small variations or idiosyncrasies in the data, resulting in vastly different hypotheses.

---

[5]What we call bias is sometimes called bias^2 in the literature.

Example 2.8. Consider a target function $f(x) = \sin(\pi x)$ and a data set of size $N = 2$. We sample x uniformly in $[-1, 1]$ to generate a data set $(x_1, y_1), (x_2, y_2)$; and fit the data using one of two models:

$$\mathcal{H}_0: \quad \text{Set of all lines of the form } h(x) = b;$$
$$\mathcal{H}_1: \quad \text{Set of all lines of the form } h(x) = ax + b.$$

For $\mathcal{H}_0$, we choose the constant hypothesis that best fits the data (the horizontal line at the midpoint, $b = \frac{y_1 + y_2}{2}$). For $\mathcal{H}_1$, we choose the line that passes through the two data points (x_1, y_1) and (x_2, y_2). Repeating this process with many data sets, we can estimate the bias and the variance. The figures which follow show the resulting fits on the same (random) data sets for both models.

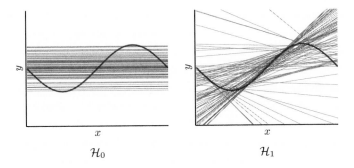

$$\mathcal{H}_0 \qquad\qquad\qquad\qquad \mathcal{H}_1$$

With $\mathcal{H}_1$, the learned hypothesis is wilder and varies extensively depending on the data set. The bias-var analysis is summarized in the next figures.

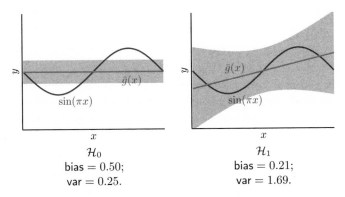

$$\mathcal{H}_0 \qquad\qquad\qquad\qquad \mathcal{H}_1$$
$$\text{bias} = 0.50; \qquad\qquad\qquad \text{bias} = 0.21;$$
$$\text{var} = 0.25. \qquad\qquad\qquad\quad \text{var} = 1.69.$$

Average hypothesis $\bar{g}$ (red) with var(x) indicated by the gray shaded region that is $\bar{g}(x) \pm \sqrt{\text{var}(x)}$.

For $\mathcal{H}_1$, the average hypothesis $\bar{g}$ (red line) is a reasonable fit with a fairly small bias of 0.21. However, the large variability leads to a high var of 1.69 resulting in a large expected out-of-sample error of 1.90. With the simpler model $\mathcal{H}_0$, the fits are much less volatile and we have a significantly lower var of 0.25, as indicated by the shaded region. However, the average fit is now the zero function, resulting in a higher bias of 0.50. The total out-of-sample error has a much smaller expected value of 0.75. The simpler model wins by significantly decreasing the var at the expense of a smaller increase in bias.

Notice that we are not comparing how well the red curves (the average hypotheses) fit the sine. These curves are only conceptual, since in real learning we do not have access to the multitude of data sets needed to generate them. We have one data set, and the simpler model results in a better out-of-sample error on average as we fit our model to just this one data. However, the var term decreases as N increases, so if we get a bigger and bigger data set, the bias term will be the dominant part of E_{out}, and $\mathcal{H}_1$ will win. $\square$

The learning algorithm plays a role in the bias-variance analysis that it did not play in the VC analysis. Two points are worth noting.

1. By design, the VC analysis is based purely on the hypothesis set $\mathcal{H}$, independently of the learning algorithm $\mathcal{A}$. In the bias-variance analysis, both $\mathcal{H}$ and the algorithm $\mathcal{A}$ matter. With the same $\mathcal{H}$, using a different learning algorithm can produce a different $g^{(\mathcal{D})}$. Since $g^{(\mathcal{D})}$ is the building block of the bias-variance analysis, this may result in different bias and var terms.

2. Although the bias-variance analysis is based on squared-error measure, the learning algorithm itself does not have to be based on minimizing the squared error. It can use any criterion to produce $g^{(\mathcal{D})}$ based on $\mathcal{D}$. However, once the algorithm produces $g^{(\mathcal{D})}$, we measure its bias and variance using squared error.

Unfortunately, the bias and variance cannot be computed in practice, since they depend on the target function and the input probability distribution (both unknown). Thus, the bias-variance decomposition is a conceptual tool which is helpful when it comes to developing a model. There are two typical goals when we consider bias and variance. The first is to try to lower the variance without significantly increasing the bias, and the second is to lower the bias without significantly increasing the variance. These goals are achieved by different techniques, some principled and some heuristic. Regularization is one of these techniques that we will discuss in Chapter 4. Reducing the bias without increasing the variance requires some prior information regarding the target function to steer the selection of $\mathcal{H}$ in the direction of f, and this task is largely application-specific. On the other hand, reducing the variance without compromising the bias can be done through general techniques.

2.3.2   The Learning Curve

We close this chapter with an important plot that illustrates the tradeoffs that we have seen so far. The *learning curves* summarize the behavior of the in-sample and out-of-sample errors as we vary the size of the training set.

After learning with a particular data set $\mathcal{D}$ of size N, the final hypothesis $g^{(\mathcal{D})}$ has in-sample error $E_{in}(g^{(\mathcal{D})})$ and out-of-sample error $E_{out}(g^{(\mathcal{D})})$, both of which depend on $\mathcal{D}$. As we saw in the bias-variance analysis, the expectation with respect to all data sets of size N gives the expected errors: $\mathbb{E}_{\mathcal{D}}[E_{in}(g^{(\mathcal{D})})]$ and $\mathbb{E}_{\mathcal{D}}[E_{out}(g^{(\mathcal{D})})]$. These expected errors are functions of N, and are called the learning curves of the model. We illustrate the learning curves for a simple learning model and a complex one, based on actual experiments.

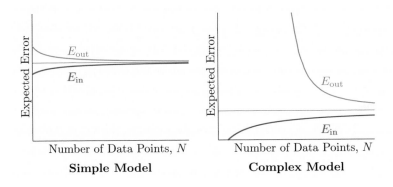

Notice that for the simple model, the learning curves converge more quickly but to worse ultimate performance than for the complex model. This behavior is typical in practice. For both simple and complex models, the out-of-sample learning curve is decreasing in N, while the in-sample learning curve is increasing in N. Let us take a closer look at these curves and interpret them in terms of the different approaches to generalization that we have discussed.

In the VC analysis, E_{out} was expressed as the sum of E_{in} and a generalization error that was bounded by Ω, the penalty for model complexity. In the bias-variance analysis, E_{out} was expressed as the sum of a bias and a variance. The following learning curves illustrate these two approaches side by side.

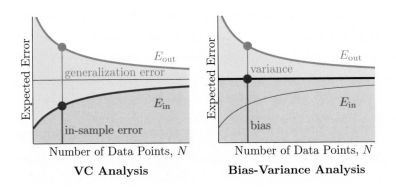

The VC analysis bounds the generalization error which is illustrated on the left.[6] The bias-variance analysis is illustrated on the right. The bias-variance illustration is somewhat idealized, since it assumes that, for every N, the average learned hypothesis $\bar{g}$ has the same performance as the best approximation to f in the learning model.

When the number of data points increases, we move to the right on the learning curves and both the generalization error and the variance term shrink, as expected. The learning curve also illustrates an important point about E_{in}. As N increases, E_{in} edges toward the smallest error that the learning model can achieve in approximating f. For small N, the value of E_{in} is actually smaller than that 'smallest possible' error. This is because the learning model has an easier task for smaller N; it only needs to approximate f on the N points regardless of what happens outside those points. Therefore, it can achieve a superior fit on those points, albeit at the expense of an inferior fit on the rest of the points as shown by the corresponding value of E_{out}.

---

[6]For the learning curve, we take the expected values of all quantities with respect to $\mathcal{D}$ of size N.

2.4 Problems

Problem 2.1   In Equation (2.1), set $\delta = 0.03$ and let

$$\epsilon(M, N, \delta) = \sqrt{\frac{1}{2N} \ln \frac{2M}{\delta}}.$$

(a) For $M = 1$, how many examples do we need to make $\epsilon \leq 0.05$?

(b) For $M = 100$, how many examples do we need to make $\epsilon \leq 0.05$?

(c) For $M = 10,000$, how many examples do we need to make $\epsilon \leq 0.05$?

Problem 2.2   Show that for the learning model of positive rectangles (aligned horizontally or vertically), $m_\mathcal{H}(4) = 2^4$ and $m_\mathcal{H}(5) < 2^5$. Hence, give a bound for $m_\mathcal{H}(N)$.

Problem 2.3   Compute the maximum number of dichotomies, $m_\mathcal{H}(N)$, for these learning models, and consequently compute d_{vc}, the VC dimension.

(a) Positive or negative ray: $\mathcal{H}$ contains the functions which are $+1$ on $[a, \infty)$ (for some a) together with those that are $+1$ on $(-\infty, a]$ (for some a).

(b) Positive or negative interval: $\mathcal{H}$ contains the functions which are $+1$ on an interval $[a, b]$ and -1 elsewhere or -1 on an interval $[a, b]$ and $+1$ elsewhere.

(c) Two concentric spheres in $\mathbb{R}^d$: $\mathcal{H}$ contains the functions which are $+1$ for $a \leq \sqrt{x_1^2 + \ldots + x_d^2} \leq b$.

Problem 2.4   Show that $B(N, k) = \sum_{i=0}^{k-1} \binom{N}{i}$ by showing the other direction to Lemma 2.3, namely that

$$B(N, k) \geq \sum_{i=0}^{k-1} \binom{N}{i}.$$

To do so, construct a specific set of $\sum_{i=0}^{k-1} \binom{N}{i}$ dichotomies that does not shatter any subset of k variables. *[Hint: Try limiting the number of -1's in each dichotomy.]*

Problem 2.5   Prove by induction that $\sum_{i=0}^{D} \binom{N}{i} \leq N^D + 1$, hence

$$m_\mathcal{H}(N) \leq N^{d_{\text{vc}}} + 1.$$

Problem 2.6   Prove that for $N \geq d$,

$$\sum_{i=0}^{d} \binom{N}{i} \leq \left(\frac{eN}{d}\right)^{d}.$$

We suggest you first show the following intermediate steps.

(a) $\sum_{i=0}^{d} \binom{N}{i} \leq \sum_{i=0}^{d} \binom{N}{i} \left(\frac{N}{d}\right)^{d-i} \leq \left(\frac{N}{d}\right)^{d} \sum_{i=0}^{N} \binom{N}{i} \left(\frac{d}{N}\right)^{i}.$

(b) $\sum_{i=0}^{N} \binom{N}{i} \left(\frac{d}{N}\right)^{i} \leq e^{d}.$ *[Hints: Binomial theorem;* $\left(1 + \frac{1}{x}\right)^{x} \leq e$ *for* $x > 0.]$

Hence, argue that $m_{\mathcal{H}}(N) \leq \left(\frac{eN}{d_{\text{vc}}}\right)^{d_{\text{vc}}}.$

Problem 2.7   Plot the bounds for $m_{\mathcal{H}}(N)$ given in Problems 2.5 and 2.6 for $d_{\text{vc}} = 2$ and $d_{\text{vc}} = 5$. When do you prefer one bound over the other?

Problem 2.8   Which of the following are possible growth functions $m_{\mathcal{H}}(N)$ for some hypothesis set:

$$1+N; \quad 1+N+\frac{N(N-1)}{2}; \quad 2^{N}; \quad 2^{\lfloor \sqrt{N} \rfloor}; \quad 2^{\lfloor N/2 \rfloor}; \quad 1+N+\frac{N(N-1)(N-2)}{6}.$$

Problem 2.9   [hard] For the perceptron in d dimensions, show that

$$m_{\mathcal{H}}(N) = 2 \sum_{i=0}^{d} \binom{N-1}{i}.$$
[Hint: Cover(1965) in Further Reading.]

Use this formula to verify that $d_{\text{vc}} = d + 1$ by evaluating $m_{\mathcal{H}}(d+1)$ and $m_{\mathcal{H}}(d+2)$. Plot $m_{\mathcal{H}}(N)/2^{N}$ for $d = 10$ and $N \in [1, 40]$. If you generate a random dichotomy on N points in 10 dimensions, give an upper bound on the probability that the dichotomy will be separable for $N = 10, 20, 40$.

Problem 2.10   Show that $m_{\mathcal{H}}(2N) \leq m_{\mathcal{H}}(N)^{2}$, and hence obtain a generalization bound which only involves $m_{\mathcal{H}}(N)$.

Problem 2.11   Suppose $m_{\mathcal{H}}(N) = N + 1$, so $d_{\text{vc}} = 1$. You have 100 training examples. Use the generalization bound to give a bound for E_{out} with confidence 90%. Repeat for $N = 10,000$.

Problem 2.12   For an $\mathcal{H}$ with $d_{\mathrm{vc}} = 10$, what sample size do you need (as prescribed by the generalization bound) to have a 95% confidence that your generalization error is at most 0.05?

Problem 2.13

(a) Let $\mathcal{H} = \{h_1, h_2, \ldots, h_M\}$ with some finite M. Prove that $d_{\mathrm{vc}}(\mathcal{H}) \leq \log_2 M$.

(b) For hypothesis sets $\mathcal{H}_1, \mathcal{H}_2, \cdots, \mathcal{H}_K$ with finite VC dimensions $d_{\mathrm{vc}}(\mathcal{H}_k)$, derive and prove the tightest upper and lower bound that you can get on $d_{\mathrm{vc}}\left(\cap_{k=1}^{K} \mathcal{H}_k\right)$.

(c) For hypothesis sets $\mathcal{H}_1, \mathcal{H}_2, \cdots, \mathcal{H}_K$ with finite VC dimensions $d_{\mathrm{vc}}(\mathcal{H}_k)$, derive and prove the tightest upper and lower bounds that you can get on $d_{\mathrm{vc}}\left(\cup_{k=1}^{K} \mathcal{H}_k\right)$.

Problem 2.14   Let $\mathcal{H}_1, \mathcal{H}_2, \ldots, \mathcal{H}_K$ be K hypothesis sets with finite VC dimension d_{vc}. Let $\mathcal{H} = \mathcal{H}_1 \cup \mathcal{H}_2 \cup \cdots \cup \mathcal{H}_K$ be the union of these models.

(a) Show that $d_{\mathrm{vc}}(\mathcal{H}) < K(d_{\mathrm{vc}} + 1)$.

(b) Suppose that ℓ satisfies $2^{\ell} > 2K\ell^{d_{\mathrm{vc}}}$. Show that $d_{\mathrm{vc}}(\mathcal{H}) \leq \ell$.

(c) Hence, show that

$$d_{\mathrm{vc}}(\mathcal{H}) \quad \leq \quad \min\left(K(d_{\mathrm{vc}} + 1), 7(d_{\mathrm{vc}} + K)\log_2(d_{\mathrm{vc}}K)\right).$$

That is, $d_{\mathrm{vc}}(\mathcal{H}) = O\left(\max(d_{\mathrm{vc}}, K)\log_2 \max(d_{\mathrm{vc}}, K)\right)$ is not too bad.

Problem 2.15   The monotonically increasing hypothesis set is

$$\mathcal{H} = \{h \mid \mathbf{x}_1 \geq \mathbf{x}_2 \implies h(\mathbf{x}_1) \geq h(\mathbf{x}_2)\},$$

where $\mathbf{x}_1 \geq \mathbf{x}_2$ if and only if the inequality is satisfied for every component.

(a) Give an example of a monotonic classifier in two dimensions, clearly showing the $+1$ and -1 regions.

(b) Compute $m_{\mathcal{H}}(N)$ and hence the VC dimension. *[Hint: Consider a set of N points generated by first choosing one point, and then generating the next point by increasing the first component and decreasing the second component until N points are obtained.]*

Problem 2.16   In this problem, we will consider $\mathcal{X} = \mathbb{R}$. That is, $\mathbf{x} = x$ is a one-dimensional variable. For a hypothesis set

$$\mathcal{H} = \left\{ h_{\mathbf{c}} \ \middle| \ h_{\mathbf{c}}(x) = \text{sign} \left(\sum_{i=0}^{D} c_i x^i \right) \right\},$$

prove that the VC dimension of $\mathcal{H}$ is exactly $(D + 1)$ by showing that

(a) There are $(D + 1)$ points which are shattered by $\mathcal{H}$.

(b) There are no $(D + 2)$ points which are shattered by $\mathcal{H}$.

Problem 2.17   The VC dimension depends on the input space as well as $\mathcal{H}$. For a fixed $\mathcal{H}$, consider two input spaces $\mathcal{X}_1 \subseteq \mathcal{X}_2$. Show that the VC dimension of $\mathcal{H}$ with respect to input space $\mathcal{X}_1$ is at most the VC dimension of $\mathcal{H}$ with respect to input space $\mathcal{X}_2$.

How can the result of this problem be used to answer part (b) in Problem 2.16? *[Hint: How is Problem 2.16 related to a perceptron in D dimensions?]*

Problem 2.18   The VC dimension of the perceptron hypothesis set corresponds to the number of parameters $(w_0, w_1, \cdots, w_d)$ of the set, and this observation is 'usually' true for other hypothesis sets. However, we will present a counter-example here. Prove that the following hypothesis set for $x \in \mathbb{R}$ has an infinite VC dimension:

$$\mathcal{H} = \left\{ h_\alpha \ \middle| \ h_\alpha(x) = (-1)^{\lfloor \alpha x \rfloor}, \text{ where } \alpha \in \mathbb{R} \right\},$$

where $\lfloor A \rfloor$ is the biggest integer $\leq A$ (the floor function). This hypothesis has only one parameter α but 'enjoys' an infinite VC dimension. *[Hint: Consider $x_1, \ldots, x_N$, where $x_n = 10^n$, and show how to implement an arbitrary dichotomy $y_1, \ldots, y_N$.]*

Problem 2.19   This problem derives a bound for the VC dimension of a complex hypothesis set that is built from simpler hypothesis sets via composition. Let $\mathcal{H}_1, \ldots, \mathcal{H}_K$ be hypothesis sets with VC dimension $d_1, \ldots, d_K$. Fix $h_1, \ldots, h_K$, where $h_i \in \mathcal{H}_i$. Define a vector $\mathbf{z}$ obtained from $\mathbf{x}$ to have components $h_i(\mathbf{x})$. Note that $\mathbf{x} \in \mathbb{R}^d$, but $\mathbf{z} \in \{-1, +1\}^K$. Let $\tilde{\mathcal{H}}$ be a hypothesis set of functions that take inputs in $\mathbb{R}^K$. So

$$\tilde{h} \in \tilde{\mathcal{H}} \colon \mathbf{z} \in \mathbb{R}^K \mapsto \{+1, -1\},$$

and suppose that $\tilde{\mathcal{H}}$ has VC dimension $\tilde{d}$.

We can apply a hypothesis in $\tilde{\mathcal{H}}$ to the $\mathbf{z}$ constructed from $(h_1, \ldots, h_K)$. This is the composition of the hypothesis set $\tilde{\mathcal{H}}$ with $(\mathcal{H}_1, \ldots, \mathcal{H}_K)$. More formally, the composed hypothesis set $\mathcal{H} = \tilde{\mathcal{H}} \circ (\mathcal{H}_1, \ldots, \mathcal{H}_K)$ is defined by $h \in \mathcal{H}$ if

$$h(\mathbf{x}) = \tilde{h}(h_1(\mathbf{x}), \ldots, h_K(\mathbf{x})), \qquad \tilde{h} \in \tilde{\mathcal{H}}; \ h_i \in \mathcal{H}_i.$$

(a) Show that

$$m_{\mathcal{H}}(N) \leq m_{\tilde{\mathcal{H}}}(N) \prod_{i=1}^{K} m_{\mathcal{H}_i}(N). \tag{2.18}$$

[Hint: Fix N points $\mathbf{x}_1, \ldots, \mathbf{x}_N$ and fix $h_1, \ldots, h_K$. This generates N transformed points $\mathbf{z}_1, \ldots, \mathbf{z}_N$. These $\mathbf{z}_1, \ldots, \mathbf{z}_N$ can be dichotomized in at most $m_{\tilde{\mathcal{H}}}(N)$ ways, hence for fixed $(h_1, \ldots, h_K)$, $(\mathbf{x}_1, \ldots, \mathbf{x}_N)$ can be dichotomized in at most $m_{\tilde{\mathcal{H}}}(N)$ ways. Through the eyes of $\mathbf{x}_1, \ldots, \mathbf{x}_N$, at most how many hypotheses are there (effectively) in $\mathcal{H}_i$? Use this bound to bound the effective number of K-tuples $(h_1, \ldots, h_K)$ that need to be considered. Finally, argue that you can bound the number of dichotomies that can be implemented by the product of the number of possible K-tuples $(h_1, \ldots, h_K)$ and the number of dichotomies per K-tuple.]

(b) Use the bound $m(N) \leq \left(\frac{eN}{d_{vc}}\right)^{d_{vc}}$ to get a bound for $m_{\mathcal{H}}(N)$ in terms of $\tilde{d}, d_1, \ldots, d_K$.

(c) Let $D = \tilde{d} + \sum_{i=1}^{K} d_i$, and assume that $D > 2e \log_2 D$. Show that

$$d_{vc}(\mathcal{H}) \leq 2D \log_2 D.$$

(d) If $\mathcal{H}_i$ and $\tilde{\mathcal{H}}$ are all perceptron hypothesis sets, show that

$$d_{vc}(\mathcal{H}) = O(dK \log(dK)).$$

In the next chapter, we will further develop the simple linear model. This linear model is the building block of many other models, such as neural networks. The results of this problem show how to bound the VC dimension of the more complex models built in this manner.

Problem 2.20   There are a number of bounds on the generalization error ϵ, all holding with probability at least $1 - \delta$.

(a) Original VC-bound:

$$\epsilon \leq \sqrt{\frac{8}{N} \ln \frac{4m_{\mathcal{H}}(2N)}{\delta}}.$$

(b) Rademacher Penalty Bound:

$$\epsilon \leq \sqrt{\frac{2 \ln(2N m_{\mathcal{H}}(N))}{N}} + \sqrt{\frac{2}{N} \ln \frac{1}{\delta}} + \frac{1}{N}.$$

(continued on next page)

(c) Parrondo and Van den Broek:

$$\epsilon \leq \sqrt{\frac{1}{N}\left(2\epsilon + \ln\frac{6m_{\mathcal{H}}(2N)}{\delta}\right)}.$$

(d) Devroye:

$$\epsilon \leq \sqrt{\frac{1}{2N}\left(4\epsilon(1+\epsilon) + \ln\frac{4m_{\mathcal{H}}(N^2)}{\delta}\right)}.$$

Note that (c) and (d) are implicit bounds in ϵ. Fix $d_{\text{vc}} = 50$ and $\delta = 0.05$ and plot these bounds as a function of N. Which is best?

Problem 2.21   Assume the following theorem to hold

Theorem

$$\mathbb{P}\left[\frac{E_{\text{out}}(g) - E_{\text{in}}(g)}{\sqrt{E_{\text{out}}(g)}} > \epsilon\right] \leq c \cdot m_{\mathcal{H}}(2N) \exp\left(-\frac{\epsilon^2 N}{4}\right),$$

where c is a constant that is a little bigger than 6.

This bound is useful because sometimes what we care about is not the absolute generalization error but instead a relative generalization error (one can imagine that a generalization error of 0.01 is more significant when $E_{\text{out}} = 0.01$ than when $E_{\text{out}} = 0.5$). Convert this to a generalization bound by showing that with probability at least $1 - \delta$,

$$E_{\text{out}}(g) \leq E_{\text{in}}(g) + \frac{\xi}{2}\left[1 + \sqrt{1 + \frac{4E_{\text{in}}(g)}{\xi}}\right],$$

where $\xi = \frac{4}{N}\log\frac{c \cdot m_{\mathcal{H}}(2N)}{\delta}$.

Problem 2.22   When there is noise in the data, $E_{\text{out}}(g^{(\mathcal{D})}) = \mathbb{E}_{\mathbf{x},y}[(g^{(\mathcal{D})}(\mathbf{x}) - y(\mathbf{x}))^2]$, where $y(\mathbf{x}) = f(\mathbf{x}) + \epsilon$. If ϵ is a zero-mean noise random variable with variance σ^2, show that the bias-variance decomposition becomes

$$\mathbb{E}_{\mathcal{D}}[E_{\text{out}}(g^{(\mathcal{D})})] = \sigma^2 + \text{bias} + \text{var}.$$

Problem 2.23   Consider the learning problem in Example 2.8, where the input space is $\mathcal{X} = [-1, +1]$, the target function is $f(x) = \sin(\pi x)$, and the input probability distribution is uniform on $\mathcal{X}$. Assume that the training set $\mathcal{D}$ has only two data points (picked independently), and that the learning algorithm picks the hypothesis that minimizes the in-sample mean squared error. In this problem, we will dig deeper into this case.

For each of the following learning models, find (analytically or numerically) (i) the best hypothesis that approximates f in the mean-squared-error sense (assume that f is known for this part), (ii) the expected value (with respect to $\mathcal{D}$) of the hypothesis that the learning algorithm produces, and (iii) the expected out-of-sample error and its bias and var components.

(a) The learning model consists of all hypotheses of the form $h(x) = ax + b$ (if you need to deal with the infinitesimal-probability case of two identical data points, choose the hypothesis tangential to f).

(b) The learning model consists of all hypotheses of the form $h(x) = ax$. This case was not covered in Example 2.8.

(c) The learning model consists of all hypotheses of the form $h(x) = b$.

Problem 2.24   Consider a simplified learning scenario. Assume that the input dimension is one. Assume that the input variable x is uniformly distributed in the interval $[-1, 1]$. The data set consists of 2 points $\{x_1, x_2\}$ and assume that the target function is $f(x) = x^2$. Thus, the full data set is $\mathcal{D} = \{(x_1, x_1^2), (x_2, x_2^2)\}$. The learning algorithm returns the line fitting these two points as g ($\mathcal{H}$ consists of functions of the form $h(x) = ax + b$). We are interested in the test performance (E_{out}) of our learning system with respect to the squared error measure, the bias and the var.

(a) Give the analytic expression for the average function $\bar{g}(x)$.

(b) Describe an experiment that you could run to determine (numerically) $\bar{g}(x)$, E_{out}, bias, and var.

(c) Run your experiment and report the results. Compare E_{out} with bias+var. Provide a plot of your $\bar{g}(x)$ and $f(x)$ (on the same plot).

(d) Compute analytically what E_{out}, bias and var should be.

Chapter 3

The Linear Model

We often wonder how to draw a line between two categories; right versus wrong, personal versus professional life, useful email versus spam, to name a few. A line is intuitively our first choice for a decision boundary. In learning, as in life, a line is also a good first choice.

In Chapter 1, we (and the machine ☺) learned a procedure to 'draw a line' between two categories based on data (the perceptron learning algorithm). We started by taking the hypothesis set $\mathcal{H}$ that included all possible lines (actually hyperplanes). The algorithm then searched for a good line in $\mathcal{H}$ by iteratively correcting the errors made by the current candidate line, in an attempt to improve E_{in}. As we saw in Chapter 2, the linear model – set of lines – has a small VC dimension and so is able to generalize well from E_{in} to E_{out}.

The aim of this chapter is to further develop the basic linear model into a powerful tool for learning from data. We branch into three important problems: the classification problem that we have seen and two other important problems called *regression* and *probability estimation*. The three problems come with different but related algorithms, and cover a lot of territory in learning from data. As a rule of thumb, when faced with learning problems, it is generally a winning strategy to try a linear model first.

3.1 Linear Classification

The linear model for classifying data into two classes uses a hypothesis set of linear classifiers, where each h has the form

$$h(\mathbf{x}) = \text{sign}(\mathbf{w}^{\text{T}}\mathbf{x}),$$

for some column vector $\mathbf{w} \in \mathbb{R}^{d+1}$, where d is the dimensionality of the input space, and the added coordinate $x_0 = 1$ corresponds to the bias 'weight' w_0 (recall that the input space $\mathcal{X} = \{1\} \times \mathbb{R}^d$ is considered d-dimensional since the added coordinate $x_0 = 1$ is fixed). We will use h and $\mathbf{w}$ interchangeably to refer to the hypothesis when the context is clear. When we left Chapter 1, we had two basic criteria for learning:

1. Can we make sure that $E_{\text{out}}(g)$ is close to $E_{\text{in}}(g)$? This ensures that what we have learned in sample will generalize out of sample.

2. Can we make $E_{\text{in}}(g)$ small? This ensures that what we have learned in sample is a good hypothesis.

The first criterion was studied in Chapter 2. Specifically, the VC dimension of the linear model is only $d + 1$ (Exercise 2.4). Using the VC generalization bound (2.12), and the bound (2.10) on the growth function in terms of the VC dimension, we conclude that with high probability,

$$E_{\text{out}}(g) = E_{\text{in}}(g) + O\left(\sqrt{\frac{d}{N}\ln N}\right). \tag{3.1}$$

Thus, when N is sufficiently large, E_{in} and E_{out} will be close to each other (see the definition of $O(\cdot)$ in the Notation table), and the first criterion for learning is fulfilled.

The second criterion, making sure that E_{in} is small, requires first and foremost that there is *some* linear hypothesis that has small E_{in}. If there isn't such a linear hypothesis, then learning certainly can't find one. So, let's suppose for the moment that there is a linear hypothesis with small E_{in}. In fact, let's suppose that the data is linearly separable, which means there is some hypothesis $\mathbf{w}^*$ with $E_{\text{in}}(\mathbf{w}^*) = 0$. We will deal with the case when this is not true shortly.

In Chapter 1, we introduced the perceptron learning algorithm (PLA). Start with an arbitrary weight vector $\mathbf{w}(0)$. Then, at every time step $t \geq 0$, select *any* misclassified data point $(\mathbf{x}(t), y(t))$, and update $\mathbf{w}(t)$ as follows:

$$\mathbf{w}(t+1) = \mathbf{w}(t) + y(t)\mathbf{x}(t).$$

The intuition is that the update is attempting to correct the error in classifying $\mathbf{x}(t)$. The remarkable thing is that this incremental approach of learning based on one data point at a time works. As discussed in Problem 1.3, it can be proved that the PLA will eventually stop updating, ending at a solution $\mathbf{w}_{\text{PLA}}$ with $E_{\text{in}}(\mathbf{w}_{\text{PLA}}) = 0$. Although this result applies to a restricted setting (linearly separable data), it is a significant step. The PLA is clever – it doesn't naïvely test every linear hypothesis to see if it (the hypothesis) separates the data; that would take infinitely long. Using an iterative approach, the PLA manages to search an *infinite* hypothesis set and output a linear separator in (provably) *finite* time.

As far as PLA is concerned, linear separability is a property of the *data*, not the *target*. A linearly separable $\mathcal{D}$ could have been generated either from a linearly separable target, or (by chance) from a target that is not linearly separable. The convergence proof of PLA guarantees that the algorithm will

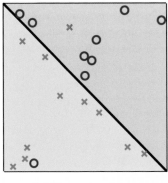
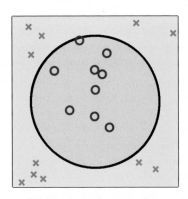

(a) Few noisy data.　　　　　　　　(b) Nonlinearly separable.

Figure 3.1: Data sets that are not linearly separable but are (a) linearly separable after discarding a few examples, or (b) separable by a more sophisticated curve.

work in both these cases, and produce a hypothesis with $E_{in} = 0$. Further, in both cases, you can be confident that this performance will generalize well out of sample, according to the VC bound.

> **Exercise 3.1**
>
> Will PLA ever stop updating if the data is not linearly separable?

3.1.1　Non-Separable Data

We now address the case where the data is not linearly separable. Figure 3.1 shows two data sets that are not linearly separable. In Figure 3.1(a), the data becomes linearly separable after the removal of just two examples, which could be considered noisy examples or outliers. In Figure 3.1(b), the data can be separated by a circle rather than a line. In both cases, there will always be a misclassified training example if we insist on using a linear hypothesis, and hence PLA will never terminate. In fact, its behavior becomes quite unstable, and can jump from a good perceptron to a very bad one within one update; the quality of the resulting E_{in} cannot be guaranteed. In Figure 3.1(a), it seems appropriate to stick with a line, but to somehow tolerate noise and output a hypothesis with a small E_{in}, not necessarily $E_{in} = 0$. In Figure 3.1(b), the linear model does not seem to be the correct model in the first place, and we will discuss a technique called nonlinear transformation for this situation in Section 3.4.

The situation in Figure 3.1(a) is actually encountered very often: even though a linear classifier seems appropriate, the data may not be linearly separable because of outliers or noise. To find a hypothesis with the minimum E_{in}, we need to solve the combinatorial optimization problem:

$$\min_{\mathbf{w}\in\mathbb{R}^{d+1}} \underbrace{\frac{1}{N}\sum_{n=1}^{N} [\![\text{sign}(\mathbf{w}^{\text{T}}\mathbf{x}_n) \neq y_n]\!]}_{E_{\text{in}}(\mathbf{w})}. \tag{3.2}$$

The difficulty in solving this problem arises from the discrete nature of both $\text{sign}(\cdot)$ and $[\![\cdot]\!]$. In fact, minimizing $E_{\text{in}}(\mathbf{w})$ in (3.2) in the general case is known to be NP-hard, which means there is no known efficient algorithm for it, and if you discovered one, you would become really, really famous ☺. Thus, one has to resort to approximately minimizing E_{in}.

One approach for getting an approximate solution is to extend PLA through a simple modification into what is called the *pocket algorithm*. Essentially, the pocket algorithm keeps 'in its pocket' the best weight vector encountered up to iteration t in PLA. At the end, the best weight vector will be reported as the final hypothesis. This simple algorithm is shown below.

The pocket algorithm:

1: Set the pocket weight vector $\hat{\mathbf{w}}$ to $\mathbf{w}(0)$ of PLA.
2: **for** $t = 0, \ldots, T-1$ **do**
3:     Run PLA for one update to obtain $\mathbf{w}(t+1)$.
4:     Evaluate $E_{\text{in}}(\mathbf{w}(t+1))$.
5:     If $\mathbf{w}(t+1)$ is better than $\hat{\mathbf{w}}$ in terms of E_{in}, set $\hat{\mathbf{w}}$ to $\mathbf{w}(t+1)$.
6: Return $\hat{\mathbf{w}}$.

The original PLA only checks *some* of the examples using $\mathbf{w}(t)$ to identify $(\mathbf{x}(t), y(t))$ in each iteration, while the pocket algorithm needs an additional step that evaluates *all* examples using $\mathbf{w}(t+1)$ to get $E_{\text{in}}(\mathbf{w}(t+1))$. The additional step makes the pocket algorithm much slower than PLA. In addition, there is no guarantee for how fast the pocket algorithm can converge to a good E_{in}. Nevertheless, it is a useful algorithm to have on hand because of its simplicity. Other, more efficient approaches for obtaining good approximate solutions have been developed based on different optimization techniques, as shown later in this chapter.

Exercise 3.2

Take $d = 2$ and create a data set $\mathcal{D}$ of size $N = 100$ that is not linearly separable. You can do so by first choosing a random line in the plane as your target function and the inputs $\mathbf{x}_n$ of the data set as random points in the plane. Then, evaluate the target function on each $\mathbf{x}_n$ to get the corresponding output y_n. Finally, flip the labels of $\frac{N}{10}$ randomly selected y_n's and the data set will likely become non-separable.

Now, try the pocket algorithm on your data set using $T = 1,000$ iterations. Repeat the experiment 20 times. Then, plot the average $E_{\text{in}}(\mathbf{w}(t))$ and the average $E_{\text{in}}(\hat{\mathbf{w}})$ (which is also a function of t) on the same figure and see how they behave when t increases. Similarly, use a test set of size $1,000$ and plot a figure to show how $E_{\text{out}}(\mathbf{w}(t))$ and $E_{\text{out}}(\hat{\mathbf{w}})$ behave.

Example 3.1 (Handwritten digit recognition). We sample some digits from the US Postal Service Zip Code Database. These 16×16 pixel images are preprocessed from the scanned handwritten zip codes. The goal is to recognize the digit in each image. We alluded to this task in part (b) of Exercise 1.1. A quick look at the images reveals that this is a non-trivial task (even for a human), and typical human E_{out} is about 2.5%. Common confusion occurs between the digits $\{4, 9\}$ and $\{2, 7\}$. A machine-learned hypothesis which can achieve such an error rate would be highly desirable.

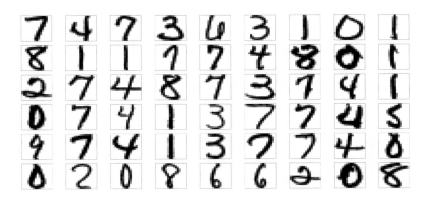

Let's first decompose the big task of separating ten digits into smaller tasks of separating two of the digits. Such a decomposition approach from *multiclass* to *binary* classification is commonly used in many learning algorithms. We will focus on digits $\{1, 5\}$ for now. A human approach to determining the digit corresponding to an image is to look at the shape (or other properties) of the black pixels. Thus, rather than carrying all the information in the 256 pixels, it makes sense to summarize the information contained in the image into a few *features*. Let's look at two important features here: intensity and symmetry. Digit 5 usually occupies more black pixels than digit 1, and hence the average pixel intensity of digit 5 is higher. On the other hand, digit 1 is symmetric while digit 5 is not. Therefore, if we define asymmetry as the average absolute difference between an image and its flipped versions, and symmetry as the negation of asymmetry, digit 1 would result in a higher symmetry value. A scatter plot for these intensity and symmetry features for some of the digits is shown next.

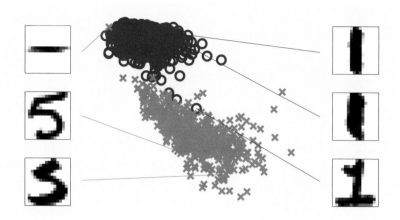

While the digits can be roughly separated by a line in the plane representing these two features, there are poorly written digits (such as the '5' depicted in the top-left corner) that prevent a perfect linear separation.

We now run PLA and pocket on the data set and see what happens. Since the data set is not linearly separable, PLA will not stop updating. In fact, as can be seen in Figure 3.2(a), its behavior can be quite unstable. When it is forcibly terminated at iteration $1,000$, PLA gives a line that has a poor $E_{in} = 2.24\%$ and $E_{out} = 6.37\%$. On the other hand, if the pocket algorithm is applied to the same data set, as shown in Figure 3.2(b), we can obtain a line that has a better $E_{in} = 0.45\%$ and a better $E_{out} = 1.89\%$.   □

3.2 Linear Regression

Linear regression is another useful linear model that applies to real-valued target functions.[1] It has a long history in statistics, where it has been studied in great detail, and has various applications in social and behavioral sciences. Here, we discuss linear regression from a learning perspective, where we derive the main results with minimal assumptions.

Let us revisit our application in credit approval, this time considering a regression problem rather than a classification problem. Recall that the bank has customer records that contain information fields related to personal credit, such as annual salary, years in residence, outstanding loans, etc. Such variables can be used to learn a linear classifier to decide on credit approval. Instead of just making a binary decision (approve or not), the bank also wants to set a proper credit limit for each approved customer. Credit limits are traditionally determined by human experts. The bank wants to automate this task, as it did with credit approval.

---

[1]Regression, a term inherited from earlier work in statistics, means y is real-valued.

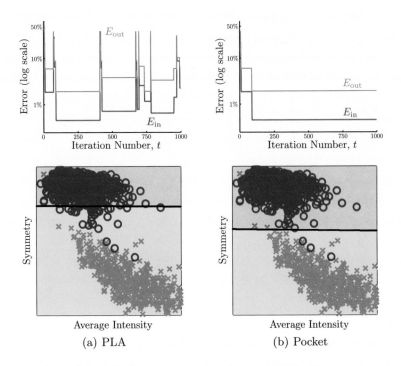

Figure 3.2: Comparison of two linear classification algorithms for separating digits 1 and 5. E_{in} and E_{out} are plotted versus iteration number and below that is the learned hypothesis g. (a) A version of the PLA which selects a random training example and updates $\mathbf{w}$ if that example is misclassified (hence the flat regions when no update is made). This version avoids searching all the data at every iteration. (b) The pocket algorithm.

This is a regression learning problem. The bank uses historical records to construct a data set $\mathcal{D}$ of examples $(\mathbf{x}_1, y_1), (\mathbf{x}_2, y_2), \ldots, (\mathbf{x}_N, y_N)$, where $\mathbf{x}_n$ is customer information and y_n is the credit limit set by one of the human experts in the bank. Note that y_n is now a real number (positive in this case) instead of just a binary value ± 1. The bank wants to use learning to find a hypothesis g that replicates how human experts determine credit limits.

Since there is more than one human expert, and since each expert may not be perfectly consistent, our target will not be a deterministic function $y = f(\mathbf{x})$. Instead, it will be a noisy target formalized as a distribution of the random variable y that comes from the different views of different experts as well as the variation within the views of each expert. That is, the label y_n comes from some distribution $P(y \mid \mathbf{x})$ instead of a deterministic function $f(\mathbf{x})$. Nonetheless, as we discussed in previous chapters, the nature of the problem is not changed. We have an *unknown* distribution $P(\mathbf{x}, y)$ that generates each $(\mathbf{x}_n, y_n)$, and we want to find a hypothesis g that minimizes the error between $g(\mathbf{x})$ and y with respect to that distribution.

The choice of a linear model for this problem presumes that there is a linear combination of the customer information fields that would properly approximate the credit limit as determined by human experts. If this assumption does not hold, we cannot achieve a small error with a linear model. We will deal with this situation when we discuss nonlinear transformation later in the chapter.

3.2.1 The Algorithm

The linear regression algorithm is based on minimizing the squared error between $h(\mathbf{x})$ and y.[2]

$$E_{\text{out}}(h) = \mathbb{E}\left[(h(\mathbf{x}) - y)^2\right],$$

where the expected value is taken with respect to the joint probability distribution $P(\mathbf{x}, y)$. The goal is to find a hypothesis that achieves a small $E_{\text{out}}(h)$. Since the distribution $P(\mathbf{x}, y)$ is unknown, $E_{\text{out}}(h)$ cannot be computed. Similar to what we did in classification, we resort to the in-sample version instead,

$$E_{\text{in}}(h) = \frac{1}{N} \sum_{n=1}^{N} (h(\mathbf{x}_n) - y_n)^2.$$

In linear regression, h takes the form of a linear combination of the components of $\mathbf{x}$. That is,

$$h(\mathbf{x}) = \sum_{i=0}^{d} w_i x_i = \mathbf{w}^\mathsf{T}\mathbf{x},$$

where $x_0 = 1$ and $\mathbf{x} \in \{1\} \times \mathbb{R}^d$ as usual, and $\mathbf{w} \in \mathbb{R}^{d+1}$. For the special case of linear h, it is very useful to have a matrix representation of $E_{\text{in}}(h)$. First, define the data matrix $\mathrm{X} \in \mathbb{R}^{N \times (d+1)}$ to be the $N \times (d+1)$ matrix whose rows are the inputs $\mathbf{x}_n$ as row vectors, and define the target vector $\mathbf{y} \in \mathbb{R}^N$ to be the column vector whose components are the target values y_n. The in-sample error is a function of $\mathbf{w}$ and the data $\mathrm{X}, \mathbf{y}$:

$$
\begin{aligned}
E_{\text{in}}(\mathbf{w}) &= \frac{1}{N} \sum_{n=1}^{N} (\mathbf{w}^\mathsf{T}\mathbf{x}_n - y_n)^2 \\
&= \frac{1}{N} \|\mathrm{X}\mathbf{w} - \mathbf{y}\|^2 \qquad\qquad\qquad (3.3) \\
&= \frac{1}{N} (\mathbf{w}^\mathsf{T}\mathrm{X}^\mathsf{T}\mathrm{X}\mathbf{w} - 2\mathbf{w}^\mathsf{T}\mathrm{X}^\mathsf{T}\mathbf{y} + \mathbf{y}^\mathsf{T}\mathbf{y}), \qquad (3.4)
\end{aligned}
$$

where $\| \cdot \|$ is the Euclidean norm of a vector, and (3.3) follows because the nth component of the vector $\mathrm{X}\mathbf{w} - \mathbf{y}$ is exactly $\mathbf{w}^\mathsf{T}\mathbf{x}_n - y_n$. The linear regression

---

[2]The term 'linear regression' has been historically confined to squared error measures.

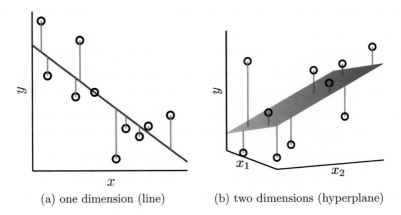

(a) one dimension (line)   (b) two dimensions (hyperplane)

Figure 3.3: The solution hypothesis (in blue) of the linear regression algorithm in one and two dimensions. The sum of squared errors is minimized.

algorithm is derived by minimizing $E_{\text{in}}(\mathbf{w})$ over all possible $\mathbf{w} \in \mathbb{R}^{d+1}$, as formalized by the following optimization problem:

$$\mathbf{w}_{\text{lin}} = \underset{\mathbf{w} \in \mathbb{R}^{d+1}}{\arg\min}\, E_{\text{in}}(\mathbf{w}). \tag{3.5}$$

Figure 3.3 illustrates the solution in one and two dimensions. Since Equation (3.4) implies that $E_{\text{in}}(\mathbf{w})$ is differentiable, we can use standard matrix calculus to find the $\mathbf{w}$ that minimizes $E_{\text{in}}(\mathbf{w})$ by requiring that the gradient of E_{in} with respect to $\mathbf{w}$ is the zero vector, i.e., $\nabla E_{\text{in}}(\mathbf{w}) = \mathbf{0}$. The gradient is a (column) vector whose ith component is $[\nabla E_{\text{in}}(\mathbf{w})]_i = \frac{\partial}{\partial w_i} E_{\text{in}}(\mathbf{w})$. By explicitly computing $\frac{\partial}{\partial w_i}$, the reader can verify the following gradient identities,

$$\nabla_{\mathbf{w}}(\mathbf{w}^{\mathsf{T}}\mathrm{A}\mathbf{w}) = (\mathrm{A} + \mathrm{A}^{\mathsf{T}})\mathbf{w}, \qquad \nabla_{\mathbf{w}}(\mathbf{w}^{\mathsf{T}}\mathbf{b}) = \mathbf{b}.$$

These identities are the matrix analog of ordinary differentiation of quadratic and linear functions. To obtain the gradient of E_{in}, we take the gradient of each term in (3.4) to obtain

$$\nabla E_{\text{in}}(\mathbf{w}) = \frac{2}{N}(\mathrm{X}^{\mathsf{T}}\mathrm{X}\mathbf{w} - \mathrm{X}^{\mathsf{T}}\mathbf{y}).$$

Note that both $\mathbf{w}$ and $\nabla E_{\text{in}}(\mathbf{w})$ are column vectors. Finally, to get $\nabla E_{\text{in}}(\mathbf{w})$ to be $\mathbf{0}$, one should solve for $\mathbf{w}$ that satisfies

$$\mathrm{X}^{\mathsf{T}}\mathrm{X}\mathbf{w} = \mathrm{X}^{\mathsf{T}}\mathbf{y}.$$

If $\mathrm{X}^{\mathsf{T}}\mathrm{X}$ is invertible, $\mathbf{w} = \mathrm{X}^{\dagger}\mathbf{y}$ where $\mathrm{X}^{\dagger} = (\mathrm{X}^{\mathsf{T}}\mathrm{X})^{-1}\mathrm{X}^{\mathsf{T}}$ is the *pseudo-inverse* of X. The resulting $\mathbf{w}$ is the unique optimal solution to (3.5). If $\mathrm{X}^{\mathsf{T}}\mathrm{X}$ is not invertible, a pseudo-inverse can still be defined, but the solution will not be unique (see Problem 3.15). In practice, $X^T X$ is invertible in most of the cases since N is often much bigger than $d + 1$, so there will likely be $d + 1$ linearly independent vectors $\mathbf{x}_n$. We have thus derived the following *linear regression algorithm*.

Linear regression algorithm:

1: Construct the matrix X and the vector $\mathbf{y}$ from the data set $(\mathbf{x}_1, y_1), \cdots, (\mathbf{x}_N, y_N)$, where each $\mathbf{x}$ includes the $x_0 = 1$ bias coordinate, as follows

$$
X = \begin{bmatrix} -\mathbf{x}_1^T- \\ -\mathbf{x}_2^T- \\ \vdots \\ -\mathbf{x}_N^T- \end{bmatrix}, \qquad \mathbf{y} = \begin{bmatrix} y_1 \\ y_2 \\ \vdots \\ y_N \end{bmatrix}.
$$

$\underbrace{\qquad\qquad}_{\text{input data matrix}} \qquad \underbrace{\qquad\qquad}_{\text{target vector}}$

2: Compute the pseudo-inverse $X^\dagger$ of the matrix X. If $X^T X$ is invertible,

$$
X^\dagger = (X^T X)^{-1} X^T.
$$

3: Return $\mathbf{w}_{\text{lin}} = X^\dagger \mathbf{y}$.

This algorithm is sometimes referred to as *ordinary least squares* (OLS). It may seem that, compared with the perceptron learning algorithm, linear regression doesn't really look like 'learning', in the sense that the hypothesis $\mathbf{w}_{\text{lin}}$ comes from an analytic solution (matrix inversion and multiplications) rather than from iterative learning steps. Well, as long as the hypothesis $\mathbf{w}_{\text{lin}}$ has a decent out-of-sample error, then learning *has* occurred. Linear regression is a rare case where we have an analytic formula for learning that is easy to evaluate. This is one of the reasons why the technique is so widely used. It should be noted that there are methods for computing the pseudo-inverse directly without inverting a matrix, and that these methods are numerically more stable than matrix inversion.

Linear regression has been analyzed in great detail in statistics. We would like to mention one of the analysis tools here since it relates to in-sample and out-of-sample errors, and that is the *hat matrix* H. Here is how H is defined. The linear regression weight vector $\mathbf{w}_{\text{lin}}$ is an attempt to map the inputs X to the outputs $\mathbf{y}$. However, $\mathbf{w}_{\text{lin}}$ does not produce $\mathbf{y}$ exactly, but produces an estimate

$$
\hat{\mathbf{y}} = X\mathbf{w}_{\text{lin}}
$$

which differs from $\mathbf{y}$ due to in-sample error. Substituting the expression for $\mathbf{w}_{\text{lin}}$ (assuming $X^T X$ is invertible), we get

$$
\hat{\mathbf{y}} = X(X^T X)^{-1} X^T \mathbf{y}.
$$

Therefore the estimate $\hat{\mathbf{y}}$ is a linear transformation of the actual $\mathbf{y}$ through matrix multiplication with H, where

$$H = X(X^{\mathsf{T}}X)^{-1}X^{\mathsf{T}}. \tag{3.6}$$

Since $\hat{\mathbf{y}} = H\mathbf{y}$, the matrix H 'puts a hat' on $\mathbf{y}$, hence the name. The hat matrix is a very special matrix. For one thing, $H^2 = H$, which can be verified using the above expression for H. This and other properties of H will facilitate the analysis of in-sample and out-of-sample errors of linear regression.

Exercise 3.3

Consider the hat matrix $H = X(X^{\mathsf{T}}X)^{-1}X^{\mathsf{T}}$, where X is an N by $d+1$ matrix, and $X^{\mathsf{T}}X$ is invertible.

(a) Show that H is symmetric.

(b) Show that $H^K = H$ for any positive integer K.

(c) If I is the identity matrix of size N, show that $(I - H)^K = I - H$ for any positive integer K.

(d) Show that $\text{trace}(H) = d + 1$, where the trace is the sum of diagonal elements. *[Hint: $\text{trace}(AB) = \text{trace}(BA)$.]*

3.2.2 Generalization Issues

Linear regression looks for the optimal weight vector in terms of the in-sample error E_{in}, which leads to the usual generalization question: Does this guarantee decent out-of-sample error E_{out}? The short answer is yes. There is a regression version of the VC generalization bound (3.1) that similarly bounds E_{out}. In the case of linear regression in particular, there are also exact formulas for the expected E_{out} and E_{in} that can be derived under simplifying assumptions. The general form of the result is

$$E_{\text{out}}(g) = E_{\text{in}}(g) + O\left(\frac{d}{N}\right),$$

where $E_{\text{out}}(g)$ and $E_{\text{in}}(g)$ are the expected values. This is comparable to the classification bound in (3.1).

Exercise 3.4

Consider a noisy target $y = \mathbf{w}^{*\mathsf{T}}\mathbf{x} + \epsilon$ for generating the data, where ϵ is a noise term with zero mean and σ^2 variance, independently generated for every example $(\mathbf{x}, y)$. The expected error of the best possible linear fit to this target is thus σ^2.

For the data $\mathcal{D} = \{(\mathbf{x}_1, y_1), \ldots, (\mathbf{x}_N, y_N)\}$, denote the noise in y_n as ϵ_n and let $\epsilon = [\epsilon_1, \epsilon_2, \ldots, \epsilon_N]^{\mathsf{T}}$; assume that $X^{\mathsf{T}}X$ is invertible. By following

(continued on next page)

---

the steps below, show that the expected in-sample error of linear regression with respect to $\mathcal{D}$ is given by

$$\mathbb{E}_{\mathcal{D}}[E_{\text{in}}(\mathbf{w}_{\text{lin}})] = \sigma^2 \left(1 - \frac{d+1}{N}\right).$$

(a) Show that the in-sample estimate of $\mathbf{y}$ is given by $\hat{\mathbf{y}} = X\mathbf{w}^* + H\epsilon$.

(b) Show that the in-sample error vector $\hat{\mathbf{y}} - \mathbf{y}$ can be expressed by a matrix times ϵ. What is the matrix?

(c) Express $E_{\text{in}}(\mathbf{w}_{\text{lin}})$ in terms of ϵ using (b), and simplify the expression using Exercise 3.3(c).

(d) Prove that $\mathbb{E}_{\mathcal{D}}[E_{\text{in}}(\mathbf{w}_{\text{lin}})] = \sigma^2 \left(1 - \frac{d+1}{N}\right)$ using (c) and the independence of $\epsilon_1, \cdots, \epsilon_N$. *[Hint: The sum of the diagonal elements of a matrix (the trace) will play a role. See Exercise 3.3(d).]*

For the expected out-of-sample error, we take a special case which is easy to analyze. Consider a test data set $\mathcal{D}_{\text{test}} = \{(\mathbf{x}_1, y_1'), \ldots, (\mathbf{x}_N, y_N')\}$, which shares the same input vectors $\mathbf{x}_n$ with $\mathcal{D}$ but with a different realization of the noise terms. Denote the noise in y_n' as ϵ_n' and let $\epsilon' = [\epsilon_1', \epsilon_2', \ldots, \epsilon_N']^{\text{T}}$. Define $E_{\text{test}}(\mathbf{w}_{\text{lin}})$ to be the average squared error on $\mathcal{D}_{\text{test}}$.

(e) Prove that $\mathbb{E}_{\mathcal{D},\epsilon'}[E_{\text{test}}(\mathbf{w}_{\text{lin}})] = \sigma^2 \left(1 + \frac{d+1}{N}\right)$.

The special test error E_{test} is a very restricted case of the general out-of-sample error. Some detailed analysis shows that similar results can be obtained for the general case, as shown in Problem 3.11.

Figure 3.4 illustrates the learning curve of linear regression under the assumptions of Exercise 3.4. The best possible linear fit has expected error σ^2. The expected in-sample error is smaller, equal to $\sigma^2(1 - \frac{d+1}{N})$ for $N \geq d+1$. The learned linear fit has eaten into the in-sample noise as much as it could with the $d+1$ degrees of freedom that it has at its disposal. This occurs because the fitting cannot distinguish the noise from the 'signal.' On the other hand, the expected out-of-sample error is $\sigma^2(1 + \frac{d+1}{N})$, which is more than the unavoidable error of σ^2. The additional error reflects the drift in $\mathbf{w}_{\text{lin}}$ due to fitting the in-sample noise.

3.3 Logistic Regression

The core of the linear model is the 'signal' $s = \mathbf{w}^{\text{T}}\mathbf{x}$ that combines the input variables linearly. We have seen two models based on this signal, and we are now going to introduce a third. In linear regression, the signal itself is taken as the output, which is appropriate if you are trying to predict a real response that could be unbounded. In linear classification, the signal is thresholded at zero to produce a ± 1 output, appropriate for binary decisions. A third possibility, which has wide application in practice, is to output a *probability*,

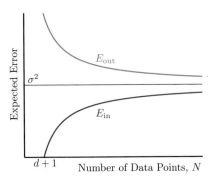

Figure 3.4: The learning curve for linear regression.

a value between 0 and 1. Our new model is called *logistic* regression. It has similarities to both previous models, as the output is real (like regression) but bounded (like classification).

Example 3.2 (Prediction of heart attacks). Suppose we want to predict the occurrence of heart attacks based on a person's cholesterol level, blood pressure, age, weight, and other factors. Obviously, we cannot predict a heart attack with any certainty, but we may be able to predict how likely it is to occur given these factors. Therefore, an output that varies continuously between 0 and 1 would be a more suitable model than a binary decision. The closer y is to 1, the more likely that the person will have a heart attack. □

3.3.1 Predicting a Probability

Linear classification uses a hard threshold on the signal $s = \mathbf{w}^\mathsf{T}\mathbf{x}$,

$$h(\mathbf{x}) = \text{sign}(\mathbf{w}^\mathsf{T}\mathbf{x}),$$

while linear regression uses no threshold at all,

$$h(\mathbf{x}) = \mathbf{w}^\mathsf{T}\mathbf{x}.$$

In our new model, we need something in between these two cases that smoothly restricts the output to the probability range $[0, 1]$. One choice that accomplishes this goal is the logistic regression model,

$$h(\mathbf{x}) = \theta(\mathbf{w}^\mathsf{T}\mathbf{x}),$$

where θ is the so-called *logistic* function $\theta(s) = \frac{e^s}{1+e^s}$ whose output is between 0 and 1.

The output can be interpreted as a probability for a binary event (heart attack or no heart attack, digit '1' versus digit '5', etc.). Linear classification also deals with a binary event, but the difference is that the 'classification' in logistic regression is allowed to be uncertain, with intermediate values between 0 and 1 reflecting

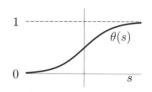

this uncertainty. The logistic function θ is referred to as a *soft threshold*, in contrast to the hard threshold in classification. It is also called a *sigmoid* because its shape looks like a flattened out 's'.

Exercise 3.5

Another popular soft threshold is the hyperbolic tangent

$$\tanh(s) = \frac{e^s - e^{-s}}{e^s + e^{-s}}.$$

(a) How is tanh related to the logistic function θ? *[Hint: shift and scale]*

(b) Show that $\tanh(s)$ converges to a hard threshold for large $|s|$, and converges to no threshold for small $|s|$. *[Hint: Formalize the figure below.]*

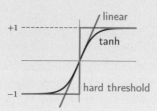

The specific formula of $\theta(s)$ will allow us to define an error measure for learning that has analytical and computational advantages, as we will see shortly. Let us first look at the target that logistic regression is trying to learn. The target is a probability, say of a patient being at risk for heart attack, that depends on the input $\mathbf{x}$ (the characteristics of the patient). Formally, we are trying to learn the target function

$$f(\mathbf{x}) = \mathbb{P}[y = +1 \mid \mathbf{x}].$$

The data does not give us the value of f explicitly. Rather, it gives us samples generated by this probability, e.g., patients who had heart attacks and patients who didn't. Therefore, the data is in fact generated by a noisy target $P(y \mid \mathbf{x})$,

$$P(y \mid \mathbf{x}) = \begin{cases} f(\mathbf{x}) & \text{for } y = +1; \\ 1 - f(\mathbf{x}) & \text{for } y = -1. \end{cases} \qquad (3.7)$$

To learn from such data, we need to define a proper error measure that gauges how close a given hypothesis h is to f in terms of these noisy ± 1 examples.

Error measure. The standard error measure $e(h(\mathbf{x}), y)$ used in logistic regression is based on the notion of *likelihood*; how 'likely' is it that we would get this output y from the input $\mathbf{x}$ if the target distribution $P(y \mid \mathbf{x})$ was indeed captured by our hypothesis $h(\mathbf{x})$? Based on (3.7), that likelihood would be

$$P(y \mid \mathbf{x}) = \begin{cases} h(\mathbf{x}) & \text{for } y = +1; \\ 1 - h(\mathbf{x}) & \text{for } y = -1. \end{cases}$$

We substitute for $h(\mathbf{x})$ by its value $\theta(\mathbf{w}^{\mathsf{T}}\mathbf{x})$, and use the fact that $1 - \theta(s) = \theta(-s)$ (easy to verify) to get

$$P(y \mid \mathbf{x}) = \theta(y \, \mathbf{w}^{\mathsf{T}}\mathbf{x}). \tag{3.8}$$

One of our reasons for choosing the mathematical form $\theta(s) = e^s/(1 + e^s)$ is that it leads to this simple expression for $P(y \mid \mathbf{x})$.

Since the data points $(\mathbf{x}_1, y_1), \ldots, (\mathbf{x}_N, y_N)$ are independently generated, the probability of getting all the y_n's in the data set from the corresponding $\mathbf{x}_n$'s would be the product

$$\prod_{n=1}^{N} P(y_n \mid \mathbf{x}_n).$$

The method of *maximum likelihood* selects the hypothesis h which maximizes this probability.[3] We can equivalently minimize a more convenient quantity,

$$-\frac{1}{N} \ln \left(\prod_{n=1}^{N} P(y_n \mid \mathbf{x}_n) \right) = \frac{1}{N} \sum_{n=1}^{N} \ln \left(\frac{1}{P(y_n \mid \mathbf{x}_n)} \right),$$

since '$-\frac{1}{N} \ln(\cdot)$' is a monotonically decreasing function. Substituting with Equation (3.8), we would be minimizing

$$\frac{1}{N} \sum_{n=1}^{N} \ln \left(\frac{1}{\theta(y_n \mathbf{w}^{\mathsf{T}}\mathbf{x}_n)} \right)$$

with respect to the weight vector $\mathbf{w}$. The fact that we are *minimizing* this quantity allows us to treat it as an 'error measure.' Substituting the functional form for $\theta(y_n \mathbf{w}^{\mathsf{T}}\mathbf{x}_n)$ produces the in-sample error measure for logistic regression,

$$E_{\text{in}}(\mathbf{w}) = \frac{1}{N} \sum_{n=1}^{N} \ln \left(1 + e^{-y_n \mathbf{w}^{\mathsf{T}}\mathbf{x}_n} \right). \tag{3.9}$$

The implied pointwise error measure is $e(h(\mathbf{x}_n), y_n) = \ln(1 + e^{-y_n \mathbf{w}^{\mathsf{T}}\mathbf{x}_n})$. Notice that this error measure is small when $y_n \mathbf{w}^{\mathsf{T}}\mathbf{x}_n$ is large and *positive*, which would imply that $\text{sign}(\mathbf{w}^{\mathsf{T}}\mathbf{x}_n) = y_n$. Therefore, as our intuition would expect, the error measure encourages $\mathbf{w}$ to 'classify' each $\mathbf{x}_n$ correctly.

---

[3] Although the method of maximum likelihood is intuitively plausible, its rigorous justification as an inference tool continues to be discussed in the statistics community.

Exercise 3.6 [Cross-entropy error measure]

(a) More generally, if we are learning from ± 1 data to predict a noisy target $P(y \mid \mathbf{x})$ with candidate hypothesis h, show that the maximum likelihood method reduces to the task of finding h that minimizes

$$E_{\text{in}}(\mathbf{w}) = \sum_{n=1}^{N} [\![y_n = +1]\!] \ln \frac{1}{h(\mathbf{x}_n)} + [\![y_n = -1]\!] \ln \frac{1}{1 - h(\mathbf{x}_n)}.$$

(b) For the case $h(\mathbf{x}) = \theta(\mathbf{w}^{\mathsf{T}}\mathbf{x})$, argue that minimizing the in-sample error in part (a) is equivalent to minimizing the one in (3.9).

For two probability distributions $\{p, 1-p\}$ and $\{q, 1-q\}$ with binary outcomes, the cross-entropy (from information theory) is

$$p \log \frac{1}{q} + (1-p) \log \frac{1}{1-q}.$$

The in-sample error in part (a) corresponds to a cross-entropy error measure on the data point $(\mathbf{x}_n, y_n)$, with $p = [\![y_n = +1]\!]$ and $q = h(\mathbf{x}_n)$.

For linear classification, we saw that minimizing E_{in} for the perceptron is a combinatorial optimization problem; to solve it, we introduced a number of algorithms such as the perceptron learning algorithm and the pocket algorithm. For linear regression, we saw that training can be done using the analytic pseudo-inverse algorithm for minimizing E_{in} by setting $\nabla E_{\text{in}}(\mathbf{w}) = \mathbf{0}$. These algorithms were developed based on the specific form of linear classification or linear regression, so none of them would apply to logistic regression.

To train logistic regression, we will take an approach similar to linear regression in that we will try to set $\nabla E_{\text{in}}(\mathbf{w}) = \mathbf{0}$. Unfortunately, unlike the case of linear regression, the mathematical form of the gradient of E_{in} for logistic regression is not easy to manipulate, so an analytic solution is not feasible.

Exercise 3.7

For logistic regression, show that

$$\nabla E_{\text{in}}(\mathbf{w}) = -\frac{1}{N} \sum_{n=1}^{N} \frac{y_n \mathbf{x}_n}{1 + e^{y_n \mathbf{w}^{\mathsf{T}} \mathbf{x}_n}}$$

$$= \frac{1}{N} \sum_{n=1}^{N} -y_n \mathbf{x}_n \theta(-y_n \mathbf{w}^{\mathsf{T}} \mathbf{x}_n).$$

Argue that a 'misclassified' example contributes more to the gradient than a correctly classified one.

Instead of analytically setting the gradient to zero, we will *iteratively* set it to zero. To do so, we will introduce a new algorithm, *gradient descent*. Gradient descent is a very general algorithm that can be used to train many other learning models with smooth error measures. For logistic regression, gradient descent has particularly nice properties.

3.3.2   Gradient Descent

Gradient descent is a general technique for minimizing a twice-differentiable function, such as $E_{in}(\mathbf{w})$ in logistic regression. A useful physical analogy of gradient descent is a ball rolling down a hilly surface. If the ball is placed on a hill, it will roll down, coming to rest at the bottom of a valley. The same basic idea underlies gradient descent. $E_{in}(\mathbf{w})$ is a 'surface' in a high-dimensional space. At step 0, we start somewhere on this surface, at $\mathbf{w}(0)$, and try to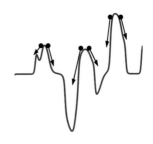
roll down this surface, thereby decreasing E_{in}. One thing which you immediately notice from the physical analogy is that the ball will not necessarily come to rest in the lowest valley of the entire surface. Depending on where you start the ball rolling, you will end up at the bottom of one of the valleys – a *local minimum*. In general, the same applies to gradient descent. Depending on your starting weights, the path of descent will take you to a local minimum in the error surface.

A particular advantage for logistic regression with the cross-entropy error is that the picture looks much nicer. There is only one valley! So, it does not matter where you start your ball rolling, it will always roll down to the same (unique) *global minimum*. This is a consequence of the fact that $E_{in}(\mathbf{w})$ is a *convex* function of $\mathbf{w}$, a mathematical property that implies a single 'valley' as shown to the right. This means that gradient descent will not be trapped in local minima when minimizing such convex error measures.[4]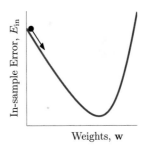

Let's now determine how to 'roll' down the E_{in}-surface. We would like to take a step in the direction of steepest descent, to gain the biggest bang for our buck. Suppose that we take a small step of size η in the direction of a unit vector $\hat{\mathbf{v}}$. The new weights are $\mathbf{w}(0) + \eta\hat{\mathbf{v}}$. Since η is small, using the Taylor expansion to first order, we compute the change in E_{in} as

$$
\begin{aligned}
\Delta E_{in} &= E_{in}(\mathbf{w}(0) + \eta\hat{\mathbf{v}}) - E_{in}(\mathbf{w}(0)) \\
&= \eta \nabla E_{in}(\mathbf{w}(0))^{\mathsf{T}} \hat{\mathbf{v}} + O(\eta^2) \\
&\geq -\eta \|\nabla E_{in}(\mathbf{w}(0))\|,
\end{aligned}
$$

---

[4]In fact, the squared in-sample error in linear regression is also convex, which is why the analytic solution found by the pseudo-inverse is guaranteed to have optimal in-sample error.

where we have ignored the small term $O(\eta^2)$. Since $\hat{\mathbf{v}}$ is a unit vector, equality holds if and only if

$$\hat{\mathbf{v}} = -\frac{\nabla E_{\text{in}}(\mathbf{w}(0))}{\|\nabla E_{\text{in}}(\mathbf{w}(0))\|}. \qquad (3.10)$$

This direction, specified by $\hat{\mathbf{v}}$, leads to the largest decrease in E_{in} for a given step size η.

Exercise 3.8

The claim that $\hat{\mathbf{v}}$ is the direction which gives largest decrease in E_{in} only holds for small η. Why?

There is nothing to prevent us from continuing to take steps of size η, re-evaluating the direction $\hat{\mathbf{v}}_t$ at each iteration $t = 0, 1, 2, \ldots$. How large a step should one take at each iteration? This is a good question, and to gain some insight, let's look at the following examples.

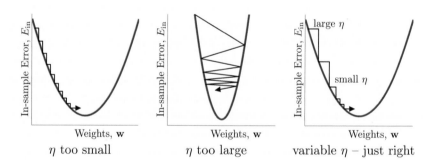

A fixed step size (if it is too small) is inefficient when you are far from the local minimum. On the other hand, too large a step size when you are close to the minimum leads to bouncing around, possibly even increasing E_{in}. Ideally, we would like to take large steps when far from the minimum to get in the right ballpark quickly, and then small (more careful) steps when close to the minimum. A simple heuristic can accomplish this: far from the minimum, the norm of the gradient is typically large, and close to the minimum, it is small. Thus, we could set $\eta_t = \eta\|\nabla E_{\text{in}}\|$ to obtain the desired behavior for the variable step size; choosing the step size proportional to the norm of the gradient will also conveniently cancel the term normalizing the unit vector $\hat{\mathbf{v}}$ in Equation (3.10), leading to the *fixed learning rate gradient descent* algorithm for minimizing E_{in} (with redefined η):

Fixed learning rate gradient descent:

1: Initialize the weights at time step $t = 0$ to $\mathbf{w}(0)$.

2: **for** $t = 0, 1, 2, \ldots$ **do**

3:    Compute the gradient $\mathbf{g}_t = \nabla E_{\text{in}}(\mathbf{w}(t))$.

4:    Set the direction to move, $\mathbf{v}_t = -\mathbf{g}_t$.

5:    Update the weights: $\mathbf{w}(t+1) = \mathbf{w}(t) + \eta\mathbf{v}_t$.

6:    Iterate to the next step until it is time to stop.

7: Return the final weights.

In the algorithm, $\mathbf{v}_t$ is a direction that is no longer restricted to unit length. The parameter η (the *learning rate*) has to be specified. A typically good choice for η is around 0.1 (a purely practical observation). To use gradient descent, one must compute the gradient. This can be done explicitly for logistic regression (see Exercise 3.7).

Example 3.3. Gradient descent is a general algorithm for minimizing twice-differentiable functions. We can apply it to the logistic regression in-sample error to return weights that approximately minimize

$$E_{\text{in}}(\mathbf{w}) = \frac{1}{N} \sum_{n=1}^{N} \ln\left(1 + e^{-y_n \mathbf{w}^{\mathsf{T}} \mathbf{x}_n}\right).$$

Logistic regression algorithm:

1: Initialize the weights at time step $t = 0$ to $\mathbf{w}(0)$.

2: **for** $t = 0, 1, 2, \ldots$ **do**

3:    Compute the gradient

$$\mathbf{g}_t = -\frac{1}{N} \sum_{n=1}^{N} \frac{y_n \mathbf{x}_n}{1 + e^{y_n \mathbf{w}^{\mathsf{T}}(t)\mathbf{x}_n}}.$$

4:    Set the direction to move, $\mathbf{v}_t = -\mathbf{g}_t$.

5:    Update the weights: $\mathbf{w}(t+1) = \mathbf{w}(t) + \eta\mathbf{v}_t$.

6:    Iterate to the next step until it is time to stop.

7: Return the final weights $\mathbf{w}$.

$\square$

Initialization and termination. We have two more loose ends to tie: the first is how to choose $\mathbf{w}(0)$, the initial weights, and the second is how to set the criterion for "... until it is time to stop" in step 6 of the gradient descent algorithm. In some cases, such as logistic regression, initializing the weights $\mathbf{w}(0)$ as zeros works well. However, in general, it is safer to initialize the weights randomly, so as to avoid getting stuck on a perfectly symmetric hilltop. Choosing each weight independently from a Normal distribution with zero mean and small variance usually works well in practice.

That takes care of initialization, so we now move on to termination. How do we decide when to stop? Termination is a non-trivial topic in optimization. One simple approach, as we encountered in the pocket algorithm, is to set an upper bound on the number of iterations, where the upper bound is typically in the thousands, depending on the amount of training time we have. The problem with this approach is that there is no guarantee on the quality of the final weights.

Another plausible approach is based on the gradient being zero at any minimum. A natural termination criterion would be to stop once $\|\mathbf{g}_t\|$ drops below a certain threshold. Eventually this must happen, but we do not know when it will happen. For logistic regression, a combination of the two conditions (setting a large upper bound for the number of iterations, and a small lower bound for the size of the gradient) usually works well in practice.

There is a problem with relying solely on the size of the gradient to stop, which is that you might stop prematurely as illustrated on the right. When the iteration reaches a relatively flat region (which is more common than you might suspect), the algorithm will prematurely stop when we may want to continue. So one solution is to require that termination occurs only

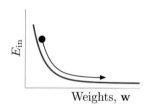

Weights, $\mathbf{w}$

if the error change is small and the error itself is small. Ultimately a combination of termination criteria (a maximum number of iterations, marginal error improvement, coupled with small value for the error itself) works reasonably well.

Example 3.4. By way of summarizing linear models, we revisit our old friend the credit example. If the goal is to decide whether to approve or deny, then we are in the realm of classification; if you want to assign an amount of credit line, then linear regression is appropriate; if you want to predict the probability that someone will default, use logistic regression.

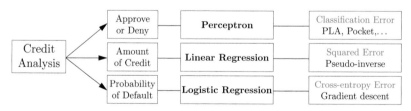

The three linear models have their respective goals, error measures, and algorithms. Nonetheless, they not only share similar sets of linear hypotheses, but are in fact related in other ways. We would like to point out one important relationship: Both logistic regression and linear regression can be used in linear classification. Here is how.

Logistic regression produces a final hypothesis $g(\mathbf{x})$ which is our estimate of $\mathbb{P}[y = +1 \mid \mathbf{x}]$. Such an estimate can easily be used for classification by

96

setting a threshold on $g(\mathbf{x})$; a natural threshold is $\frac{1}{2}$, which corresponds to classifying $+1$ if $+1$ is more likely. This choice for threshold corresponds to using the logistic regression weights as weights in the perceptron for classification. Not only can logistic regression weights be used for classification in this way, but they can also be used as a way to train the perceptron model. The perceptron learning problem (3.2) is a very hard combinatorial optimization problem. The convexity of E_{in} in logistic regression makes the optimization problem much easier to solve. Since the logistic function is a soft version of a hard threshold, the logistic regression weights should be good weights for classification using the perceptron.

A similar relationship exists between classification and linear regression. Linear regression can be used with any real-valued target function, which includes real values that are ± 1. If $\mathbf{w}_{\text{lin}}^{\mathrm{T}}\mathbf{x}$ is fit to ± 1 values, $\text{sign}(\mathbf{w}_{\text{lin}}^{\mathrm{T}}\mathbf{x})$ will likely agree with these values and make good classification predictions. In other words, the linear regression weights $\mathbf{w}_{\text{lin}}$, which are easily computed using the pseudo-inverse, are also an approximate solution for the perceptron model. The weights can be directly used for classification, or used as an initial condition for the pocket algorithm to give it a head start. ☐

Exercise 3.9

Consider pointwise error measures $e_{\text{class}}(s, y) = [\![y \neq \text{sign}(s)]\!]$, $e_{\text{sq}}(s, y) = (y - s)^2$, and $e_{\text{log}}(s, y) = \ln(1 + \exp(-ys))$, where the signal $s = \mathbf{w}^{\mathrm{T}}\mathbf{x}$.

(a) For $y = +1$, plot e_{class}, e_{sq} and $\frac{1}{\ln 2}e_{\text{log}}$ versus s, on the same plot.

(b) Show that $e_{\text{class}}(s, y) \leq e_{\text{sq}}(s, y)$, and hence that the classification error is upper bounded by the squared error.

(c) Show that $e_{\text{class}}(s, y) \leq \frac{1}{\ln 2}e_{\text{log}}(s, y)$, and, as in part (b), get an upper bound (up to a constant factor) using the logistic regression error.

These bounds indicate that minimizing the squared or logistic regression error should also decrease the classification error, which justifies using the weights returned by linear or logistic regression as approximations for classification.

Stochastic gradient descent. The version of gradient descent we have described so far is known as *batch* gradient descent – the gradient is computed for the error on the whole data set before a weight update is done. A sequential version of gradient descent known as *stochastic gradient descent* (SGD) turns out to be very efficient in practice. Instead of considering the full batch gradient on all N training data points, we consider a stochastic version of the gradient. First, pick a training data point $(\mathbf{x}_n, y_n)$ uniformly at random (hence the name 'stochastic'), and consider only the error on that data point (in the case of logistic regression),

$$\mathsf{e}_n(\mathbf{w}) = \ln\left(1 + e^{-y_n \mathbf{w}^\mathsf{T} \mathbf{x}_n}\right).$$

The gradient of this single data point's error is used for the weight update in exactly the same way that the gradient was used in batch gradient descent. The gradient needed for the weight update of SGD is (see Exercise 3.7)

$$\nabla \mathsf{e}_n(\mathbf{w}) = \frac{-y_n \mathbf{x}_n}{1 + e^{y_n \mathbf{w}^\mathsf{T} \mathbf{x}_n}},$$

and the weight update is $\mathbf{w} \leftarrow \mathbf{w} - \eta \nabla \mathsf{e}_n(\mathbf{w})$. Insight into why SGD works can be gained by looking at the expected value of the change in the weight (the expectation is with respect to the random point that is selected). Since n is picked uniformly at random from $\{1, \ldots, N\}$, the expected weight change is

$$-\eta \cdot \frac{1}{N} \sum_{n=1}^{N} \nabla \mathsf{e}_n(\mathbf{w}).$$

This is exactly the same as the deterministic weight change from the batch gradient descent weight update. That is, 'on average' the minimization proceeds in the right direction, but is a bit wiggly. In the long run, these random fluctuations cancel out. The computational cost is cheaper by a factor of N, though, since we compute the gradient for only one point per iteration, rather than for all N points as we do in batch gradient descent.

Notice that SGD is similar to PLA in that it decreases the error with respect to one data point at a time. Minimizing the error on one data point may interfere with the error on the rest of the data points that are not considered at that iteration. However, also similar to PLA, the interference cancels out on average as we have just argued.

Exercise 3.10

(a) Define an error for a single data point $(\mathbf{x}_n, y_n)$ to be

$$\mathsf{e}_n(\mathbf{w}) = \max(0, -y_n \mathbf{w}^\mathsf{T} \mathbf{x}_n).$$

Argue that PLA can be viewed as SGD on e_n with learning rate $\eta = 1$.

(b) For logistic regression with a very large $\mathbf{w}$, argue that minimizing E_{in} using SGD is similar to PLA. This is another indication that the logistic regression weights can be used as a good approximation for classification.

SGD is successful in practice, often beating the batch version and other more sophisticated algorithms. In fact, SGD was an important part of the algorithm that won the million-dollar Netflix competition, discussed in Section 1.1. It scales well to large data sets, and is naturally suited to online learning, where a stream of data present themselves to the learning algorithm sequentially. The randomness introduced by processing one data point at a time can be a plus, helping the algorithm to avoid flat regions and local minima in the case of a complicated error surface. However, it is challenging to choose a suitable termination criterion for SGD. A good stopping criterion should consider the total error on all the data, which can be computationally demanding to evaluate at each iteration.

3.4 Nonlinear Transformation

All formulas for the linear model have used the sum

$$\mathbf{w}^{\mathrm{T}}\mathbf{x} = \sum_{i=0}^{d} w_i x_i \tag{3.11}$$

as the main quantity in computing the hypothesis output. This quantity is linear, not only in the x_i's but also in the w_i's. A closer inspection of the corresponding learning algorithms shows that *the linearity in w_i's is the key property for deriving these algorithms*; the x_i's are just constants as far as the algorithm is concerned. This observation opens the possibility for allowing nonlinear versions of x_i's while still remaining in the analytic realm of linear models, because the form of Equation (3.11) remains linear in the w_i parameters.

Consider the credit limit problem for instance. It makes sense that the 'years in residence' field would affect a person's credit since it is correlated with stability. However, it is less plausible that the credit limit would grow *linearly* with the number of years in residence. More plausibly, there is a threshold (say 1 year) below which the credit limit is affected negatively and another threshold (say 5 years) above which the credit limit is affected positively. If x_i is the input variable that measures years in residence, then two nonlinear 'features' derived from it, namely $[\![x_i < 1]\!]$ and $[\![x_i > 5]\!]$, would allow a linear formula to reflect the credit limit better.

We have already seen the use of features in the classification of handwritten digits, where intensity and symmetry features were derived from input pixels. Nonlinear transforms can be further applied to those features, as we will see shortly, creating more elaborate features and improving the performance. The scope of linear methods expands significantly when we represent the input by a set of appropriate features.

3.4.1 The $\mathcal{Z}$ Space

Consider the situation in Figure 3.1(b) where a linear classifier can't fit the data. By transforming the inputs x_1, x_2 in a nonlinear fashion, we will be able to separate the data with more complicated boundaries while still using the simple PLA as a building block. Let's start by looking at the circle in Figure 3.5(a), which is a replica of the non-separable case in Figure 3.1(b). The circle represents the following equation:

$$x_1^2 + x_2^2 = 0.6.$$

That is, the nonlinear hypothesis $h(\mathbf{x}) = \text{sign}(-0.6 + x_1^2 + x_2^2)$ separates the data set perfectly. We can view the hypothesis as a *linear* one after applying a nonlinear transformation on $\mathbf{x}$. In particular, consider $z_0 = 1$, $z_1 = x_1^2$ and $z_2 = x_2^2$,

$$h(\mathbf{x}) \;=\; \text{sign}\left(\underbrace{(-0.6)}_{\tilde{w}_0} \cdot \underbrace{1}_{z_0} \;+\; \underbrace{1}_{\tilde{w}_1} \cdot \underbrace{x_1^2}_{z_1} \;+\; \underbrace{1}_{\tilde{w}_2} \cdot \underbrace{x_2^2}_{z_2}\right)$$

$$\;=\; \text{sign}\left(\underbrace{[\tilde{w}_0 \ \tilde{w}_1 \ \tilde{w}_2]}_{\tilde{\mathbf{w}}^{\mathsf{T}}} \underbrace{\begin{bmatrix} 1 \\ z_1 \\ z_2 \end{bmatrix}}_{\mathbf{z}}\right).$$

where the vector $\mathbf{z}$ is obtained from $\mathbf{x}$ through a nonlinear transform Φ,

$$\mathbf{z} = \Phi(\mathbf{x}).$$

We can plot the data in terms of $\mathbf{z}$ instead of $\mathbf{x}$, as depicted in Figure 3.5(b). For instance, the point $\mathbf{x}_1$ in Figure 3.5(a) is transformed to the point $\mathbf{z}_1$ in Figure 3.5(b) and the point $\mathbf{x}_2$ is transformed to the point $\mathbf{z}_2$. The space $\mathcal{Z}$, which contains the $\mathbf{z}$ vectors, is referred to as the *feature space* since its coordinates are higher-level features derived from the raw input $\mathbf{x}$. We designate different quantities in $\mathcal{Z}$ with a tilde version of their counterparts in $\mathcal{X}$, e.g., the dimensionality of $\mathcal{Z}$ is $\tilde{d}$ and the weight vector is $\tilde{\mathbf{w}}$.[5] The transform Φ that takes us from $\mathcal{X}$ to $\mathcal{Z}$ is called a *feature transform*, which in this case is

$$\Phi(\mathbf{x}) = (1, x_1^2, x_2^2). \tag{3.12}$$

In general, some points in the $\mathcal{Z}$ space may not be valid transforms of any $\mathbf{x} \in \mathcal{X}$, and multiple points in $\mathcal{X}$ may be transformed to the same $\mathbf{z} \in \mathcal{Z}$, depending on the nonlinear transform Φ.

The usefulness of the transform above is that the nonlinear hypothesis h (circle) in the $\mathcal{X}$ space can be represented by a linear hypothesis (line) in the $\mathcal{Z}$ space. Indeed, any linear hypothesis $\tilde{h}$ in $\mathbf{z}$ corresponds to a (possibly nonlinear) hypothesis of $\mathbf{x}$ given by

$$h(\mathbf{x}) = \tilde{h}(\Phi(\mathbf{x})).$$

---

[5] $\mathcal{Z} = \{1\} \times \mathbb{R}^{\tilde{d}}$, where $\tilde{d} = 2$ in this case. We treat $\mathcal{Z}$ as $\tilde{d}$-dimensional since the added coordinate $z_0 = 1$ is fixed.

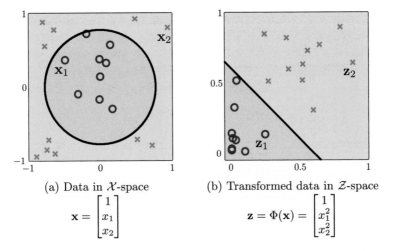

(a) Data in $\mathcal{X}$-space   (b) Transformed data in $\mathcal{Z}$-space

$$\mathbf{x} = \begin{bmatrix} 1 \\ x_1 \\ x_2 \end{bmatrix} \qquad \mathbf{z} = \Phi(\mathbf{x}) = \begin{bmatrix} 1 \\ x_1^2 \\ x_2^2 \end{bmatrix}$$

Figure 3.5: (a) The original data set that is not linearly separable, but separable by a circle. (b) The transformed data set that is linearly separable in the $\mathcal{Z}$ space. In the figure, $\mathbf{x}_1$ maps to $\mathbf{z}_1$ and $\mathbf{x}_2$ maps to $\mathbf{z}_2$; the circular separator in the $\mathcal{X}$-space maps to the linear separator in the $\mathcal{Z}$-space.

The set of these hypotheses h is denoted by $\mathcal{H}_\Phi$. For instance, when using the feature transform in (3.12), each $h \in \mathcal{H}_\Phi$ is a quadratic curve in $\mathcal{X}$ that corresponds to some line $\tilde{h}$ in $\mathcal{Z}$.

Exercise 3.11

Consider the feature transform Φ in (3.12). What kind of boundary in $\mathcal{X}$ does a hyperplane $\tilde{\mathbf{w}}$ in $\mathcal{Z}$ correspond to in the following cases? Draw a picture that illustrates an example of each case.

(a) $\tilde{w}_1 > 0, \tilde{w}_2 < 0$

(b) $\tilde{w}_1 > 0, \tilde{w}_2 = 0$

(c) $\tilde{w}_1 > 0, \tilde{w}_2 > 0, \tilde{w}_0 < 0$

(d) $\tilde{w}_1 > 0, \tilde{w}_2 > 0, \tilde{w}_0 > 0$

Because the transformed data set $(\mathbf{z}_1, y_1), \cdots, (\mathbf{z}_N, y_N)$ in Figure 3.5(b) is linearly separable in the feature space $\mathcal{Z}$, we can apply PLA on the transformed data set to obtain $\tilde{\mathbf{w}}_{\text{PLA}}$, the PLA solution, which gives us a final hypothesis $g(\mathbf{x}) = \text{sign}(\tilde{\mathbf{w}}_{\text{PLA}}^{\mathsf{T}} \mathbf{z})$ in the $\mathcal{X}$ space, where $\mathbf{z} = \Phi(\mathbf{x})$. The whole process of applying the feature transform before running PLA for linear classification is depicted in Figure 3.6.

The in-sample error in the input space $\mathcal{X}$ is the same as in the feature space $\mathcal{Z}$, so $E_{\text{in}}(g) = 0$. Hyperplanes that achieve $E_{\text{in}}(\tilde{\mathbf{w}}_{\text{PLA}}) = 0$ in $\mathcal{Z}$ correspond to separating curves in the original input space $\mathcal{X}$. For instance,

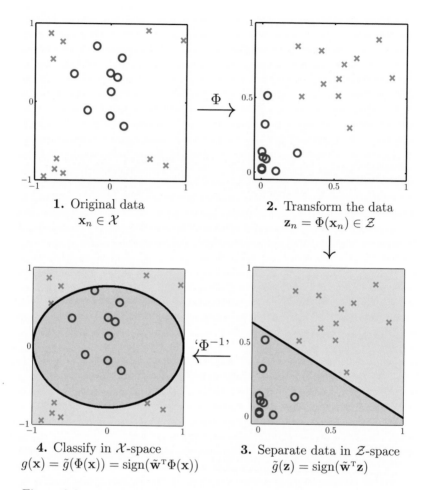

1. Original data
$\mathbf{x}_n \in \mathcal{X}$

2. Transform the data
$\mathbf{z}_n = \Phi(\mathbf{x}_n) \in \mathcal{Z}$

4. Classify in $\mathcal{X}$-space
$g(\mathbf{x}) = \tilde{g}(\Phi(\mathbf{x})) = \text{sign}(\tilde{\mathbf{w}}^{\mathsf{T}}\Phi(\mathbf{x}))$

3. Separate data in $\mathcal{Z}$-space
$\tilde{g}(\mathbf{z}) = \text{sign}(\tilde{\mathbf{w}}^{\mathsf{T}}\mathbf{z})$

Figure 3.6: The nonlinear transform for separating non-separable data.

as shown in Figure 3.6, the PLA may select the line $\tilde{\mathbf{w}}_{\text{PLA}} = (-0.6, 0.6, 1)$ that separates the transformed data $(\mathbf{z}_1, y_1), \cdots, (\mathbf{z}_N, y_N)$. The corresponding hypothesis $g(\mathbf{x}) = \text{sign}(-0.6 + 0.6 \cdot x_1^2 + x_2^2)$ will separate the original data $(\mathbf{x}_1, y_1), \cdots, (\mathbf{x}_N, y_N)$. In this case, the decision boundary is an ellipse in $\mathcal{X}$.

How does the feature transform affect the VC bound (3.1)? If we honestly decide on the transform Φ before seeing the data, then with probability at least $1 - \delta$, the bound (3.1) remains true by using $d_{\text{vc}}(\mathcal{H}_\Phi)$ as the VC dimension. For instance, consider the feature transform Φ in (3.12). We know that $\mathcal{Z} = \{1\} \times \mathbb{R}^2$. Since $\mathcal{H}_\Phi$ is the perceptron in $\mathcal{Z}$, $d_{\text{vc}}(\mathcal{H}_\Phi) \leq 3$ (the $\leq$ is because some points $\mathbf{z} \in \mathcal{Z}$ may not be valid transforms of any $\mathbf{x}$, so some dichotomies may not be realizable). We can then substitute N, $d_{\text{vc}}(\mathcal{H}_\Phi)$, and δ into the VC bound. After running PLA on the transformed data set, if we succeed in getting some g with $E_{\text{in}}(g) = 0$, we can claim that g will perform well out of sample.

It is very important to understand that the claim above is valid only if you decide on Φ *before* seeing the data or trying any algorithms. What if we first try using lines to separate the data, fail, and then use the circles? Then we are effectively using a model that contains both lines and circles, and d_{vc} is no longer 3.

Exercise 3.12

We know that in the Euclidean plane, the perceptron model $\mathcal{H}$ cannot implement all 16 dichotomies on 4 points. That is, $m_{\mathcal{H}}(4) < 16$. Take the feature transform Φ in (3.12).

(a) Show that $m_{\mathcal{H}_\Phi}(3) = 8$.

(b) Show that $m_{\mathcal{H}_\Phi}(4) < 16$.

(c) Show that $m_{\mathcal{H} \cup \mathcal{H}_\Phi}(4) = 16$.

That is, if you used lines, $d_{\text{vc}} = 3$; if you used elipses, $d_{\text{vc}} = 3$; if you used lines and elipses, $d_{\text{vc}} > 3$.

Worse yet, if you actually *look* at the data (e.g., look at the points in Figure 3.1(a)) before deciding on a suitable Φ, you forfeit most of what you learned in Chapter 2 ☺. You have inadvertently explored a huge hypothesis space in your mind to come up with a specific Φ that would work *for this data set*. If you invoke a generalization bound now, you will be charged for the VC dimension of the full space that you explored in your mind, not just the space that Φ creates.

This does not mean that Φ should be chosen blindly. In the credit limit problem for instance, we suggested nonlinear features based on the 'years in residence' field that may be more suitable for linear regression than the raw input. This was based on our understanding of the problem, not on 'snooping' into the training data. Therefore, we pay no price in terms of generalization, and we may well gain a dividend in performance because of a good choice of features.

The feature transform Φ can be general, as long as it is chosen before seeing the data set (as if we cannot emphasize this enough). For instance, you may have noticed that the feature transform in (3.12) only allows us to get very limited types of quadratic curves. Ellipses that do not center at the origin in $\mathcal{X}$ cannot correspond to a hyperplane in $\mathcal{Z}$. To get all possible quadratic curves in $\mathcal{X}$, we could consider the more general feature transform $\mathbf{z} = \Phi_2(\mathbf{x})$,

$$\Phi_2(\mathbf{x}) = (1, x_1, x_2, x_1^2, x_1 x_2, x_2^2), \qquad (3.13)$$

which gives us the flexibility to represent any quadratic curve in $\mathcal{X}$ by a hyperplane in $\mathcal{Z}$ (the subscript 2 of Φ is for polynomials of degree 2 - quadratic curves). The price we pay is that $\mathcal{Z}$ is now five-dimensional instead of two-dimensional, and hence d_{vc} is doubled from 3 to 6.

Exercise 3.13

Consider the feature transform $z = \Phi_2(x)$ in (3.13). How can we use a hyperplane $\tilde{w}$ in $\mathcal{Z}$ to represent the following boundaries in $\mathcal{X}$?

(a) The parabola $(x_1 - 3)^2 + x_2 = 1$.

(b) The circle $(x_1 - 3)^2 + (x_2 - 4)^2 = 1$.

(c) The ellipse $2(x_1 - 3)^2 + (x_2 - 4)^2 = 1$.

(d) The hyperbola $(x_1 - 3)^2 - (x_2 - 4)^2 = 1$.

(e) The ellipse $2(x_1 + x_2 - 3)^2 + (x_1 - x_2 - 4)^2 = 1$.

(f) The line $2x_1 + x_2 = 1$.

One may further extend Φ_2 to a feature transform Φ_3 for cubic curves in $\mathcal{X}$, or more generally define the feature transform Φ_Q for degree-Q curves in $\mathcal{X}$. The feature transform Φ_Q is called the *Qth order polynomial transform*.

The power of the feature transform should be used with care. It may not be worth it to insist on linear separability and employ a highly complex surface to achieve that. Consider the case of Figure 3.1(a). If we insist on a feature transform that linearly separates the data, it may lead to a significant increase of the VC dimension. As we see in Figure 3.7, no line can separate the training examples perfectly, and neither can any quadratic nor any third-order polynomial curves. Thus, we need to use a fourth-order polynomial transform:

$$\Phi_4(x) = (1, x_1, x_2, x_1^2, x_1 x_2, x_2^2, x_1^3, x_1^2 x_2, x_1 x_2^2, x_2^3, x_1^4, x_1^3 x_2, x_1^2 x_2^2, x_1 x_2^3, x_2^4).$$

If you look at the fourth-order decision boundary in Figure 3.7(b), you don't need the VC analysis to tell you that this is an overkill that is unlikely to generalize well to new data. A better option would have been to ignore the two misclassified examples in Figure 3.7(a), separate the other examples perfectly with the line, and accept the small but nonzero E_{in}. Indeed, sometimes our best bet is to go with a simpler hypothesis set while tolerating a small E_{in}.

While our discussion of feature transforms has focused on classification problems, these transforms can be applied equally to regression problems. Both linear regression and logistic regression can be implemented in the feature space $\mathcal{Z}$ instead of the input space $\mathcal{X}$. For instance, linear regression is often coupled with a feature transform to perform nonlinear regression. The N by $d + 1$ input matrix X in the algorithm is replaced with the N by $\tilde{d} + 1$ matrix Z, while the output vector y remains the same.

3.4.2 Computation and Generalization

Although using a larger Q gives us more flexibility in terms of the shape of decision boundaries in $\mathcal{X}$, there is a price to be paid. Computation is one issue, and generalization is the other.

Computation is an issue because the feature transform Φ_Q maps a two-dimensional vector x to $\tilde{d} = \frac{Q(Q+3)}{2}$ dimensions, which increases the memory

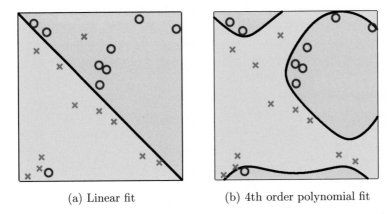

(a) Linear fit   (b) 4th order polynomial fit

Figure 3.7: Illustration of the nonlinear transform using a data set that is not linearly separable; (a) a line separates the data after omitting a few points, (b) a fourth-order polynomial separates all the points.

and computational costs. Things could get worse if $\mathbf{x}$ is in a higher dimension to begin with.

Exercise 3.14

Consider the Qth order polynomial transform Φ_Q for $\mathcal{X} = \mathbb{R}^d$. What is the dimensionality $\tilde{d}$ of the feature space $\mathcal{Z}$ (excluding the fixed coordinate $z_0 = 1$). Evaluate your result on $d \in \{2, 3, 5, 10\}$ and $Q \in \{2, 3, 5, 10\}$.

The other important issue is generalization. If Φ_Q is the feature transform of a two-dimensional input space, there will be $\tilde{d} = \frac{Q(Q+3)}{2}$ dimensions in $\mathcal{Z}$, and $d_{\mathrm{vc}}(\mathcal{H}_\Phi)$ can be as high as $\frac{Q(Q+3)}{2} + 1$. This means that the second term in the VC bound (3.1) can grow significantly. In other words, we would have a weaker guarantee that E_{out} will be small. For instance, if we use $\Phi = \Phi_{50}$, the VC dimension of $\mathcal{H}_\Phi$ could be as high as $\frac{(50)(53)}{2} + 1 = 1326$ instead of the original $d_{\mathrm{vc}} = 3$. Applying the rule of thumb that the amount of data needed is proportional to the VC dimension, we would need hundreds of times more data than we would if we didn't use a feature transform, in order to achieve the same level of generalization error.

Exercise 3.15

High-dimensional feature transforms are by no means the only transforms that we can use. We can take the tradeoff in the other direction, and use low-dimensional feature transforms as well (to achieve an even lower generalization error bar).

(continued on next page)

Consider the following feature transform, which maps a d-dimensional $\mathbf{x}$ to a one-dimensional $\mathbf{z}$, keeping only the kth coordinate of $\mathbf{x}$.

$$\Phi_{(k)}(\mathbf{x}) = (1, x_k). \qquad (3.14)$$

Let $\mathcal{H}_k$ be the set of perceptrons in the feature space.

(a) Prove that $d_{\mathrm{vc}}(\mathcal{H}_k) = 2$.

(b) Prove that $d_{\mathrm{vc}}(\cup_{k=1}^{d}\mathcal{H}_k) \leq 2(\log_2 d + 1)$.

$\mathcal{H}_k$ is called the *decision stump* model on dimension k.

The problem of generalization when we go to high-dimensional space is sometimes balanced by the advantage we get in approximating the target better. As we have seen in the case of using quadratic curves instead of lines, the transformed data became linearly separable, reducing E_{in} to 0. In general, when choosing the appropriate dimension for the feature transform, we cannot avoid the approximation-generalization tradeoff,

higher $\tilde{d}$	better chance of being linearly separable ($E_{\mathrm{in}} \downarrow$)	$d_{\mathrm{vc}} \uparrow$
lower $\tilde{d}$	possibly not linearly separable ($E_{\mathrm{in}} \uparrow$)	$d_{\mathrm{vc}} \downarrow$

Therefore, choosing a feature transform before seeing the data is a non-trivial task. When we apply learning to a particular problem, some understanding of the problem can help in choosing features that work well. More generally, there are some guidelines for choosing a suitable transform, or a suitable model, which we will discuss in Chapter 4.

Exercise 3.16

Write down the steps of the algorithm that combines Φ_3 with linear regression. How about using Φ_{10} instead? Where is the main computational bottleneck of the resulting algorithm?

Example 3.5. Let's revisit the handwritten digit recognition example. We can try a different way of decomposing the big task of separating ten digits to smaller tasks. One decomposition is to separate digit 1 from all the other digits. Using intensity and symmetry as our input variables like we did before, the scatter plot of the training data is shown next. A line can roughly separate digit 1 from the rest, but a more complicated curve might do better.

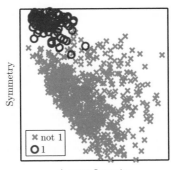

We use linear regression (for classification), first without any feature transform. The results are shown below (LHS). We get $E_{in} = 2.13\%$ and $E_{out} = 2.38\%$.

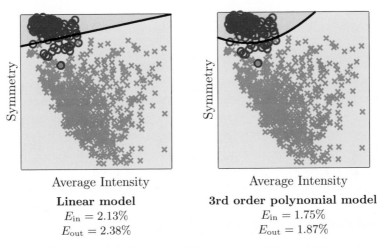

Average Intensity	Average Intensity
Linear model	**3rd order polynomial model**
$E_{in} = 2.13\%$	$E_{in} = 1.75\%$
$E_{out} = 2.38\%$	$E_{out} = 1.87\%$

Classification of the digits data ('1' versus 'not 1') using linear and third order polynomial models.

When we run linear regression with Φ_3, the third-order polynomial transform, we obtain a better fit to the data, with a lower $E_{in} = 1.75\%$. The result is depicted in the RHS of the figure. In this case, the better in-sample fit also resulted in a better out-of-sample performance, with $E_{out} = 1.87\%$. $\qquad\square$

Linear models, a final pitch. The linear model (for classification or regression) is an often overlooked resource in the arena of learning from data. Since efficient learning algorithms exist for linear models, they are low overhead. They are also very robust and have good generalization properties. A sound policy to follow when learning from data is to *first* try a linear model. Because of the good generalization properties of linear models, not much can go wrong. If you get a good fit to the data (low E_{in}), then you are done. If you do not get a good enough fit to the data and decide to go for a more complex model, you will pay a price in terms of the VC dimension as we have seen in Exercise 3.12, but the price is modest.

3.5 Problems

Problem 3.1   Consider the double semi-circle "toy" learning task below.

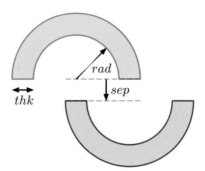

There are two semi-circles of width thk with inner radius rad, separated by sep as shown (red is -1 and blue is $+1$). The center of the top semi-circle is aligned with the middle of the edge of the bottom semi-circle. This task is linearly separable when $sep \geq 0$, and not so for $sep < 0$. Set $rad = 10$, $thk = 5$ and $sep = 5$. Then, generate $2,000$ examples uniformly, which means you will have approximately $1,000$ examples for each class.

(a) Run the PLA starting from $\mathbf{w} = \mathbf{0}$ until it converges. Plot the data and the final hypothesis.

(b) Repeat part (a) using the linear regression (for classification) to obtain $\mathbf{w}$. Explain your observations.

Problem 3.2   For the double-semi-circle task in Problem 3.1, vary sep in the range $\{0.2, 0.4, \ldots, 5\}$. Generate $2,000$ examples and run the PLA starting with $\mathbf{w} = \mathbf{0}$. Record the number of iterations PLA takes to converge.

Plot sep versus the number of iterations taken for PLA to converge. Explain your observations. *[Hint: Problem 1.3.]*

Problem 3.3   For the double-semi-circle task in Problem 3.1, set $sep = -5$ and generate $2,000$ examples.

(a) What will happen if you run PLA on those examples?

(b) Run the pocket algorithm for $100,000$ iterations and plot E_{in} versus the iteration number t.

(c) Plot the data and the final hypothesis in part (b).

(continued on next page)

(d) Use the linear regression algorithm to obtain the weights $\mathbf{w}$, and compare this result with the pocket algorithm in terms of computation time and quality of the solution.

(e) Repeat (b) – (d) with a 3rd order polynomial feature transform.

Problem 3.4   In Problem 1.5, we introduced the Adaptive Linear Neuron (Adaline) algorithm for classification. Here, we derive Adaline from an optimization perspective.

(a) Consider $E_n(\mathbf{w}) = (\max(0, 1 - y_n \mathbf{w}^{\mathsf{T}} \mathbf{x}_n))^2$. Show that $E_n(\mathbf{w})$ is continuous and differentiable. Write down the gradient $\nabla E_n(\mathbf{w})$.

(b) Show that $E_n(\mathbf{w})$ is an upper bound for $[\![\mathrm{sign}(\mathbf{w}^{\mathsf{T}}\mathbf{x}_n) \neq y_n]\!]$. Hence, $\frac{1}{N} \sum_{n=1}^{N} E_n(\mathbf{w})$ is an upper bound for the in-sample classification error $E_{\mathrm{in}}(\mathbf{w})$.

(c) Argue that the Adaline algorithm in Problem 1.5 performs stochastic gradient descent on $\frac{1}{N} \sum_{n=1}^{N} E_n(\mathbf{w})$.

Problem 3.5

(a) Consider
$$E_n(\mathbf{w}) = \max(0, 1 - y_n \mathbf{w}^{\mathsf{T}} \mathbf{x}_n).$$
Show that $E_n(\mathbf{w})$ is continuous and differentiable except when $y_n = \mathbf{w}^{\mathsf{T}} \mathbf{x}_n$.

(b) Show that $E_n(\mathbf{w})$ is an upper bound for $[\![\mathrm{sign}(\mathbf{w}^{\mathsf{T}}\mathbf{x}_n) \neq y_n]\!]$. Hence, $\frac{1}{N} \sum_{n=1}^{N} E_n(\mathbf{w})$ is an upper bound for the in-sample classification error $E_{\mathrm{in}}(\mathbf{w})$.

(c) Apply stochastic gradient descent on $\frac{1}{N} \sum_{n=1}^{N} E_n(\mathbf{w})$ (ignoring the singular case of $\mathbf{w}^{\mathsf{T}}\mathbf{x}_n = y_n$) and derive a new perceptron learning algorithm.

Problem 3.6   Derive a linear programming algorithm to fit a linear model for classification using the following steps. A linear program is an optimization problem of the following form:

$$\min_{\mathbf{z}} \quad \mathbf{c}^{\mathsf{T}}\mathbf{z}$$
$$\text{subject to} \quad A\mathbf{z} \leq \mathbf{b}.$$

A, b and c are parameters of the linear program and $\mathbf{z}$ is the optimization variable. This is such a well studied optimization problem that most mathematics software have canned optimization functions which solve linear programs.

(a) For linearly separable data, show that for some $\mathbf{w}$, $y_n(\mathbf{w}^{\mathsf{T}}\mathbf{x}_n) \geq 1$ for $n = 1, \ldots, N$.

(b) Formulate the task of finding a separating $\mathbf{w}$ for separable data as a linear program. You need to specify what the parameters $A, \mathbf{b}, \mathbf{c}$ are and what the optimization variable $\mathbf{z}$ is.

(c) If the data is not separable, the condition in (a) cannot hold for every n. Thus introduce the violation $\xi_n \geq 0$ to capture the amount of violation for example $\mathbf{x}_n$. So, for $n = 1, \ldots, N$,

$$
\begin{aligned}
y_n(\mathbf{w}^{\mathsf{T}}\mathbf{x}_n) &\geq 1 - \xi_n, \\
\xi_n &\geq 0.
\end{aligned}
$$

Naturally, we would like to minimize the amount of violation. One intuitive approach is to minimize $\sum_{n=1}^{N} \xi_n$, i.e., we want $\mathbf{w}$ that solves

$$
\begin{aligned}
&\min_{\mathbf{w}, \xi_n} \quad \sum_{n=1}^{N} \xi_n \\
&\text{subject to} \quad y_n(\mathbf{w}^{\mathsf{T}}\mathbf{x}_n) \geq 1 - \xi_n, \\
&\qquad\qquad\quad \xi_n \geq 0,
\end{aligned}
$$

where the inequalities must hold for $n = 1, \ldots, N$. Formulate this problem as a linear program.

(d) Argue that the linear program you derived in (c) and the optimization problem in Problem 3.5 are equivalent.

Problem 3.7   Use the linear programming algorithm from Problem 3.6 on the learning task in Problem 3.1 for the separable ($sep = 5$) and the non-separable ($sep = -5$) cases.

Compare your results to the linear regression approach with and without the 3rd order polynomial feature transform.

Problem 3.8   For linear regression, the out-of-sample error is

$$
E_{\text{out}}(h) = \mathbb{E}\left[(h(\mathbf{x}) - y)^2\right].
$$

Show that among *all* hypotheses, the one that minimizes E_{out} is given by

$$
h^*(\mathbf{x}) = \mathbb{E}[y \mid \mathbf{x}].
$$

The function h^* can be treated as a deterministic target function, in which case we can write $y = h^*(\mathbf{x}) + \epsilon(\mathbf{x})$ where $\epsilon(\mathbf{x})$ is an (input dependent) noise variable. Show that $\epsilon(\mathbf{x})$ has expected value zero.

Problem 3.9   Assuming that $X^T X$ is invertible, show by direct comparison with Equation (3.4) that $E_{\text{in}}(\mathbf{w})$ can be written as

$$E_{\text{in}}(\mathbf{w})$$
$$= (\mathbf{w} - (X^T X)^{-1} X^T \mathbf{y})^T (X^T X)(\mathbf{w} - (X^T X)^{-1} X^T \mathbf{y}) + \mathbf{y}^T (I - X(X^T X)^{-1} X^T) \mathbf{y}.$$

Use this expression for E_{in} to obtain $\mathbf{w}_{\text{lin}}$. What is the in-sample error? *[Hint: The matrix $X^T X$ is positive definite.]*

Problem 3.10   Exercise 3.3 studied some properties of the hat matrix $H = X(X^T X)^{-1} X^T$, where X is a N by $d + 1$ matrix, and $X^T X$ is invertible. Show the following additional properties.

  (a) Every eigenvalue of H is either 0 or 1. *[Hint: Exercise 3.3(b).]*

  (b) Show that the trace of a symmetric matrix equals the sum of its eigenvalues. *[Hint: Use the spectral theorem and the cyclic property of the trace. Note that the same result holds for non-symmetric matrices, but is a little harder to prove.]*

  (c) How many eigenvalues of H are 1?   What is the rank of H?   *[Hint: Exercise 3.3(d).]*

Problem 3.11   Consider the linear regression problem setup in Exercise 3.4, where the data comes from a genuine linear relationship with added noise. The noise for the different data points is assumed to be iid with zero mean and variance σ^2. Assume that the 2nd moment matrix $\Sigma = \mathbb{E}_{\mathbf{x}}[\mathbf{x}\mathbf{x}^T]$ is non-singular. Follow the steps below to show that, with high probability, the out-of-sample error on average is

$$E_{\text{out}}(\mathbf{w}_{\text{lin}}) = \sigma^2 \left(1 + \frac{d+1}{N} + o(\tfrac{1}{N}) \right).$$

  (a) For a test point $\mathbf{x}$, show that the error $y - g(\mathbf{x})$ is

$$\epsilon - \mathbf{x}^T (X^T X)^{-1} X^T \boldsymbol{\epsilon},$$

  where ϵ is the noise realization for the test point and $\boldsymbol{\epsilon}$ is the vector of noise realizations on the data.

  (b) Take the expectation with respect to the test point, i.e., $\mathbf{x}$ and ϵ, to obtain an expression for E_{out}. Show that

$$E_{\text{out}} = \sigma^2 + \text{trace}\left(\Sigma (X^T X)^{-1} X^T \boldsymbol{\epsilon}\boldsymbol{\epsilon}^T X (X^T X)^{-1} \right).$$

  [Hints: $a = \text{trace}(a)$ for any scalar a; $\text{trace}(AB) = \text{trace}(BA)$; expectation and trace commute.]

  (c) What is $\mathbb{E}_{\boldsymbol{\epsilon}}[\boldsymbol{\epsilon}\boldsymbol{\epsilon}^T]$?

(d) Take the expectation with respect to ϵ to show that, on average,

$$E_{\text{out}} = \sigma^2 + \frac{\sigma^2}{N} \text{trace} \left(\Sigma (\tfrac{1}{N} X^{\mathsf{T}} X)^{-1} \right).$$

Note that $\frac{1}{N} X^{\mathsf{T}} X = \frac{1}{N} \sum_{n=1}^{N} \mathbf{x}_n \mathbf{x}_n^{\mathsf{T}}$ is an N-sample estimate of Σ. So $\frac{1}{N} X^{\mathsf{T}} X \approx \Sigma$. If $\frac{1}{N} X^{\mathsf{T}} X = \Sigma$, then what is E_{out} on average?

(e) Show that (after taking the expectation over the data noise) with high probability,

$$E_{\text{out}} = \sigma^2 \left(1 + \frac{d+1}{N} + o(\tfrac{1}{N}) \right).$$

[Hint: By the law of large numbers $\frac{1}{N} X^{\mathsf{T}} X$ converges in probability to Σ, and so by continuity of the inverse at Σ, $\left(\frac{1}{N} X^{\mathsf{T}} X \right)^{-1}$ converges in probability to Σ^{-1}.]

Problem 3.12   In linear regression, the in-sample predictions are given by $\hat{\mathbf{y}} = H\mathbf{y}$, where $H = X(X^{\mathsf{T}}X)^{-1}X^{\mathsf{T}}$. Show that H is a projection matrix, i.e. $H^2 = H$. So $\hat{\mathbf{y}}$ is the projection of $\mathbf{y}$ onto some space. What is this space?

Problem 3.13   This problem creates a linear regression algorithm from a good algorithm for linear classification. As illustrated, the idea is to take the original data and shift it in one direction to get the $+1$ data points; then, shift it in the opposite direction to get the -1 data points.

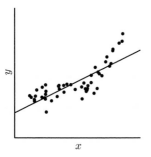

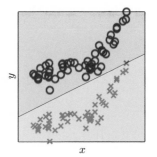

Original data for the one-dimensional regression problem

Shifted data viewed as a two-dimensional classification problem

More generally, The data $(\mathbf{x}_n, y_n)$ can be viewed as data points in $\mathbb{R}^{d+1}$ by treating the y-value as the $(d+1)$th coordinate.

(continued on next page)

Now, construct positive and negative points

$$\begin{aligned}
\mathcal{D}_+ &= (\mathbf{x}_1, y_1) + \mathbf{a}, \ldots, (\mathbf{x}_N, y_N) + \mathbf{a} \\
\mathcal{D}_- &= (\mathbf{x}_1, y_1) - \mathbf{a}, \ldots, (\mathbf{x}_N, y_N) - \mathbf{a},
\end{aligned}$$

where $\mathbf{a}$ is a perturbation parameter. You can now use the linear programming algorithm in Problem 3.6 to separate $\mathcal{D}_+$ from $\mathcal{D}_-$. The resulting separating hyperplane can be used as the regression 'fit' to the original data.

(a) How many weights are learned in the classification problem? How many weights are needed for the linear fit in the regression problem?

(b) The linear fit requires weights $\mathbf{w}$, where $h(\mathbf{x}) = \mathbf{w}^\mathsf{T}\mathbf{x}$. Suppose the weights returned by solving the classification problem are $\mathbf{w}_{\text{class}}$. Derive an expression for $\mathbf{w}$ as a function of $\mathbf{w}_{\text{class}}$.

(c) Generate a data set $y_n = x_n^2 + \sigma\epsilon_n$ with $N = 50$, where x_n is uniform on $[0, 1]$ and ϵ_n is zero mean Gaussian noise; set $\sigma = 0.1$. Plot $\mathcal{D}_+$ and $\mathcal{D}_-$ for $\mathbf{a} = \begin{bmatrix} 0 \\ 0.1 \end{bmatrix}$.

(d) Give comparisons of the resulting fits from running the classification approach and the analytic pseudo-inverse algorithm for linear regression.

Problem 3.14   In a regression setting, assume the target function is linear, so $f(\mathbf{x}) = \mathbf{x}^\mathsf{T}\mathbf{w}_f$, and $\mathbf{y} = \mathrm{X}\mathbf{w}_f + \boldsymbol{\epsilon}$, where the entries in $\boldsymbol{\epsilon}$ are zero mean, iid with variance σ^2. In this problem derive the bias and variance as follows.

(a) Show that the average function is $\bar{g}(\mathbf{x}) = f(\mathbf{x})$, no matter what the size of the data set, as long as $\mathrm{X}^\mathsf{T}\mathrm{X}$ is invertible. What is the bias?

(b) What is the variance? *[Hint: Problem 3.11]*

Problem 3.15   In the text we derived that the linear regression solution weights must satisfy $\mathrm{X}^\mathsf{T}\mathrm{X}\mathbf{w} = \mathrm{X}^\mathsf{T}\mathbf{y}$. If $\mathrm{X}^\mathsf{T}\mathrm{X}$ is not invertible, the solution $\mathbf{w}_{\text{lin}} = (\mathrm{X}^\mathsf{T}\mathrm{X})^{-1}\mathrm{X}^\mathsf{T}\mathbf{y}$ won't work. In this event, there will be many solutions for $\mathbf{w}$ that minimize E_{in}. Here, you will derive one such solution. Let ρ be the rank of X. Assume that the singular value decomposition (SVD) of X is $\mathrm{X} = \mathrm{U}\Gamma\mathrm{V}^\mathsf{T}$, where $\mathrm{U} \in \mathbb{R}^{N\times\rho}$ satisfies $\mathrm{U}^\mathsf{T}\mathrm{U} = \mathrm{I}_\rho$, $\mathrm{V} \in \mathbb{R}^{(d+1)\times\rho}$ satisfies $\mathrm{V}^\mathsf{T}\mathrm{V} = \mathrm{I}_\rho$, and $\Gamma \in \mathbb{R}^{\rho\times\rho}$ is a positive diagonal matrix.

(a) Show that $\rho < d + 1$.

(b) Show that $\mathbf{w}_{\text{lin}} = \mathrm{V}\Gamma^{-1}\mathrm{U}^\mathsf{T}\mathbf{y}$ satisfies $\mathrm{X}^\mathsf{T}\mathrm{X}\mathbf{w}_{\text{lin}} = \mathrm{X}^\mathsf{T}\mathbf{y}$, and hence is a solution.

(c) Show that for any other solution that satisfies $\mathrm{X}^\mathsf{T}\mathrm{X}\mathbf{w} = \mathrm{X}^\mathsf{T}\mathbf{y}$, $\|\mathbf{w}_{\text{lin}}\| < \|\mathbf{w}\|$. That is, the solution we have constructed is the minimum norm set of weights that minimizes E_{in}.

114

Problem 3.16   In Example 3.4, it is mentioned that the output of the final hypothesis $g(\mathbf{x})$ learned using logistic regression can be thresholded to get a 'hard' (± 1) classification. This problem shows how to use the risk matrix introduced in Example 1.1 to obtain such a threshold.

Consider fingerprint verification, as in Example 1.1. After learning from the data using logistic regression, you produce the final hypothesis

$$g(\mathbf{x}) = \mathbb{P}[y = +1 \mid \mathbf{x}],$$

which is your estimate of the probability that $y = +1$. Suppose that the cost matrix is given by

		True classification	
		$+1$ (correct person)	-1 (intruder)
you say	$+1$	0	c_a
	-1	c_r	0

For a new person with fingerprint $\mathbf{x}$, you compute $g(\mathbf{x})$ and you now need to decide whether to accept or reject the person (i.e., you need a hard classification). So, you will accept if $g(\mathbf{x}) \geq \kappa$, where κ is the threshold.

(a) Define the cost(accept) as your expected cost if you accept the person. Similarly define cost(reject). Show that

$$\begin{aligned} \text{cost(accept)} &= (1 - g(\mathbf{x}))c_a, \\ \text{cost(reject)} &= g(\mathbf{x})c_r. \end{aligned}$$

(b) Use part (a) to derive a condition on $g(\mathbf{x})$ for accepting the person and hence show that

$$\kappa = \frac{c_a}{c_a + c_r}.$$

(c) Use the cost-matrices for the Supermarket and CIA applications in Example 1.1 to compute the threshold κ for each of these two cases. Give some intuition for the thresholds you get.

Problem 3.17   Consider a function

$$E(u, v) = e^u + e^{2v} + e^{uv} + u^2 - 3uv + 4v^2 - 3u - 5v,$$

(a) Approximate $E(u + \Delta u, v + \Delta v)$ by $\hat{E}_1(\Delta u, \Delta v)$, where $\hat{E}_1$ is the first-order Taylor's expansion of E around $(u, v) = (0, 0)$. Suppose $\hat{E}_1(\Delta u, \Delta v) = a_u \Delta u + a_v \Delta v + a$. What are the values of a_u, a_v, and a?

(continued on next page)

(b) Minimize $\hat{E}_1$ over all possible $(\Delta u, \Delta v)$ such that $\|(\Delta u, \Delta v)\| = 0.5$. In this chapter, we proved that the optimal column vector $\begin{bmatrix} \Delta u \\ \Delta v \end{bmatrix}$ is parallel to the column vector $-\nabla E(u, v)$, which is called the *negative gradient direction*. Compute the optimal $(\Delta u, \Delta v)$ and the resulting $E(u + \Delta u, v + \Delta v)$.

(c) Approximate $E(u+\Delta u, v+\Delta v)$ by $\hat{E}_2(\Delta u, \Delta v)$, where $\hat{E}_2$ is the second-order Taylor's expansion of E around $(u, v) = (0, 0)$. Suppose

$$\hat{E}_2(\Delta u, \Delta v) = b_{uu}(\Delta u)^2 + b_{vv}(\Delta v)^2 + b_{uv}(\Delta u)(\Delta v) + b_u \Delta u + b_v \Delta v + b.$$

What are the values of b_{uu}, b_{vv}, b_{uv}, b_u, b_v, and b?

(d) Minimize $\hat{E}_2$ over all possible $(\Delta u, \Delta v)$ (regardless of length). Use the fact that $\nabla^2 E(u, v)\big|_{(0,0)}$ (the Hessian matrix at $(0, 0)$) is positive definite to prove that the optimal column vector

$$\begin{bmatrix} \Delta u^* \\ \Delta v^* \end{bmatrix} = -\left(\nabla^2 E(u, v)\right)^{-1} \nabla E(u, v),$$

which is called the *Newton direction*.

(e) Numerically compute the following values:

  (i) the vector $(\Delta u, \Delta v)$ of length 0.5 along the Newton direction, and the resulting $E(u + \Delta u, v + \Delta v)$.

  (ii) the vector $(\Delta u, \Delta v)$ of length 0.5 that minimizes $E(u+\Delta u, v+\Delta v)$, and the resulting $E(u + \Delta u, v + \Delta v)$. (*Hint: Let $\Delta u = 0.5 \sin \theta$.*)

  Compare the values of $E(u+\Delta u, v+\Delta v)$ in (b), (e-i), and (e-ii). Briefly state your findings.

The negative gradient direction and the Newton direction are quite fundamental for designing optimization algorithms. It is important to understand these directions and put them in your toolbox for designing learning algorithms.

Problem 3.18   Take the feature transform Φ_2 in Equation (3.13) as Φ.

(a) Show that $d_{\text{vc}}(\mathcal{H}_\Phi) \leq 6$.

(b) Show that $d_{\text{vc}}(\mathcal{H}_\Phi) > 4$. [*Hint: Exercise 3.12*]

(c) Give an upper bound on $d_{\text{vc}}(\mathcal{H}_{\Phi_k})$ for $\mathcal{X} = \mathbb{R}^d$.

(d) Define

$$\tilde{\Phi}_2 \colon \mathbf{x} \to (1, x_1, x_2, x_1 + x_2, x_1 - x_2, x_1^2, x_1 x_2, x_2 x_1, x_2^2) \text{ for } \mathbf{x} \in \mathbb{R}^2.$$

Argue that $d_{\text{vc}}(\mathcal{H}_{\Phi_2}) = d_{\text{vc}}(\mathcal{H}_{\tilde{\Phi}_2})$. In other words, while $\tilde{\Phi}_2(\mathcal{X}) \in \mathbb{R}^9$, $d_{\text{vc}}(\mathcal{H}_{\tilde{\Phi}_2}) \leq 6 < 9$. Thus, the dimension of $\Phi(\mathcal{X})$ only gives an upper bound of $d_{\text{vc}}(\mathcal{H}_\Phi)$, and the exact value of $d_{\text{vc}}(\mathcal{H}_\Phi)$ can depend on the components of the transform.

Problem 3.19   A Transformer thinks the following procedures would work well in learning from two-dimensional data sets of any size. Please point out if there are any potential problems in the procedures:

(a) Use the feature transform

$$\Phi(\mathbf{x}) = \begin{cases} \underbrace{(0,\cdots,0,1,0,\cdots)}_{n-1} & \text{if } \mathbf{x} = \mathbf{x}_n \\ (0,0,\cdots,0) & \text{otherwise .} \end{cases}$$

before running PLA.

(b) Use the feature transform Φ with

$$\phi_n(\mathbf{x}) = \exp\left(-\frac{\|\mathbf{x} - \mathbf{x}_n\|^2}{2\gamma^2}\right)$$

using some very small γ.

(c) Use the feature transform Φ that consists of all

$$\phi_{i,j}(\mathbf{x}) = \exp\left(-\frac{\|\mathbf{x} - (i,j)\|^2}{2\gamma^2}\right),$$

before running PLA, with $i \in \{0, \frac{1}{100}, \ldots, 1\}$ and $j \in \{0, \frac{1}{100}, \ldots, 1\}$.

Chapter 4

Overfitting

Paraskavedekatriaphobia[1] (fear of Friday the 13th), and superstitions in general, are perhaps the most illustrious cases of the human ability to overfit. Unfortunate events are memorable, and given a few such memorable events, it is natural to *try* and find an explanation. In the future, will there be more unfortunate events on Friday the 13th's than on any other day?

Overfitting is the phenomenon where fitting the observed facts (data) well no longer indicates that we will get a decent out-of-sample error, and may actually lead to the opposite effect. You have probably seen cases of overfitting when the learning model is more complex than is necessary to represent the target function. The model uses its additional degrees of freedom to fit idiosyncrasies in the data (for example, noise), yielding a final hypothesis that is inferior. Overfitting can occur even when the hypothesis set contains only functions which are *far simpler* than the target function, and so the plot thickens ☺.

The ability to deal with overfitting is what separates professionals from amateurs in the field of learning from data. We will cover three themes: When does overfitting occur? What are the tools to combat overfitting? How can one estimate the degree of overfitting and 'certify' that a model is good, or better than another? Our emphasis will be on techniques that work well in practice.

4.1   When Does Overfitting Occur?

Overfitting literally means "Fitting the data more than is warranted." The main case of overfitting is when you pick the hypothesis with lower E_{in}, and it results in higher E_{out}. This means that E_{in} alone is no longer a good guide for learning. Let us start by identifying the cause of overfitting.

---

[1]from the Greek *paraskevi* (Friday), *dekatreis* (thirteen), *phobia* (fear)

Consider a simple one-dimensional regression problem with five data points. We do not know the target function, so let's select a general model, maximizing our chance to capture the target function. Since 5 data points can be fit by a 4th order polynomial, we select 4th order polynomials.

The result is shown on the right. The target function is a 2nd order polynomial (blue curve), with a *little* added noise in the data points. Though the target is simple, the learning algorithm used the full power of the 4th order polynomial to fit the data exactly, but the result does not look anything like the target function. The data has been 'overfit.' The little noise in the data has misled the learning, for if there were no noise, the fitted red

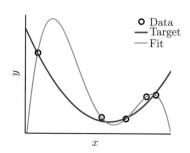

curve would exactly match the target. This is a typical overfitting scenario, in which a complex model uses its additional degrees of freedom to 'learn' the noise.

The fit has zero in-sample error but huge out-of-sample error, so this is a case of bad generalization (as discussed in Chapter 2) – a likely outcome when overfitting is occurring. However, our definition of overfitting goes beyond bad generalization for any given hypothesis. Instead, overfitting applies to a *process*: in this case, the process of picking a hypothesis with lower and lower E_{in} resulting in higher and higher E_{out}.

4.1.1 A Case Study: Overfitting with Polynomials

Let's dig deeper to gain a better understanding of when overfitting occurs. We will illustrate the main concepts using data in one-dimension and polynomial regression, a special case of a linear model that uses the feature transform $x \mapsto (1, x, x^2, \cdots)$. Consider the two regression problems below:

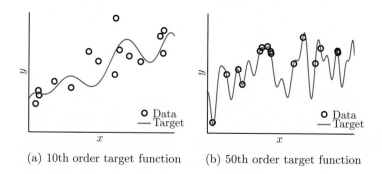

(a) 10th order target function   (b) 50th order target function

In both problems, the target function is a polynomial and the data set $\mathcal{D}$ contains 15 data points. In (a), the target function is a 10th order polynomial

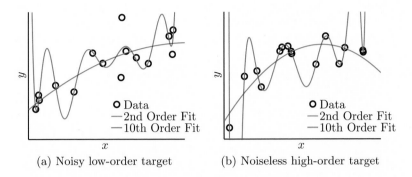

(a) Noisy low-order target   (b) Noiseless high-order target

Figure 4.1: Fits using 2nd and 10th order polynomials to 15 data points. In (a), the data are noisy and the target is a 10th order polynomial. In (b) the data are noiseless and the the target is a 50th order polynomial.

and the sampled data are noisy (the data do not lie on the target function curve). In (b), the target function is a 50th order polynomial and the data are noiseless.

The best 2nd and 10th order fits are shown in Figure 4.1, and the in-sample and out-of-sample errors are given in the following table.

	10th order noisy target			50th order noiseless target	
	2nd Order	10th Order		2nd Order	10th Order
E_{in}	0.050	0.034	E_{in}	0.029	10^{-5}
E_{out}	0.127	**9.00**	E_{out}	0.120	**7680**

What the learning algorithm sees is the data, not the target function. In both cases, the 10th order polynomial heavily overfits the data, and results in a nonsensical final hypothesis which does not resemble the target function. The 2nd order fits do not capture the full nature of the target function either, but they do at least capture its general trend, resulting in significantly lower out-of-sample error. The 10th order fits have lower in-sample error and higher out-of-sample error, so this is indeed a case of overfitting that results in pathologically bad generalization.

Exercise 4.1

Let $\mathcal{H}_2$ and $\mathcal{H}_{10}$ be the 2nd and 10th order hypothesis sets respectively. Specify these sets as parameterized sets of functions. Show that $\mathcal{H}_2 \subset \mathcal{H}_{10}$.

These two examples reveal some surprising phenomena. Let's consider first the 10th order target function, Figure 4.1(a). Here is the scenario. Two learners, O (for overfitted) and R (for restricted), know that the target function is a 10th order polynomial, and that they will receive 15 noisy data points. Learner O

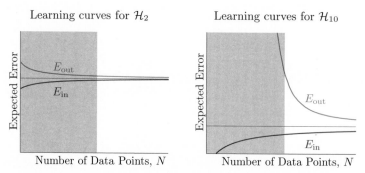

Figure 4.2: Overfitting is occurring for N in the shaded gray region because by choosing $\mathcal{H}_{10}$ which has *better* E_{in}, you get *worse* E_{out}.

uses model $\mathcal{H}_{10}$, which is known to contain the target function, and finds the best fitting hypothesis to the data. Learner R uses model $\mathcal{H}_2$, and similarly finds the best fitting hypothesis to the data.

The surprising thing is that learner R wins (lower out-of-sample error) by using the smaller model, even though she has *knowingly* given up the ability to implement the true target function. Learner R trades off a worse in-sample error for a huge gain in the generalization error, ultimately resulting in lower out-of-sample error. What is funny here? A folklore belief about learning is that best results are obtained by incorporating as much information about the target function as is available. But as we see here, even if we *know* the order of the target and naively incorporate this knowledge by choosing the model accordingly ($\mathcal{H}_{10}$), the performance is inferior to that demonstrated by the more 'stable' 2nd order model.

The models $\mathcal{H}_2$ and $\mathcal{H}_{10}$ were in fact the ones used to generate the learning curves in Chapter 2, and we use those same learning curves to illustrate overfitting in Figure 4.2. If you mentally superimpose the two plots, you can see that there is a range of N for which $\mathcal{H}_{10}$ has lower E_{in} but higher E_{out} than $\mathcal{H}_2$ does, a case in point of overfitting.

Is learner R always going to prevail? Certainly not. For example, if the data was noiseless, then indeed learner O would recover the target function exactly from 15 data points, while learner R would have no hope. This brings us to the second example, Figure 4.1(b). Here, the data *is* noiseless, but the target function is very complex (50th order polynomial). Again learner R wins, and again because learner O heavily overfits the data. Overfitting is not a disease inflicted only upon complex models with many more degrees of freedom than warranted by the complexity of the target function. In fact the reverse is true here, and overfitting is just as bad. What matters is how the model complexity matches the *quantity and quality of the data* we have, not how it matches the target function.

4.1.2   Catalysts for Overfitting

A skeptical reader should ask whether the examples in Figure 4.1 are just pathological constructions created by the authors, or is overfitting a real phenomenon which has to be considered carefully when learning from data? The next exercise guides you through an experimental design for studying overfitting within our current setup. We will use the results from this experiment to serve two purposes: to convince you that overfitting is not the result of some rare pathological construction, and to unravel some of the conditions conducive to overfitting.

> **Exercise 4.2 [Experimental design for studying overfitting]**
>
> This is a reading exercise that sets up an experimental framework to study various aspects of overfitting. The reader interested in implementing the experiment can find the details fleshed out in Problem 4.4. The input space is $\mathcal{X} = [-1, 1]$, with uniform input probability density, $P(x) = \frac{1}{2}$. We consider the two models $\mathcal{H}_2$ and $\mathcal{H}_{10}$.
>
> The target is a degree-Q_f polynomial, which we write $f(x) = \sum_{q=0}^{Q_f} a_q L_q(x)$, where $L_i(x)$ are polynomials of increasing complexity (the Legendre polynomials). The data set is $\mathcal{D} = (x_1, y_1), \ldots, (x_N, y_N)$, where $y_n = f(x_n) + \sigma \epsilon_n$ and ϵ_n are *iid* (independent and identically distributed) standard Normal random variates.
>
> For a single experiment, with specified values for Q_f, N, σ, generate a random degree-Q_f target function by selecting coefficients a_i independently from a standard Normal, rescaling them so that $\mathbb{E}_{a,x}\left[f^2\right] = 1$. Generate a data set, selecting $x_1, \ldots, x_N$ independently according to $P(x)$ and $y_n = f(x_n) + \sigma \epsilon_n$. Let g_2 and g_{10} be the best fit hypotheses to the data from $\mathcal{H}_2$ and $\mathcal{H}_{10}$ respectively, with out-of-sample errors $E_{\text{out}}(g_2)$ and $E_{\text{out}}(g_{10})$.
>
> Vary Q_f, N, σ, and for each combination of parameters, run a large number of experiments, each time computing $E_{\text{out}}(g_2)$ and $E_{\text{out}}(g_{10})$. Averaging these out-of-sample errors gives estimates of the expected out-of-sample error for the given learning scenario (Q_f, N, σ) using $\mathcal{H}_2$ and $\mathcal{H}_{10}$.

Exercise 4.2 set up an experiment to study how the noise level σ^2, the target complexity Q_f, and the number of data points N relate to overfitting. We compare the final hypothesis $g_{10} \in \mathcal{H}_{10}$ (larger model) to the final hypothesis $g_2 \in \mathcal{H}_2$ (smaller model). Clearly, $E_{\text{in}}(g_{10}) \leq E_{\text{in}}(g_2)$ since g_{10} has more degrees of freedom to fit the data. What is surprising is how often g_{10} overfits the data, resulting in $E_{\text{out}}(g_{10}) > E_{\text{out}}(g_2)$. Let us define the overfit measure as $E_{\text{out}}(g_{10}) - E_{\text{out}}(g_2)$. The more positive this measure is, the more severe overfitting would be.

Figure 4.3 shows how the extent of overfitting depends on certain parameters of the learning problem (the results are from our implementation of Exercise 4.2). In the figure, the colors map to the level of overfitting, with redder

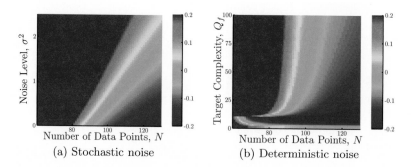

Figure 4.3: How overfitting depends on the noise σ^2, the target function complexity Q_f, and the number of data points N. The colors map to the overfit measure $E_{\text{out}}(\mathcal{H}_{10}) - E_{\text{out}}(\mathcal{H}_2)$. In (a) we see how overfitting depends on σ^2 and N, with $Q_f = 20$. As σ^2 increases we are adding stochastic noise to the data. In (b) we see how overfitting depends on Q_f and N, with $\sigma^2 = 0.1$. As Q_f increases we are adding deterministic noise to the data.

regions showing worse overfitting. These red regions are large—overfitting is real, and here to stay.

Figure 4.3(a) reveals that there is less overfitting when the noise level σ^2 drops or when the number of data points N increases (the linear pattern in Figure 4.3(a) is typical). Since the 'signal' f is normalized to $\mathbb{E}[f^2] = 1$, the noise level σ^2 is automatically calibrated to the signal level. Noise leads the learning astray, and the larger, more complex model is more susceptible to noise than the simpler one because it has more ways to go astray. Figure 4.3(b) reveals that target function complexity Q_f affects overfitting in a similar way to noise, albeit nonlinearly. To summarize,

Number of data points	↑	Overfitting	↓
Noise	↑	Overfitting	↑
Target complexity	↑	Overfitting	↑

Deterministic noise. Why does a higher target complexity lead to more overfitting when comparing the same two models? The intuition is that for a given learning model, there is a best approximation to the target function. The part of the target function 'outside' this best fit acts like noise in the data. We can call this *deterministic noise* to differentiate it from the random *stochastic noise*. Just as stochastic noise cannot be modeled, the deterministic noise is that part of the target function which cannot be modeled. The learning algorithm should not attempt to fit the noise; however, it cannot distinguish noise from signal. On a finite data set, the algorithm inadvertently uses some

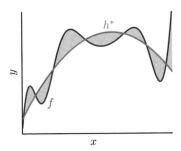

Figure 4.4: Deterministic noise. h^* is the best fit to f in $\mathcal{H}_2$. The shading illustrates deterministic noise for this learning problem.

of the degrees of freedom to fit the noise, which can result in overfitting and a spurious final hypothesis.

Figure 4.4 illustrates deterministic noise for a quadratic model fitting a more complex target function. While stochastic and deterministic noise have similar effects on overfitting, there are two basic differences between the two types of noise. First, if we generated the same data ($\mathbf{x}$ values) again, the deterministic noise would not change but the stochastic noise would. Second, different models capture different 'parts' of the target function, hence the same data set will have different deterministic noise depending on which model we use. In reality, we work with one model at a time and have only one data set on hand. Hence, we have one realization of the noise to work with and the algorithm cannot differentiate between the two types of noise.

Exercise 4.3

Deterministic noise depends on $\mathcal{H}$, as some models approximate f better than others.

(a) Assume $\mathcal{H}$ is fixed and we increase the complexity of f. Will deterministic noise in general go up or down? Is there a higher or lower tendency to overfit?

(b) Assume f is fixed and we decrease the complexity of $\mathcal{H}$. Will deterministic noise in general go up or down? Is there a higher or lower tendency to overfit? *[Hint: There is a race between two factors that affect overfitting in opposite ways, but one wins.]*

The bias-variance decomposition, which we discussed in Section 2.3.1 (see also Problem 2.22) is a useful tool for understanding how noise affects performance:

$$\mathbb{E}_{\mathcal{D}}[E_{\text{out}}] = \sigma^2 + \text{bias} + \text{var}.$$

The first two terms reflect the direct impact of the stochastic and deterministic noise. The variance of the stochastic noise is σ^2 and the bias is directly related to the deterministic noise in that it captures the model's inability to approximate f. The var term is indirectly impacted by both types of noise, capturing a model's susceptibility to being led astray by the noise.

4.2   Regularization

Regularization is our first weapon to combat overfitting. It constrains the learning algorithm to improve out-of-sample error, especially when noise is present. To whet your appetite, look at what a little regularization can do for our first overfitting example in Section 4.1. Though we only used a very small 'amount' of regularization, the fit improves dramatically.

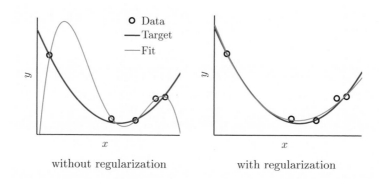

without regularization   with regularization

Now that we have your attention, we would like to come clean. Regularization is as much an art as it is a science. Most of the methods used successfully in practice are heuristic methods. However, these methods are grounded in a mathematical framework that is developed for special cases. We will discuss both the mathematical and the heuristic, trying to maintain a balance that reflects the reality of the field.

Speaking of heuristics, one view of regularization is through the lens of the VC bound, which bounds E_{out} using a model complexity penalty $\Omega(\mathcal{H})$:

$$E_{\text{out}}(h) \leq E_{\text{in}}(h) + \Omega(\mathcal{H}) \qquad \text{for all } h \in \mathcal{H}. \tag{4.1}$$

So, we are better off if we fit the data using a simple $\mathcal{H}$. Extrapolating one step further, we should be better off by fitting the data using a 'simple' h from $\mathcal{H}$. The essence of regularization is to concoct a measure $\Omega(h)$ for the complexity of an individual hypothesis. Instead of minimizing $E_{\text{in}}(h)$ alone, one minimizes a combination of $E_{\text{in}}(h)$ and $\Omega(h)$. This avoids overfitting by constraining the learning algorithm to fit the data well using a simple hypothesis.

Example 4.1. One popular regularization technique is *weight decay*, which measures the complexity of a hypothesis h by the size of the coefficients used to represent h (e.g. in a linear model). This heuristic prefers mild lines with small offset and slope, to wild lines with bigger offset and slope. We will get to the mechanics of weight decay shortly, but for now let's focus on the outcome.

We apply weight decay to fitting the target $f(x) = \sin(\pi x)$ using $N = 2$ data points (as in Example 2.8). We sample x uniformly in $[-1, 1]$, generate a data set and fit a line to the data (our model is $\mathcal{H}_1$). The figures below show the resulting fits on the same (random) data sets with and without regularization.

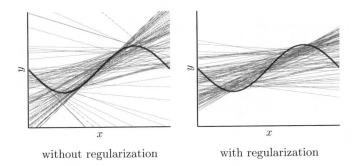

without regularization   with regularization

Without regularization, the learned function varies extensively depending on the data set. As we have seen in Example 2.8, a constant model scored $E_{\text{out}} = 0.75$, handily beating the performance of the (unregularized) linear model that scored $E_{\text{out}} = 1.90$. With a little weight decay regularization, the fits to *the same data sets* are considerably less volatile. This results in a significantly lower $E_{\text{out}} = 0.56$ that beats both the constant model and the unregularized linear model.

The bias-variance decomposition helps us to understand how the regularized version beat both the unregularized version as well as the constant model.

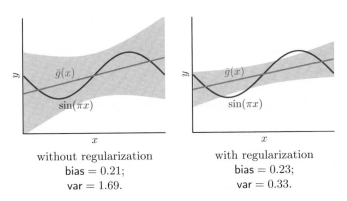

without regularization   with regularization
bias = 0.21;   bias = 0.23;
var = 1.69.   var = 0.33.

Average hypothesis $\bar{g}$ (red) with $\text{var}(x)$ indicated by the gray shaded region that is $\bar{g}(x) \pm \sqrt{\text{var}(x)}$.

As expected, regularization reduced the var term rather dramatically from 1.69 down to 0.33. The price paid in terms of the bias (quality of the average fit) was

127

modest, only slightly increasing from 0.21 to 0.23. The result was a significant decrease in the expected out-of-sample error because bias+var decreased. This is the crux of regularization. By constraining the learning algorithm to select 'simpler' hypotheses from $\mathcal{H}$, we sacrifice a little bias for a significant gain in the var. $\square$

This example also illustrates why regularization is needed. The linear model is *too sophisticated for the amount of data we have*, since a line can perfectly fit any 2 points. This need would persist even if we changed the target function, as long as we have either stochastic or deterministic noise. The need for regularization depends on the *quantity and quality of the data*. Given our meager data set, our choices were either to take a simpler model, such as the model with constant functions, or to constrain the linear model. It turns out that using the complex model but constraining the algorithm toward simpler hypotheses gives us more flexibility, and ends up giving the best E_{out}. In practice, this is the rule not the exception.

Enough heuristics. Let's develop the mathematics of regularization.

4.2.1 A Soft Order Constraint

In this section, we derive a regularization method that applies to a wide variety of learning problems. To simplify the math, we will use the concrete setting of regression using Legendre polynomials, the polynomials of increasing complexity used in Exercise 4.2. So, let's first formally introduce you to the Legendre polynomials.

Consider a learning model where $\mathcal{H}$ is the set of polynomials in one variable $x \in [-1, 1]$. Instead of expressing the polynomials in terms of consecutive powers of x, we will express them as a combination of Legendre polynomials in x. Legendre polynomials are a standard set of polynomials with nice analytic properties that result in simpler derivations. The zeroth-order Legendre polynomial is the constant $L_0(x) = 1$, and the first few Legendre polynomials are illustrated below.

As you can see, when the order of the Legendre polynomial increases, the curve gets more complex. Legendre polynomials are orthogonal to each other within $x \in [-1, 1]$, and any regular polynomial can be written as a linear combination of Legendre polynomials, just like it can be written as a linear combination of powers of x.

128

Polynomial models are a special case of linear models in a space $\mathcal{Z}$, under a nonlinear transformation $\Phi \colon \mathcal{X} \to \mathcal{Z}$. Here, for the Qth order polynomial model, Φ transforms x into a vector $\mathbf{z}$ of Legendre polynomials,

$$
\mathbf{z} = \begin{bmatrix} 1 \\ L_1(x) \\ \vdots \\ L_Q(x) \end{bmatrix}.
$$

Our hypothesis set $\mathcal{H}_Q$ is a linear combination of these polynomials,

$$
\mathcal{H}_Q = \left\{ h \;\middle|\; h(x) = \mathbf{w}^\mathsf{T}\mathbf{z} = \sum_{q=0}^{Q} w_q L_q(x) \right\}_{\mathbf{w} \in \mathbb{R}^{Q+1}},
$$

where $L_0(x) = 1$. As usual, we will sometimes refer to the hypothesis h by its weight vector $\mathbf{w}$.[2] Since each h is linear in $\mathbf{w}$, we can use the machinery of linear regression from Chapter 3 to minimize the squared error

$$
E_{\text{in}}(\mathbf{w}) = \frac{1}{N} \sum_{n=1}^{N} (\mathbf{w}^\mathsf{T}\mathbf{z}_n - y_n)^2. \tag{4.2}
$$

The case of polynomial regression with squared-error measure illustrates the main ideas of regularization well, and facilitates a solid mathematical derivation. Nonetheless, our discussion will generalize in practice to non-linear, multi-dimensional settings with more general error measures. The baseline algorithm (without regularization) is to minimize E_{in} over the hypotheses in $\mathcal{H}_Q$ to produce the final hypothesis $g(x) = \mathbf{w}_{\text{lin}}^\mathsf{T}\mathbf{z}$, where $\mathbf{w}_{\text{lin}} = \underset{\mathbf{w}}{\operatorname{argmin}}\, E_{\text{in}}(\mathbf{w})$.

Exercise 4.4

Let $Z = \begin{bmatrix} \mathbf{z}_1 & \cdots & \mathbf{z}_N \end{bmatrix}^\mathsf{T}$ be the data matrix (assume Z has full column rank); let $\mathbf{w}_{\text{lin}} = (Z^\mathsf{T}Z)^{-1}Z^\mathsf{T}\mathbf{y}$; and let $H = Z(Z^\mathsf{T}Z)^{-1}Z^\mathsf{T}$ (the hat matrix of Exercise 3.3). Show that

$$
E_{\text{in}}(\mathbf{w}) = \frac{(\mathbf{w} - \mathbf{w}_{\text{lin}})^\mathsf{T}Z^\mathsf{T}Z(\mathbf{w} - \mathbf{w}_{\text{lin}}) + \mathbf{y}^\mathsf{T}(I - H)\mathbf{y}}{N}, \tag{4.3}
$$

where I is the identity matrix.

(a) What value of $\mathbf{w}$ minimizes E_{in}?

(b) What is the minimum in-sample error?

The task of regularization, which results in a final hypothesis $\mathbf{w}_{\text{reg}}$ instead of the simple $\mathbf{w}_{\text{lin}}$, is to constrain the learning so as to prevent overfitting the

---

[2] We used $\tilde{\mathbf{w}}$ and $\tilde{d}$ for the weight vector and dimension in $\mathcal{Z}$. Since we are explicitly dealing with polynomials and $\mathcal{Z}$ is the only space around, we use $\mathbf{w}$ and Q for simplicity.

data. We have already seen an example of constraining the learning; the set $\mathcal{H}_2$ can be thought of as a constrained version of $\mathcal{H}_{10}$ in the sense that some of the $\mathcal{H}_{10}$ weights are required to be zero. That is, $\mathcal{H}_2$ is a subset of $\mathcal{H}_{10}$ defined by $\mathcal{H}_2 = \{\mathbf{w} \mid \mathbf{w} \in \mathcal{H}_{10}; w_q = 0 \text{ for } q \geq 3\}$. Requiring some weights to be 0 is a *hard* constraint. We have seen that such a hard constraint on the order can help, for example $\mathcal{H}_2$ is better than $\mathcal{H}_{10}$ when there is a lot of noise and N is small. Instead of requiring some weights to be zero, we can force the weights to be small but not necessarily zero through a softer constraint such as

$$\sum_{q=0}^{Q} w_q^2 \leq C.$$

This is a 'soft order' constraint because it only encourages each weight to be small, without changing the order of the polynomial by explicitly setting some weights to zero. The in-sample optimization problem becomes:

$$\min_{\mathbf{w}} E_{\text{in}}(\mathbf{w}) \quad \text{subject to} \quad \mathbf{w}^{\mathsf{T}} \mathbf{w} \leq C. \tag{4.4}$$

The data determines the optimal weight sizes, given the total budget C which determines the amount of regularization; the larger C is, the weaker the constraint and the smaller the amount of regularization. We can define the soft-order-constrained hypothesis set $\mathcal{H}(C)$ by

$$\mathcal{H}(C) = \{h \mid h(x) = \mathbf{w}^{\mathsf{T}} \mathbf{z} , \ \mathbf{w}^{\mathsf{T}} \mathbf{w} \leq C\}.$$

Equation (4.4) is equivalent to minimizing E_{in} over $\mathcal{H}(C)$. If $C_1 < C_2$, then $\mathcal{H}(C_1) \subset \mathcal{H}(C_2)$ and so $d_{\text{vc}}(\mathcal{H}(C_1)) \leq d_{\text{vc}}(\mathcal{H}(C_2))$, and we expect better generalization with $\mathcal{H}(C_1)$. Let the regularized weights $\mathbf{w}_{\text{reg}}$ be the solution to (4.4).

Solving for $\mathbf{w}_{\text{reg}}$. If $\mathbf{w}_{\text{lin}}^{\mathsf{T}} \mathbf{w}_{\text{lin}} \leq C$ then $\mathbf{w}_{\text{reg}} = \mathbf{w}_{\text{lin}}$ because $\mathbf{w}_{\text{lin}} \in \mathcal{H}(C)$. If $\mathbf{w}_{\text{lin}} \notin \mathcal{H}(C)$, then not only is $\mathbf{w}_{\text{reg}}^{\mathsf{T}} \mathbf{w}_{\text{reg}} \leq C$, but in fact $\mathbf{w}_{\text{reg}}^{\mathsf{T}} \mathbf{w}_{\text{reg}} = C$ ($\mathbf{w}_{\text{reg}}$ uses the entire budget C; see Problem 4.10).

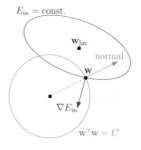

We thus need to minimize E_{in} subject to the *equality* constraint $\mathbf{w}^{\mathsf{T}} \mathbf{w} = C$. The situation is illustrated to the right. The weights $\mathbf{w}$ must lie on the surface of the sphere $\mathbf{w}^{\mathsf{T}} \mathbf{w} = C$; the normal vector to this surface at $\mathbf{w}$ is the vector $\mathbf{w}$ itself (also in red). A surface of constant E_{in} is shown in blue; this surface is a quadratic surface (see Exercise 4.4) and the normal to this surface is $\nabla E_{\text{in}}(\mathbf{w})$. In this case, $\mathbf{w}$ cannot be optimal because $\nabla E_{\text{in}}(\mathbf{w})$ is not parallel to the red normal vector. This means that $\nabla E_{\text{in}}(\mathbf{w})$ has some non-zero component along the constraint surface, and by moving a small amount in the opposite direction of this component we can improve E_{in}, while still remaining on the surface. If $\mathbf{w}_{\text{reg}}$ is to be optimal, then for some positive parameter λ_C

$$\nabla E_{\text{in}}(\mathbf{w}_{\text{reg}}) = -2\lambda_C \mathbf{w}_{\text{reg}},$$

i.e., ∇E_{in} must be parallel to $\mathbf{w}_{\text{reg}}$, the normal vector to the constraint surface (the scaling by 2 is for mathematical convenience and the negative sign is because ∇E_{in} and $\mathbf{w}$ are in opposite directions). Equivalently, $\mathbf{w}_{\text{reg}}$ satisfies

$$\nabla \left(E_{\text{in}}(\mathbf{w}) + \lambda_C \mathbf{w}^{\mathsf{T}} \mathbf{w} \right)\big|_{\mathbf{w}=\mathbf{w}_{\text{reg}}} = \mathbf{0},$$

because $\nabla(\mathbf{w}^{\mathsf{T}}\mathbf{w}) = 2\mathbf{w}$. So, for some $\lambda_C > 0$, $\mathbf{w}_{\text{reg}}$ locally minimizes

$$E_{\text{in}}(\mathbf{w}) + \lambda_C \mathbf{w}^{\mathsf{T}} \mathbf{w}. \tag{4.5}$$

The parameter λ_C and the vector $\mathbf{w}_{\text{reg}}$ (both of which depend on C and the data) must be chosen so as to simultaneously satisfy the gradient equality and the weight norm constraint $\mathbf{w}_{\text{reg}}^{\mathsf{T}}\mathbf{w}_{\text{reg}} = C$.[3] That $\lambda_C > 0$ is intuitive since we are enforcing smaller weights, and minimizing $E_{\text{in}}(\mathbf{w}) + \lambda_C \mathbf{w}^{\mathsf{T}} \mathbf{w}$ would not lead to smaller weights if λ_C were negative. Note that if $\mathbf{w}_{\text{lin}}^{\mathsf{T}}\mathbf{w}_{\text{lin}} \leq C$, $\mathbf{w}_{\text{reg}} = \mathbf{w}_{\text{lin}}$ and minimizing (4.5) still holds with $\lambda_C = 0$. Therefore, we have an equivalence between solving the constrained problem (4.4) and the unconstrained minimization of (4.5). This equivalence means that minimizing (4.5) is similar to minimizing E_{in} using a smaller hypothesis set, which in turn means that we can expect better generalization by minimizing (4.5) than by just minimizing E_{in}.

Other variations of the constraint in (4.4) can be used to emphasize some weights over the others. Consider the constraint $\sum_{q=0}^{Q} \gamma_q w_q^2 \leq C$. The importance γ_q given to weight w_q determines the type of regularization. For example, $\gamma_q = q$ or $\gamma_q = e^q$ encourages a low-order fit, and $\gamma_q = (1+q)^{-1}$ or $\gamma_q = e^{-q}$ encourages a high-order fit. In extreme cases, one recovers hard-order constraints by choosing some $\gamma_q = 0$ and some $\gamma_q \to \infty$.

Exercise 4.5 [Tikhonov regularizer]

A more general soft constraint is the *Tikhonov* regularization constraint

$$\mathbf{w}^{\mathsf{T}} \Gamma^{\mathsf{T}} \Gamma \mathbf{w} \leq C$$

which can capture relationships among the w_i (the matrix Γ is the Tikhonov regularizer).

(a) What should Γ be to obtain the constraint $\sum_{q=0}^{Q} w_q^2 \leq C$?

(b) What should Γ be to obtain the constraint $(\sum_{q=0}^{Q} w_q)^2 \leq C$?

---

[3]λ_C is known as a Lagrange multiplier and an alternate derivation of these same results can be obtained via the theory of Lagrange multipliers for constrained optimization.

4.2.2 Weight Decay and Augmented Error

The soft-order constraint for a given value of C is a constrained minimization of E_{in}. Equation (4.5) suggests that we may equivalently solve an unconstrained minimization of a different function. Let's define the *augmented error*,

$$E_{\text{aug}}(\mathbf{w}) = E_{\text{in}}(\mathbf{w}) + \lambda \mathbf{w}^{\mathsf{T}}\mathbf{w}, \qquad (4.6)$$

where $\lambda \geq 0$ is now a free parameter at our disposal. The augmented error has two terms. The first is the in-sample error which we are used to minimizing, and the second is a *penalty term*. Notice that this fits the heuristic view of regularization that we discussed earlier, where the penalty for complexity is defined for each individual h instead of $\mathcal{H}$ as a whole. When $\lambda = 0$, we have the usual in-sample error. For $\lambda > 0$, minimizing the augmented error corresponds to minimizing a penalized in-sample error. The value of λ controls the amount of regularization. The penalty term $\mathbf{w}^{\mathsf{T}}\mathbf{w}$ enforces a tradeoff between making the in-sample error small and making the weights small, and has become known as *weight decay*. As discussed in Problem 4.8, if we minimize the augmented error using an iterative method like gradient descent, we will have a reduction of the in-sample error together with a gradual shrinking of the weights, hence the name weight 'decay.' In the statistics community, this type of penalty term is a form of *ridge regression*.

There is an equivalence between the soft order constraint and augmented error minimization. In the soft-order constraint, the amount of regularization is controlled by the parameter C. From (4.5), there is a particular λ_C (depending on C and the data $\mathcal{D}$), for which minimizing the augmented error $E_{\text{aug}}(\mathbf{w})$ leads to the same final hypothesis $\mathbf{w}_{\text{reg}}$. A larger C allows larger weights and is a weaker soft-order constraint; this corresponds to smaller λ, i.e., less emphasis on the penalty term $\mathbf{w}^{\mathsf{T}}\mathbf{w}$ in the augmented error. For a particular data set, the optimal value C^* leading to minimum out-of-sample error with the soft-order constraint corresponds to an optimal value λ^* in the augmented error minimization. If we can find λ^*, we can get the minimum E_{out}.

Have we gained from the augmented error view? Yes, because augmented error minimization is unconstrained, which is generally easier than constrained minimization. For example, we can obtain a closed form solution for linear models or use a method like stochastic gradient descent to carry out the minimization. However, augmented error minimization is not so easy to interpret. There are no values for the weights which are explicitly forbidden, as there are in the soft-order constraint. For a given C, the soft-order constraint corresponds to selecting a hypothesis from the smaller set $\mathcal{H}(C)$, and so from our VC analysis we should expect better generalization when C decreases (λ increases). It is through the relationship between λ and C that one has a theoretical justification of weight decay as a method for regularization.

We focused on the soft-order constraint $\mathbf{w}^{\mathsf{T}}\mathbf{w} \leq C$ with corresponding augmented error $E_{\text{aug}}(\mathbf{w}) = E_{\text{in}}(\mathbf{w}) + \lambda \mathbf{w}^{\mathsf{T}}\mathbf{w}$. However, our discussion applies more generally. There is a duality between the minimization of the in-sample error over a constrained hypothesis set and the unconstrained minimization of an augmented error. We may choose to live in either world, but more often than not, the unconstrained minimization of the augmented error is more convenient.

In our definition of $E_{\text{aug}}(\mathbf{w})$ in Equation (4.6), we only highlighted the dependence on $\mathbf{w}$. There are two other quantities under our control, namely the amount of regularization, λ, and the nature of the regularizer which we chose to be $\mathbf{w}^{\text{T}}\mathbf{w}$. In general, the augmented error for a hypothesis $h \in \mathcal{H}$ is

$$E_{\text{aug}}(h, \lambda, \Omega) = E_{\text{in}}(h) + \frac{\lambda}{N}\Omega(h). \tag{4.7}$$

For weight decay, $\Omega(h) = \mathbf{w}^{\text{T}}\mathbf{w}$, which penalizes large weights. The penalty term has two components: the regularizer $\Omega(h)$ (the type of regularization) which penalizes a particular property of h; and the *regularization parameter* λ (the amount of regularization). The need for regularization goes down as the number of data points goes up, so we factored out $\frac{1}{N}$; this allows the optimal choice for λ to be less sensitive to N. This is just a redefinition of the λ that we have been using, in order to make it a more stable parameter that is easier to interpret. Notice how Equation (4.7) resembles the VC bound (4.1) as we anticipated in the heuristic view of regularization. This is why we use the same notation Ω for both the penalty on individual hypotheses $\Omega(h)$ and the penalty on the whole set $\Omega(\mathcal{H})$. The correspondence between the complexity of $\mathcal{H}$ and the complexity of an individual h will be discussed further in Section 5.1.

The regularizer Ω is typically fixed ahead of time, before seeing the data; sometimes the problem itself can dictate an appropriate regularizer.

Exercise 4.6

We have seen both the hard-order constraint and the soft-order constraint. Which do you expect to be more useful for binary classification using the perceptron model? *[Hint: $sign(\mathbf{w}^{\text{T}}\mathbf{x}) = sign(\alpha\mathbf{w}^{\text{T}}\mathbf{x})$ for any $\alpha > 0$.]*

The optimal regularization parameter, however, typically depends on the data. The choice of the optimal λ is one of the applications of *validation*, which we will discuss shortly.

Example 4.2. Linear models with weight decay. Linear models are important enough that it is worthwhile to spell out the details of augmented error minimization in this case. From Exercise 4.4, the augmented error is

$$E_{\text{aug}}(\mathbf{w}) = \frac{(\mathbf{w} - \mathbf{w}_{\text{lin}})^{\text{T}}Z^{\text{T}}Z(\mathbf{w} - \mathbf{w}_{\text{lin}}) + \lambda\mathbf{w}^{\text{T}}\mathbf{w} + \mathbf{y}^{\text{T}}(I - H)\mathbf{y}}{N},$$

where Z is the transformed data matrix and $\mathbf{w}_{\text{lin}} = (Z^{\text{T}}Z)^{-1}Z^{\text{T}}\mathbf{y}$. The reader may verify, after taking the derivatives of E_{aug} and setting $\nabla_{\mathbf{w}}E_{\text{aug}} = \mathbf{0}$, that

$$\mathbf{w}_{\text{reg}} = (Z^{\text{T}}Z + \lambda I)^{-1}Z^{\text{T}}\mathbf{y}.$$

As expected, $\mathbf{w}_{\text{reg}}$ will go to zero as $\lambda \to \infty$, due to the λI term. The predictions on the in-sample data are given by $\hat{\mathbf{y}} = Z\mathbf{w}_{\text{reg}} = H(\lambda)\mathbf{y}$, where

$$H(\lambda) = Z(Z^\mathsf{T}Z + \lambda I)^{-1}Z^\mathsf{T}.$$

The matrix $H(\lambda)$ plays an important role in defining the effective complexity of a model. When $\lambda = 0$, H is the hat matrix of Exercises 3.3 and 4.4, which satisfies $H^2 = H$ and $\text{trace}(H) = d + 1$. The vector of in-sample errors, which are also called residuals, is $\mathbf{y} - \hat{\mathbf{y}} = (I - H(\lambda))\mathbf{y}$, and the in-sample error E_{in} is $E_{\text{in}}(\mathbf{w}_{\text{reg}}) = \frac{1}{N}\mathbf{y}^\mathsf{T}(I - H(\lambda))^2\mathbf{y}$. $\qquad\square$

We can now apply weight decay regularization to the first overfitting example that opened this chapter. The results for different λ's are shown in Figure 4.5.

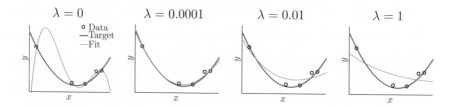

Figure 4.5: Weight decay applied to Example 4.2 with different values for the regularization parameter λ. The red fit gets flatter as we increase λ.

As you can see, even very little regularization goes a long way, but too much regularization results in an overly flat curve at the expense of in-sample fit. Another case we saw earlier is Example 4.1, where we fit a linear model to a sinusoid. The regularization used there was also weight decay, with $\lambda = 0.1$.

4.2.3 Choosing a Regularizer: Pill or Poison?

We have presented a number of ways to constrain a model: hard-order constraints where we simply use a lower-order model, soft-order constraints where we constrain the parameters of the model, and augmented error where we add a penalty term to an otherwise unconstrained minimization of error. Augmented error is the most popular form of regularization, for which we need to choose the regularizer $\Omega(h)$ and the regularization parameter λ.

In practice, the choice of Ω is largely heuristic. Finding a perfect Ω is as difficult as finding a perfect $\mathcal{H}$. It depends on information that, by the very nature of learning, we don't have. However, there are regularizers we can work with that have stood the test of time, such as weight decay. Some forms of regularization work and some do not, depending on the specific application and the data. Figure 4.5 illustrated that even the amount of regularization

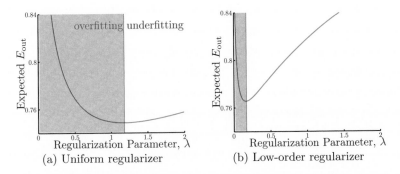

(a) Uniform regularizer   (b) Low-order regularizer

Figure 4.6: Out-of-sample performance for the uniform and low-order regularizers using model $\mathcal{H}_{15}$, with $\sigma^2 = 0.5$, $Q_f = 15$ and $N = 30$. Overfitting occurs in the shaded region because lower E_{in} (lower λ) leads to higher E_{out}. Underfitting occurs when λ is too large, because the learning algorithm has too little flexibility to fit the data.

has to be chosen carefully. Too much regularization (too harsh a constraint) leaves the learning too little flexibility to fit the data and leads to *underfitting*, which can be just as bad as overfitting.

If so many choices can go wrong, why do we bother with regularization in the first place? Regularization is a necessary evil, with the operative word being *necessary*. If our model is too sophisticated for the amount of data we have, we are doomed. By applying regularization, we have a chance. By applying the proper regularization, we are in good shape. Let us experiment with two choices of a regularizer for the model $\mathcal{H}_{15}$ of 15th order polynomials, using the experimental design in Exercise 4.2:

1. A uniform regularizer: $\Omega_{\text{unif}}(\mathbf{w}) = \sum_{q=0}^{15} w_q^2$.

2. A low-order regularizer: $\Omega_{\text{low}}(\mathbf{w}) = \sum_{q=0}^{15} q w_q^2$.

The first encourages all weights to be small, uniformly; the second pays more attention to the higher order weights, encouraging a lower order fit. Figure 4.6 shows the performance for different values of the regularization parameter λ. As you decrease λ, the optimization pays less attention to the penalty term and more to E_{in}, and so E_{in} will decrease (Problem 4.7). In the shaded region, E_{out} increases as you decrease E_{in} (decrease λ) – the regularization parameter is too small and there is not enough of a constraint on the learning, leading to decreased performance because of overfitting. In the unshaded region, the regularization parameter is too large, over-constraining the learning and not giving it enough flexibility to fit the data, leading to decreased performance because of underfitting. As can be observed from the figure, the price paid for overfitting is generally more severe than underfitting. It usually pays to be conservative.

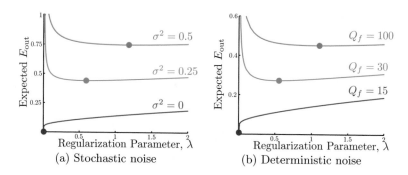

Figure 4.7: Performance of the uniform regularizer at different levels of noise. The optimal λ is highlighted for each curve.

The optimal regularization parameter for the two cases is quite different and the performance can be quite sensitive to the choice of regularization parameter. However, the promising message from the figure is that though the behaviors are quite different, the performances of the two regularizers are comparable (around 0.76), *if we choose the right λ for each.*

We can also use this experiment to study how performance with regularization depends on the noise. In Figure 4.7(a), when $\sigma^2 = 0$, no amount of regularization helps (i.e., the optimal regularization parameter is $\lambda = 0$), which is not a surprise because there is no stochastic or deterministic noise in the data (both target and model are 15th order polynomials). As we add more stochastic noise, the overall performance degrades as expected. Note that the optimal value for the regularization parameter increases with noise, which is also expected based on the earlier discussion that the potential to overfit increases as the noise increases; hence, constraining the learning more should help. Figure 4.7(b) shows what happens when we add deterministic noise, keeping the stochastic noise at zero. This is accomplished by increasing Q_f (the target complexity), thereby adding deterministic noise, but keeping everything else the same. Comparing parts (a) and (b) of Figures 4.7 provides another demonstration of how the effects of deterministic and stochastic noise are similar. When either is present, it *is* helpful to regularize, and the more noise there is, the larger the amount of regularization you need.

What happens if you pick the wrong regularizer? To illustrate, we picked a regularizer which encourages large weights (weight growth) versus weight decay which encourages small weights. As you can see, in this case, weight growth does not help the cause of overfitting. If we happened to choose weight growth as our regularizer, we would still be OK as long as we have

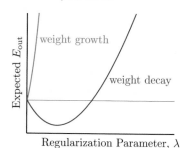

a good way to pick the regularization parameter – the optimal regularization parameter in this case is $\lambda = 0$, and we are no worse off than not regularizing. No regularizer will be ideal for all settings, or even for a specific setting since we never have perfect information, but they all tend to work with varying success, *if the amount of regularization λ is set to the correct level.* Thus, the entire burden rests on picking the right λ, a task that can be addressed by a technique called validation, which is the topic of the next section.

The lesson learned is that some form of regularization is necessary, as learning is quite sensitive to stochastic and deterministic noise. The best way to constrain the learning is in the 'direction' of the target function, and more of a constraint is needed when there is more noise. Even though we don't know either the target function or the noise, regularization helps by reducing the impact of the noise. Most common models have hypothesis sets which are naturally parameterized so that smaller parameters lead to smoother hypotheses. Thus, a weight decay type of regularizer constrains the learning towards smoother hypotheses. This helps, because stochastic noise is 'high frequency' (non-smooth). Similarly, deterministic noise (the part of the target function which cannot be modeled) also tends to be non-smooth. Thus, constraining the learning towards smoother hypotheses 'hurts' our ability to overfit the noise more than it hurts our ability to fit the useful information. These are empirical observations, not theoretically justifiable statements.

Regularization and the VC dimension. Regularization (for example soft-order selection by minimizing the augmented error) poses a problem for the VC line of reasoning. As λ goes up, the learning algorithm changes but the hypothesis set does not, so d_{vc} will not change. We argued that $\lambda \uparrow$ in the augmented error corresponds to $C \downarrow$ in the soft-order constrained model. So, more regularization corresponds to an effectively smaller model, and we expect better generalization for a small increase in E_{in} even though the VC dimension of the model we are actually using with augmented error does not change. This suggests a heuristic that works well in practice, which is to use an 'effective VC dimension' instead of the VC dimension. For linear perceptrons, the VC dimension equals the number of free parameters $d + 1$, and so an *effective number of parameters* is a good surrogate for the VC dimension in the VC bound. The effective number of parameters will go down as λ increases, and so the effective VC dimension will reflect better generalization with increased regularization. Problems 4.13, 4.14, and 4.15 explore the notion of an effective number of parameters.

4.3 Validation

So far, we have identified overfitting as a problem, noise (stochastic and deterministic) as a cause, and regularization as a cure. In this section, we introduce another cure, called *validation*. One can think of both regularization and validation as attempts at minimizing E_{out} rather than just E_{in}. Of course the true E_{out} is not available to us, so we need an estimate of E_{out} based on information available to us in sample. In some sense, this is the Holy Grail of machine learning: to find an in-sample estimate of the out-of-sample error. Regularization attempts to minimize E_{out} by working through the equation

$$E_{out}(h) = E_{in}(h) + \underbrace{\text{overfit penalty}}_{\text{regularization estimates this quantity}},$$

and concocting a heuristic term that emulates the penalty term. Validation, on the other hand, cuts to the chase and estimates the out-of-sample error directly.

$$\underbrace{E_{out}(h)}_{\text{validation estimates this quantity}} = E_{in}(h) + \text{overfit penalty}.$$

Estimating the out-of-sample error directly is nothing new to us. In Section 2.2.3, we introduced the idea of a *test set*, a subset of $\mathcal{D}$ that is not involved in the learning process and is used to evaluate the final hypothesis. The test error E_{test}, unlike the in-sample error E_{in}, is an unbiased estimate of E_{out}.

4.3.1 The Validation Set

The idea of a *validation set* is almost identical to that of a test set. We remove a subset from the data; this subset is not used in training. We then use this held-out subset to estimate the out-of-sample error. The held-out set is effectively out-of-sample, because it has not been used during the learning.

However, there is a difference between a validation set and a test set. Although the validation set will not be directly used for training, it will be used in making certain choices in the learning process. The minute a set affects the learning process in any way, it is no longer a *test* set. However, as we will see, the way the validation set is used in the learning process is so benign that its estimate of E_{out} remains almost intact.

Let us first look at how the validation set is created. The first step is to partition the data set $\mathcal{D}$ into a *training set* $\mathcal{D}_{train}$ of size $(N - K)$ and a *validation set* $\mathcal{D}_{val}$ of size K. Any partitioning method which does not depend on the values of the data points will do; for example, we can select $N - K$ points at random for training and the remaining for validation.

Now, we run the learning algorithm using the training set $\mathcal{D}_{train}$ to obtain a final hypothesis $g^- \in \mathcal{H}$, where the 'minus' superscript indicates that some data points were taken out of the training. We then compute the validation error for g^- using the validation set $\mathcal{D}_{val}$:

$$E_{val}(g^-) = \frac{1}{K} \sum_{\mathbf{x}_n \in \mathcal{D}_{val}} e\left(g^-(\mathbf{x}_n), y_n\right),$$

where $e\left(g^-(\mathbf{x}), y\right)$ is the pointwise error measure which we introduced in Section 1.4.1. For classification, $e(g(\mathbf{x}), y) = [\![g^-(\mathbf{x}) \neq y]\!]$ and for regression using squared error, $e(g(\mathbf{x}), y) = (g^-(\mathbf{x}) - y)^2$.

The validation error is an *unbiased* estimate of E_{out} because the final hypothesis g^- was created independently of the data points in the validation set. Indeed, taking the expectation of E_{val} with respect to the data points in $\mathcal{D}_{\text{val}}$,

$$
\begin{aligned}
\mathbb{E}_{\mathcal{D}_{\text{val}}}\left[E_{\text{val}}(g^-)\right] &= \frac{1}{K} \sum_{\mathbf{x}_n \in \mathcal{D}_{\text{val}}} \mathbb{E}_{\mathcal{D}_{\text{val}}}\left[e\left(g^-(\mathbf{x}_n), y_n\right)\right], \\
&= \frac{1}{K} \sum_{\mathbf{x}_n \in \mathcal{D}_{\text{val}}} E_{\text{out}}(g^-), \\
&= E_{\text{out}}(g^-).
\end{aligned}
\tag{4.8}
$$

The first step uses the linearity of expectation, and the second step follows because $e\left(g^-(\mathbf{x}_n), y_n\right)$ depends only on $\mathbf{x}_n$ and so

$$
\mathbb{E}_{\mathcal{D}_{\text{val}}}\left[e\left(g^-(\mathbf{x}_n), y_n\right)\right] = \mathbb{E}_{\mathbf{x}_n}\left[e\left(g^-(\mathbf{x}_n), y_n\right)\right] = E_{\text{out}}(g^-).
$$

How reliable is E_{val} at estimating E_{out}? In the case of classification, one can use the VC bound to predict how good the validation error is as an estimate for the out-of-sample error. We can view $\mathcal{D}_{\text{val}}$ as an 'in-sample' data set on which we computed the error of the single hypothesis g^-. We can thus apply the VC bound for a finite model with one hypothesis in it (the Hoeffding bound). With high probability,

$$
E_{\text{out}}(g^-) \leq E_{\text{val}}(g^-) + O\left(\frac{1}{\sqrt{K}}\right).
\tag{4.9}
$$

While Inequality (4.9) applies to binary target functions, we may use the variance of E_{val} as a more generally applicable measure of the reliability. The next exercise studies how the variance of E_{val} depends on K (the size of the validation set), and implies that a similar bound holds for regression. The conclusion is that the error between $E_{\text{val}}(g^-)$ and $E_{\text{out}}(g^-)$ drops as $\sigma(g^-)/\sqrt{K}$, where $\sigma(g^-)$ is bounded by a constant in the case of classification.

Exercise 4.7

Fix g^- (learned from $\mathcal{D}_{\text{train}}$) and define $\sigma_{\text{val}}^2 \overset{\text{def}}{=} \text{Var}_{\mathcal{D}_{\text{val}}}[E_{\text{val}}(g^-)]$. We consider how σ_{val}^2 depends on K. Let

$$
\sigma^2(g^-) = \text{Var}_{\mathbf{x}}[e(g^-(\mathbf{x}), y)]
$$

be the pointwise variance in the out-of-sample error of g^-.

(a) Show that $\sigma_{\text{val}}^2 = \frac{1}{K}\sigma^2(g^-)$.

(b) In a classification problem, where $e(g^-(\mathbf{x}), y) = [\![g^-(\mathbf{x}) \neq y]\!]$, express σ_{val}^2 in terms of $\mathbb{P}[g^-(\mathbf{x}) \neq y]$.

(c) Show that for any g^- in a classification problem, $\sigma_{\text{val}}^2 \leq \frac{1}{4K}$.

(continued on next page)

(d) Is there a uniform upper bound for $\text{Var}[E_{\text{val}}(g^-)]$ similar to (c) in the case of regression with squared error $e(g^-(\mathbf{x}), y) = (g^-(\mathbf{x}) - y)^2$? [Hint: The squared error is unbounded.]

(e) For regression with squared error, if we train using fewer points (smaller $N - K$) to get g^-, do you expect $\sigma^2(g^-)$ to be higher or lower? [Hint: For continuous, non-negative random variables, higher mean often implies higher variance.]

(f) Conclude that increasing the size of the validation set can result in a better or a worse estimate of E_{out}.

The expected validation error for $\mathcal{H}_2$ is illustrated in Figure 4.8, where we used the experimental design in Exercise 4.2, with $Q_f = 10$, $N = 40$ and noise level 0.4. The expected validation error equals $E_{\text{out}}(g^-)$, per Equation (4.8).

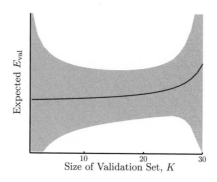

Figure 4.8: The expected validation error $\mathbb{E}[E_{\text{val}}(g^-)]$ as a function of K; the shaded area is $\mathbb{E}[E_{\text{val}}] \pm \sigma_{\text{val}}$.

The figure clearly shows that there is a price to be paid for setting aside K data points to get this unbiased estimate of E_{out}: when we set aside more data for validation, there are fewer training data points and so g^- becomes worse; $E_{\text{out}}(g^-)$, and hence the expected validation error, *increases* (the blue curve). As we expect, the uncertainty in E_{val} as measured by σ_{val} (size of the shaded region) is decreasing with K, up to the point where the variance $\sigma^2(g^-)$ gets really bad. This point comes when the number of training data points becomes critically small, as in Exercise 4.7(e). If K is neither too small nor too large, E_{val} provides a good estimate of E_{out}. A rule of thumb in practice is to set $K = \frac{N}{5}$ (set aside 20% of the data for validation).

We have established two conflicting demands on K. It has to be big enough for E_{val} to be reliable, and it has to be small enough so that the training set with $N - K$ points is big enough to get a decent g^-. Inequality (4.9) quantifies the first demand. The second demand is quantified by the learning curve discussed in Section 2.3.2 (also the blue curve in Figure 4.8, from right to left), which shows how the expected out-of-sample error goes down as the number of training data points goes up . The fact that more training data lead to a better final hypothesis has been extensively verified empirically, although it is challenging to prove theoretically.

Restoring $\mathcal{D}$. Although the learning curve suggests that taking out K data points for validation and using only $N - K$ for training will cost us in terms of E_{out}, we do not have to pay that price! The purpose of validation is to *estimate* the out-of-sample performance, and E_{val} happens to be a good estimate of $E_{\text{out}}(g^-)$. This does not mean that we have to output g^- as our final hypothesis. The primary goal is to get the best possible hypothesis, so we should output g, the hypothesis trained on the entire set $\mathcal{D}$. The secondary goal is to estimate E_{out}, which is what validation allows us to do. Based on our discussion of learning curves, $E_{\text{out}}(g) \leq E_{\text{out}}(g^-)$, so

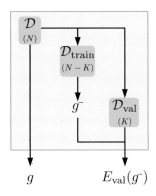

Figure 4.9: Using a validation set to estimate E_{out}.

$$E_{\text{out}}(g) \leq E_{\text{out}}(g^-) \leq E_{\text{val}}(g^-) + O\left(\frac{1}{\sqrt{K}}\right). \tag{4.10}$$

The first inequality is subdued because it was not rigorously proved. If we first train with $N - K$ data points, validate with the remaining K data points and then retrain using all the data to get g, the validation error we got will likely still be better at estimating $E_{\text{out}}(g)$ than the estimate using the VC-bound with $E_{\text{in}}(g)$, especially for large hypothesis sets with big d_{VC}.

So far, we have treated the validation set as a way to estimate E_{out}, without involving it in any decisions that affect the learning process. Estimating E_{out} is a useful role by itself – a customer would typically want to know how good the final hypothesis is (in fact, the inequalities in (4.10) suggest that the validation error is a pessimistic estimate of E_{out}, so your customer is likely to be pleasantly surprised when he tries your system on new data). However, as we will see next, an important role of a validation set is in fact to guide the learning process. That's what distinguishes a validation set from a test set.

4.3.2 Model Selection

By far, the most important use of validation is for *model selection*. This could mean the choice between a linear model and a nonlinear model, the choice of the order of polynomial in a model, the choice of the value of a regularization

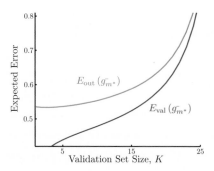

Figure 4.10: Optimistic bias of the validation error when using a validation set for the model selected.

parameter, or any other choice that affects the learning process. In almost every learning situation, there are some choices to be made and we need a principled way of making these choices.

The leap is to realize that validation can be used to estimate the out-of-sample error for more than one model. Suppose we have M models $\mathcal{H}_1, \ldots, \mathcal{H}_M$. Validation can be used to select one of these models. Use the training set $\mathcal{D}_{\text{train}}$ to learn a final hypothesis g_m^- for each model. Now evaluate each model on the validation set to obtain the validation errors $E_1, \cdots, E_M$, where

$$E_m = E_{\text{val}}(g_m^-); \quad m = 1, \ldots, M.$$

The validation errors estimate the out-of-sample error $E_{\text{out}}(g_m^-)$ for each $\mathcal{H}_m$.

Exercise 4.8

Is E_m an unbiased estimate for the out-of-sample error $E_{\text{out}}(g_m^-)$?

It is now a simple matter to select the model with lowest validation error. Let m^* be the index of the model which achieves the minimum validation error. So for $\mathcal{H}_{m^*}$, $E_{m^*} \leq E_m$ for $m = 1, \ldots, M$. The model $\mathcal{H}_{m^*}$ is the model selected based on the validation errors. Note that E_{m^*} is no longer an unbiased estimate of $E_{\text{out}}(g_{m^*}^-)$. Since we *selected* the model with minimum validation error, E_{m^*} will have an optimistic bias. This optimistic bias when selecting between $\mathcal{H}_2$ and $\mathcal{H}_5$ is illustrated in Figure 4.10, using the experimental design described in Exercise 4.2 with $Q_f = 3$, $\sigma^2 = 0.4$ and $N = 35$.

Exercise 4.9

Referring to Figure 4.10, why are both curves increasing with K? Why do they converge to each other with increasing K?

How good is the generalization error for this entire process of model selection using validation? Consider a new model $\mathcal{H}_{\text{val}}$ consisting of the final hypotheses learned from the training data using each model $\mathcal{H}_1, \ldots, \mathcal{H}_M$:

$$\mathcal{H}_{\text{val}} = \{g_1^-, g_2^-, \ldots, g_M^-\}.$$

Model selection using the validation set chose one of the hypotheses in $\mathcal{H}_{\text{val}}$ based on its performance on $\mathcal{D}_{\text{val}}$. Since the model $\mathcal{H}_{\text{val}}$ was obtained before ever looking at the data in the validation set, this process is entirely equivalent to learning a hypothesis from $\mathcal{H}_{\text{val}}$ using the data in $\mathcal{D}_{\text{val}}$. The validation errors $E_{\text{val}}(g_m^-)$ are 'in-sample' errors for this learning process and so we may apply the VC bound for finite hypothesis sets, with $|\mathcal{H}_{\text{val}}| = M$:

$$E_{\text{out}}(g_{m^*}^-) \leq E_{\text{val}}(g_{m^*}^-) + O\left(\sqrt{\frac{\ln M}{K}}\right). \qquad (4.11)$$

What if we didn't use a validation set to choose the model? One alternative would be to use the in-sample errors from each model as the model selection criterion. Specifically, pick the model which gives a final hypothesis with minimum in-sample error. This is equivalent to picking the hypothesis with minimum in-sample error from the grand model which contains all the hypotheses in each of the M original models. If we want a bound on the out-of-sample error for the final hypothesis that results from this selection, we need to apply the VC-penalty for this grand hypothesis set which is the union of the M hypothesis sets (see Problem 2.14). Since this grand hypothesis set can have a huge VC-dimension, the bound in (4.11) will generally be tighter.

The goal of model selection is to select the best model *and* output the best hypothesis from that model. Specifically, we want to select the model m for which $E_{\text{out}}(g_m)$ will be minimum when we retrain with all the data. Model selection using a validation set relies on the leap of faith that if $E_{\text{out}}(g_m^-)$ is minimum, then $E_{\text{out}}(g_m)$ is also minimum. The validation errors E_m estimate $E_{\text{out}}(g_m^-)$, so modulo our leap of faith, the validation set should pick the right model. No matter which model m^* is selected, however, based on the discussion of learning curves in the previous section, we should not output $g_{m^*}^-$ as the final hypothesis. Rather,

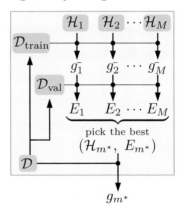

Figure 4.11: Using a validation set for model selection

once m^* is selected using validation, learn using all the data and output g_{m^*}, which satisfies

$$E_{\text{out}}(g_{m^*}) \leq E_{\text{out}}(g_{m^*}^-) \leq E_{\text{val}}(g_{m^*}^-) + O\left(\sqrt{\frac{\ln M}{K}}\right). \qquad (4.12)$$

Again, the first inequality is subdued because we didn't prove it.

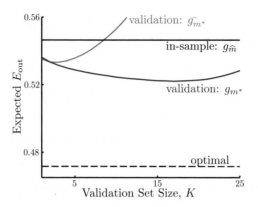

Figure 4.12: Model selection between $\mathcal{H}_2$ and $\mathcal{H}_5$ using a validation set. The solid black line uses E_{in} for model selection, which always selects $\mathcal{H}_5$. The dotted line shows the optimal model selection, if we could select the model based on the true out-of-sample error. This is unachievable, but a useful benchmark. The best performer is clearly the validation set, outputting g_{m^*}. For suitable K, even $g_{m^*}^-$ is better than in-sample selection.

Continuing our experiment from Figure 4.10, we evaluate the out-of-sample performance when using a validation set to select between the models $\mathcal{H}_2$ and $\mathcal{H}_5$. The results are shown in Figure 4.12. Validation is a clear winner over using E_{in} for model selection.

Exercise 4.10

(a) From Figure 4.12, $\mathbb{E}[E_{\text{out}}(g_{m^*}^-)]$ is initially decreasing. How can this be, if $\mathbb{E}[E_{\text{out}}(g_m^-)]$ is increasing in K for each m?

(b) From Figure 4.12 we see that $\mathbb{E}[E_{\text{out}}(g_{m^*})]$ is initially decreasing, and then it starts to increase. What are the possible reasons for this?

(c) When $K = 1$, $\mathbb{E}[E_{\text{out}}(g_{m^*}^-)] < \mathbb{E}[E_{\text{out}}(g_{m^*})]$. How can this be, if the learning curves for both models are decreasing?

Example 4.3. We can use a validation set to select the value of the regularization parameter in the augmented error of (4.6). Although the most important part of a model is the hypothesis set, every hypothesis set has an associated learning algorithm which selects the final hypothesis g. Two models may be different only in their learning algorithm, while working with the same hypothesis set. Changing the value of λ in the augmented error changes the learning algorithm (the criterion by which g is selected) and effectively changes the model.

Based on this discussion, consider the M *different* models corresponding to the same hypothesis set $\mathcal{H}$ but with M different choices for λ in the augmented error. So, we have $(\mathcal{H}, \lambda_1), (\mathcal{H}, \lambda_2), \ldots, (\mathcal{H}, \lambda_M)$ as our M different models. We may, for example, choose $\lambda_1 = 0, \lambda_2 = 0.01, \lambda_3 = 0.02, \ldots, \lambda_M = 10$. Using a validation set to choose one of these M models amounts to determining the value of λ to within a resolution of 0.01.   □

We have analyzed validation for model selection based on a finite number of models. If validation is used to choose the value of a parameter, for example λ as in the previous example, then the value of M will depend on the resolution to which we determine that parameter. In the limit, the selection is actually among an infinite number of models since the value of λ can be any real number. What happens to bounds like (4.11) and (4.12) which depend on M? Just as the Hoeffding bound for a finite hypothesis set did not collapse when we moved to infinite hypothesis sets with finite VC-dimension, bounds like (4.11) and (4.12) will not completely collapse either. We can derive VC-type bounds here too, because even though there are an infinite number of models, these models are all very similar; they differ only slightly in the value of λ. As a rule of thumb, what matters is the number of parameters we are trying to set. If we have only one or a few parameters, the estimates based on a decent-sized validation set would be reliable. The more choices we make based on the same validation set, the more 'contaminated' the validation set becomes and the less reliable its estimates will be. The more we use the validation set to fine tune the model, the more the validation set becomes like a *training* set used to 'learn the right *model*'; and we all know how limited a training set is in its ability to estimate E_{out}.

You will be hard pressed to find a serious learning problem in which validation is not used. Validation is a conceptually simple technique, easy to apply in almost any setting, and requires no specific knowledge about the details of a model. The main drawback is the reduced size of the training set, but that can be significantly mitigated through a modified version of validation which we discuss next.

4.3.3 Cross Validation

Validation relies on the following chain of reasoning,

$$E_{\text{out}}(g) \approx E_{\text{out}}(g^-) \approx E_{\text{val}}(g^-),$$
$$\text{(small } K) \quad \text{(large } K)$$

which highlights the dilemma we face in trying to select K. We are going to output g. When K is large, there is a discrepancy between the two out-of-sample errors $E_{\text{out}}(g^-)$ (which E_{val} directly estimates) and $E_{\text{out}}(g)$ (which is the final error when we learn using all the data $\mathcal{D}$). We would like to choose K as small as possible in order to minimize the discrepancy between $E_{\text{out}}(g^-)$ and $E_{\text{out}}(g)$; ideally $K = 1$. However, if we make this choice, we lose the reliability of the validation estimate as the bound on the RHS of (4.9) becomes huge. The validation error $E_{\text{val}}(g^-)$ will still be an unbiased estimate of $E_{\text{out}}(g^-)$

(g^- is trained on $N-1$ points), but it will be so unreliable as to be useless since it is based on only one data point. This brings us to the *cross validation* estimate of out-of-sample error. We will focus on the *leave-one-out* version which corresponds to a validation set of size $K = 1$, and is also the easiest case to illustrate. More popular versions typically use larger K, but the essence of the method is the same.

There are N ways to partition the data into a training set of size $N-1$ and a validation set of size 1. Specifically, let

$$\mathcal{D}_n = (\mathbf{x}_1, y_1), \dots, (\mathbf{x}_{n-1}, y_{n-1}), \cancel{(\mathbf{x}_n, y_n)}, (\mathbf{x}_{n+1}, y_{n+1}), \dots, (\mathbf{x}_N, y_N)$$

be the data set $\mathcal{D}$ after leaving out data point $(\mathbf{x}_n, y_n)$, which has been shaded in red. Denote the final hypothesis learned from $\mathcal{D}_n$ by g_n^-. Let e_n be the error made by g_n^- on its validation set which is just a single data point $\{(\mathbf{x}_n, y_n)\}$:

$$\mathsf{e}_n = E_{\mathrm{val}}(g_n^-) = \mathsf{e}\left(g_n^-(\mathbf{x}_n), y_n\right).$$

The cross validation estimate is the average value of the e_n's,

$$E_{\mathrm{cv}} = \frac{1}{N} \sum_{n=1}^{N} \mathsf{e}_n.$$

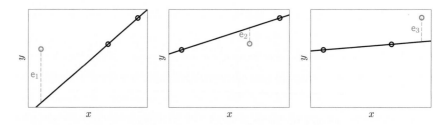

Figure 4.13: Illustration of leave-one-out cross validation for a linear fit using three data points. The average of the three red errors obtained by the linear fits leaving out one data point at a time is E_{cv}.

Figure 4.13 illustrates cross validation on a simple example. Each e_n is a wild, yet unbiased estimate for the corresponding $E_{\mathrm{out}}(g_n^-)$, which follows after setting $K = 1$ in (4.8). With cross validation, we have N functions $g_1^-, \dots, g_N^-$ together with the N error estimates $\mathsf{e}_1, \dots, \mathsf{e}_N$. The hope is that these N errors *together* would be almost equivalent to estimating E_{out} on a reliable validation set of size N, while at the same time we managed to use $N-1$ points to obtain each g_n^-. Let's try to understand why E_{cv} is a good estimator of E_{out}.

First and foremost, E_{cv} is an unbiased estimator of '$E_{\text{out}}(g^-)$'. We have to be a little careful here because we don't have a single hypothesis g^-, as we did when using a single validation set. Depending on the $(\mathbf{x}_n, y_n)$ that was taken out, each g_n^- can be a different hypothesis. To understand the sense in which E_{cv} estimates E_{out}, we need to revisit the concept of the learning curve.

Ideally, we would like to know $E_{\text{out}}(g)$. The final hypothesis g is the result of learning on a random data set $\mathcal{D}$ of size N. It is almost as useful to know the *expected* performance of your model when you learn on a data set of size N; the hypothesis g is just one such instance of learning on a data set of size N. This expected performance averaged over data sets of size N, when viewed as a function of N, is exactly the learning curve shown in Figure 4.2. More formally, for a given model, let

$$\bar{E}_{\text{out}}(N) = \mathbb{E}_{\mathcal{D}}[E_{\text{out}}(g)]$$

be the expectation (over data sets $\mathcal{D}$ of size N) of the out-of-sample error produced by the model. The expected value of E_{cv} is exactly $\bar{E}_{\text{out}}(N-1)$. This is true because it is true for each individual validation error e_n:

$$\begin{aligned} \mathbb{E}_{\mathcal{D}}[\mathsf{e}_n] &= \mathbb{E}_{\mathcal{D}_n}\, \mathbb{E}_{(\mathbf{x}_n, y_n)}\left[\mathsf{e}(g_n^-(\mathbf{x}_n), y_n)\right], \\ &= \mathbb{E}_{\mathcal{D}_n}[E_{\text{out}}(g_n^-)], \\ &= \bar{E}_{\text{out}}(N-1). \end{aligned}$$

Since this equality holds for each e_n, it also holds for the average. We highlight this result by making it a theorem.

Theorem 4.4. E_{cv} *is an unbiased estimate of* $\bar{E}_{\text{out}}(N-1)$ *(the expectation of the model performance,* $\mathbb{E}[E_{\text{out}}]$, *over data sets of size* $N-1$).

Now that we have our cross validation estimate of E_{out}, there is no need to output any of the g_n^- as our final hypothesis. We might as well squeeze every last drop of performance and retrain using the entire data set $\mathcal{D}$, outputting g as the final hypothesis and getting the benefit of going from $N-1$ to N on the learning curve. In this case, the cross validation estimate will on average be an upper estimate for the out-of-sample error: $E_{\text{out}}(g) \le E_{\text{cv}}$, so expect to be pleasantly surprised, albeit slightly.

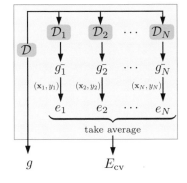

Figure 4.14: Using cross validation to estimate E_{out}

With just simple validation and a validation set of size $K = 1$, we know that the validation estimate will not be reliable. How reliable is the cross validation estimate E_{cv}? We can measure the reliability using the variance of E_{cv}.

Unfortunately, while we were able to pin down the expectation of E_{cv}, the variance is not so easy.

If the N cross validation errors $e_1, \ldots, e_N$ were equivalent to N errors on a totally separate validation set of size N, then E_{cv} would indeed be a reliable estimate, for decent-sized N. The equivalence would hold if the individual e_n's were independent of each other. Of course, this is too optimistic. Consider two validation errors e_n, e_m. The validation error e_n depends on g_n^- which was trained on data containing $(\mathbf{x}_m, y_m)$. Thus, e_n has a dependency on $(\mathbf{x}_m, y_m)$. The validation error e_m is computed using $(\mathbf{x}_m, y_m)$ directly, and so it also has a dependency on $(\mathbf{x}_m, y_m)$. Consequently, there is a possible correlation between e_n and e_m through the data point $(\mathbf{x}_m, y_m)$. That correlation wouldn't be there if we were validating a single hypothesis using N fresh (independent) data points.

How much worse is the cross validation estimate as compared to an estimate based on a truly independent set of N validation errors? A VC-type probabilistic bound, or even computation of the asymptotic variance of the cross validation estimate (Problem 4.23), is challenging. One way to quantify the reliability of E_{cv} is to compute how many fresh validation data points would have a comparable reliability to E_{cv}, and Problem 4.24 discusses one way to do this. There are two extremes for this effective size. On the high end is N, which means that the cross validation errors are essentially independent. On the low end is 1, which means that E_{cv} is only as good as any single one of the individual cross validation errors e_n, i.e., the cross validation errors are totally dependent. While one cannot prove anything theoretically, in practice the reliability of E_{cv} is much closer to the higher end.

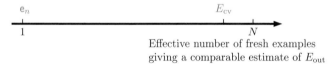

Effective number of fresh examples
giving a comparable estimate of E_{out}

Cross validation for model selection. In Figure 4.11, the estimates E_m for the out-of-sample error of model $\mathcal{H}_m$ were obtained using the validation set. Instead, we may use cross validation estimates to obtain E_m: use cross validation to obtain estimates of the out-of-sample error for each model $\mathcal{H}_1, \ldots, \mathcal{H}_M$, and select the model with the smallest cross validation error. Now, train this model selected by cross validation using all the data to output a final hypothesis, making the usual leap of faith that $E_{\text{out}}(g^-)$ tracks $E_{\text{out}}(g)$ well.

Example 4.5. In Figure 4.13, we illustrated cross validation for estimating E_{out} of a linear model $(h(x) = ax + b)$ using a simple experiment with three data points generated from a constant target function with noise. We now consider a second model, the constant model $(h(x) = b)$. We can also use cross validation to estimate E_{out} for the constant model, illustrated in Figure 4.15.

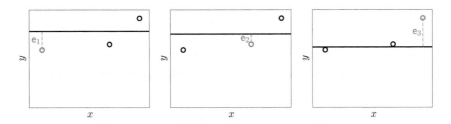

Figure 4.15: Leave-one-out cross validation error for a constant fit.

If we use the in-sample error after fitting all the data (three points), then the linear model wins because it can use its additional degree of freedom to fit the data better. The same is true with the cross validation data sets of size two – the linear model has perfect in-sample error. But, with cross validation, what matters is the error on *the outstanding point* in each of these fits. Even to the naked eye, the average of the cross validation errors is smaller for the constant model which obtained $E_{cv} = 0.065$ versus $E_{cv} = 0.184$ for the linear model. The constant model wins, according to cross validation. The constant model also has lower E_{out} and so cross validation selected the correct model in this example.   □

One important use of validation is to estimate the optimal regularization parameter λ, as described in Example 4.3. We can use cross validation for the same purpose as summarized in the algorithm below.

Cross validation for selecting λ:
1: Define M models by choosing different values for λ in the augmented error: $(\mathcal{H}, \lambda_1), (\mathcal{H}, \lambda_2), \ldots, (\mathcal{H}, \lambda_M)$
2: **for** each model $m = 1, \ldots, M$ **do**
3: Use the cross validation module in Figure 4.14 to estimate $E_{cv}(m)$, the cross validation error for model m.
4: Select the model m^* with minimum $E_{cv}(m^*)$.
5: Use model $(\mathcal{H}, \lambda_{m^*})$ and all the data $\mathcal{D}$ to obtain the final hypothesis g_{m^*}. Effectively, you have estimated the optimal λ.

We see from Figure 4.14 that estimating E_{cv} for just a single model requires N rounds of learning on $\mathcal{D}_1, \ldots, \mathcal{D}_N$, each of size $N - 1$. So the cross validation algorithm above requires MN rounds of learning. This is a formidable task. If we could analytically obtain E_{cv}, that would be a big bonus, but analytic results are often difficult to come by for cross validation. One exception is in the case of linear models, where we are able to derive an exact analytic formula for the cross validation estimate.

Analytic computation of E_{cv} for linear models. Recall that for linear regression with weight decay, $\mathbf{w}_{reg} = (Z^T Z + \lambda I)^{-1} Z^T \mathbf{y}$, and the in-sample predictions are

$$\hat{\mathbf{y}} = H(\lambda)\mathbf{y},$$

where $H(\lambda) = Z(Z^T Z + \lambda I)^{-1} Z^T$. Given H, $\hat{\mathbf{y}}$, and $\mathbf{y}$, it turns out that we can analytically compute the cross validation estimate as:

$$E_{cv} = \frac{1}{N} \sum_{n=1}^{N} \left(\frac{\hat{y}_n - y_n}{1 - H_{nn}(\lambda)} \right)^2. \tag{4.13}$$

Notice that the cross validation estimate is very similar to the in-sample error, $E_{in} = \frac{1}{N} \sum_n (\hat{y}_n - y_n)^2$, differing only by a normalization of each term in the sum by a factor $1/(1 - H_{nn}(\lambda))^2$. One use for this analytic formula is that it can be directly optimized to obtain the best regularization parameter λ. A proof of this remarkable formula is given in Problem 4.26.

Even when we cannot derive such an analytic characterization of cross validation, the technique widely results in good out-of-sample error estimates in practice, and so the computational burden is often worth enduring. Also, as with using a validation set, cross validation applies in almost any setting without requiring specific knowledge about the details of the models.

So far, we have lived in a world of unlimited computation, and all that mattered was out-of-sample error; in reality, computation time can be of consequence, especially with huge data sets. For this reason, leave-one-out cross validation may not be the method of choice.[4] A popular derivative of leave-one-out cross validation is *V-fold cross validation*.[5] In *V*-fold cross validation, the data are partitioned into *V* disjoint sets (or folds) $\mathcal{D}_1, \ldots, \mathcal{D}_V$, each of size approximately N/V; each set $\mathcal{D}_v$ in this partition serves as a validation set to compute a validation error for a hypothesis g^- learned on a training set which is the complement of the validation set, $\mathcal{D} \setminus \mathcal{D}_v$. So, you always validate a hypothesis on data that was *not* used for training that particular hypothesis. The *V*-fold cross validation error is the average of the *V* validation errors that are obtained, one from each validation set $\mathcal{D}_v$. Leave-one-out cross validation is the same as *N*-fold cross validation. The gain from choosing $V \ll N$ is computational. The drawback is that you will be estimating E_{out} for a hypothesis g^- trained on less data (as compared with leave-one-out) and so the discrepancy between $E_{out}(g)$ and $E_{out}(g^-)$ will be larger. A common choice in practice is 10-fold cross validation, and one of the folds is illustrated below.

$$\mathcal{D}$$

---

[4]Stability problems have also been reported in leave-one-out.

[5]Some authors call it K-fold cross validation, but we choose V so as not to confuse with the size of the validation set K.

4.3.4   Theory Versus Practice

Both validation and cross validation present challenges for the mathematical theory of learning, similar to the challenges presented by regularization. The theory of generalization, in particular the VC analysis, forms the foundation for learnability. It provides us with guidelines under which it is possible to make a generalization conclusion with high probability. It is not straightforward, and sometimes not possible, to rigorously carry these conclusions over to the analysis of validation, cross validation, or regularization. What is possible, and indeed quite effective, is to use the theory as a guideline. In the case of regularization, constraining the choice of a hypothesis leads to better generalization, as we would intuitively expect, even if the hypothesis set remains technically the same. In the case of validation, making a choice for few parameters does not overly contaminate the validation estimate of E_{out}, even if the VC guarantee for these estimates is too weak. In the case of cross validation, the benefit of averaging several validation errors is observed, even if the estimates are not independent.

Although these techniques were based on sound theoretical foundation, they are to be considered *heuristics* because they do not have a full mathematical justification in the general case. Learning from data is an empirical task with theoretical underpinnings. We prove what we can prove, but we use the theory as a guideline when we don't have a conclusive proof. In a practical application, heuristics may win over a rigorous approach that makes unrealistic assumptions. The only way to be convinced about what works and what doesn't in a given situation is to try out the techniques and see for yourself. The basic message in this chapter can be summarized as follows.

---

1. Noise (stochastic or deterministic) affects learning adversely, leading to overfitting.

2. Regularization helps to prevent overfitting by constraining the model, reducing the impact of the noise, while still giving us flexibility to fit the data.

3. Validation and cross validation are useful techniques for estimating E_{out}. One important use of validation is model selection, in particular to estimate the amount of regularization to use.

Example 4.6. We illustrate validation on the handwritten digit classification task of deciding whether a digit is 1 or not (see also Example 3.1) based on the two features which measure the symmetry and average intensity of the digit. The data is shown in Figure 4.16(a).

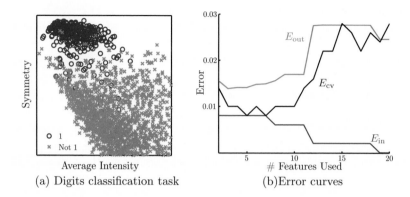

(a) Digits classification task   (b)Error curves

Figure 4.16: (a) The digits data of which 500 are selected as the training set. (b) The data are transformed via the 5th order polynomial transform to a 20-dimensional feature vector. We show the performance curves as we vary the number of these features used for classification.

We have randomly selected 500 data points as the training data and the remaining are used as a test set for evaluation. We considered a nonlinear feature transform to a 5th order polynomial feature space:

$$(1, x_1, x_2) \rightarrow (1, x_1, x_2, x_1^2, x_1 x_2, x_2^2, x_1^3, x_1^2 x_2, \ldots, x_1^5, x_1^4 x_2, x_1^3 x_2^2, x_1^2 x_2^3, x_1 x_2^4, x_2^5).$$

Figure 4.16(b) shows the in-sample error as you use more of the transformed features, increasing the dimension from 1 to 20. As you add more dimensions (increase the complexity of the model), the in-sample error drops, as expected. The out-of-sample error drops at first, and then starts to increase, as we hit the approximation-generalization tradeoff. The leave-one-out cross validation error tracks the behavior of the out-of-sample error quite well. If we were to pick a model based on the in-sample error, we would use all 20 dimensions. The cross validation error is minimized between 5-7 feature dimensions; we take 6 feature dimensions as the model selected by cross validation. The table below summarizes the resulting performance metrics:

	E_{in}	E_{out}
No Validation	0%	2.5%
Cross Validation	0.8%	1.5%

Cross validation results in a performance improvement of about 1%, which is a massive relative improvement (40% reduction in error rate).

Exercise 4.11

In this particular experiment, the black curve (E_{cv}) is sometimes below and sometimes above the the red curve (E_{out}). If we repeated this experiment many times, and plotted the average black and red curves, would you expect the black curve to lie above or below the red curve?

It is illuminating to see the actual classification boundaries learned with and without validation. These resulting classifiers, together with the 500 in-sample data points, are shown in the next figure.

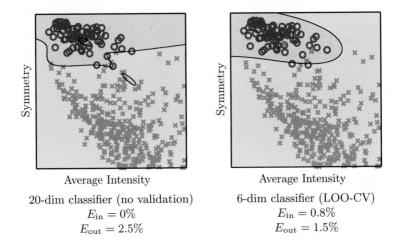

20-dim classifier (no validation)	6-dim classifier (LOO-CV)
$E_{\text{in}} = 0\%$	$E_{\text{in}} = 0.8\%$
$E_{\text{out}} = 2.5\%$	$E_{\text{out}} = 1.5\%$

It is clear that the worse out-of-sample performance of the classifier picked without validation is due to the overfitting of a few noisy points in the training data. While the training data is perfectly separated, the shape of the resulting boundary seems highly contorted, which is a symptom of overfitting. Does this remind you of the first example that opened the chapter? There, albeit in a toy example, we similarly obtained a highly contorted fit. As you can see, overfitting is real, and here to stay! □

4.4 Problems

Problem 4.1   Plot the monomials of order i, $\phi_i(x) = x^i$. As you increase the order, does this correspond to the intuitive notion of increasing complexity?

Problem 4.2   Consider the feature transform $\mathbf{z} = [L_0(x), L_1(x), L_2(x)]^{\mathsf{T}}$ and the linear model $h(x) = \mathbf{w}^{\mathsf{T}}\mathbf{z}$. For the hypothesis with $\mathbf{w} = [1, -1, 1]^{\mathsf{T}}$, what is $h(x)$ explicitly as a function of x. What is its degree?

Problem 4.3   The Legendre Polynomials are a family of orthogonal polynomials which are useful for regression. The first two Legendre Polynomials are $L_0(x) = 1$, $L_1(x) = x$. The higher order Legendre Polynomials are defined by the recursion:

$$L_k(x) = \frac{2k-1}{k} x L_{k-1}(x) - \frac{k-1}{k} L_{k-2}(x).$$

(a) What are the first six Legendre Polynomials? Use the recursion to develop an efficient algorithm to compute $L_0(x), \ldots, L_K(x)$ given x. Your algorithm should run in time linear in K. Plot the first six Legendre polynomials.

(b) Show that $L_k(x)$ is a linear combination of monomials $x^k, x^{k-2}, \ldots$ (either all odd or all even order, with highest order k). Thus,

$$L_k(-x) = (-1)^k L_k(x).$$

(c) Show that $\frac{x^2-1}{k} \frac{dL_k(x)}{dx} = x L_k(x) - L_{k-1}(x)$. *[Hint: use induction.]*

(d) Use part (c) to show that L_k satisfies *Legendre's differential equation*

$$\frac{d}{dx}(x^2 - 1) \frac{dL_k(x)}{dx} = k(k+1) L_k(x).$$

This means that the Legendre Polynomials are eigenfunctions of a Hermitian linear differential operator and, from Sturm-Liouville theory, they form an orthogonal basis for continuous functions on $[-1, 1]$.

(e) Use the recurrence to show directly the orthogonality property:

$$\int_{-1}^{1} dx \, L_k(x) L_\ell(x) = \begin{cases} 0 & \ell \neq k, \\ \frac{2}{2k+1} & \ell = k. \end{cases}$$

[Hint: use induction on k, with $\ell \leq k$. Use the recurrence for L_k and consider separately the four cases $\ell = k, k-1, k-2$ and $\ell < k-2$. For the case $\ell = k$ you will need to compute the integral $\int_{-1}^{1} dx \, x^2 L_{k-1}^2(x)$. In order to do this, you could use the differential equation in part (c), multiply by $x L_k$ and then integrate both sides (the LHS can be integrated by parts). Now solve the resulting equation for $\int_{-1}^{1} dx \, x^2 L_{k-1}^2(x)$.]

154

Problem 4.4   LAMi This problem is a detailed version of Exercise 4.2.
We set up an experimental framework which the reader may use to study various aspects of overfitting. The input space is $\mathcal{X} = [-1, 1]$, with uniform input probability density, $P(x) = \frac{1}{2}$. We consider the two models $\mathcal{H}_2$ and $\mathcal{H}_{10}$. The target function is a polynomial of degree Q_f, which we write as $f(x) = \sum_{q=0}^{Q_f} a_q L_q(x)$, where $L_q(x)$ are the Legendre polynomials. We use the Legendre polynomials because they are a convenient orthogonal basis for the polynomials on $[-1, 1]$ (see Section 4.2 and Problem 4.3 for some basic information on Legendre polynomials). The data set is $\mathcal{D} = (x_1, y_1), \ldots, (x_N, y_N)$, where $y_n = f(x_n) + \sigma\epsilon_n$ and ϵ_n are iid standard Normal random variates.

For a single experiment, with specified values for Q_f, N, σ, generate a random degree-Q_f target function by selecting coefficients a_q independently from a standard Normal, rescaling them so that $\mathbb{E}_{a,x}\left[f^2\right] = 1$. Generate a data set, selecting $x_1, \ldots, x_N$ independently from $P(x)$ and $y_n = f(x_n) + \sigma\epsilon_n$. Let g_2 and g_{10} be the best fit hypotheses to the data from $\mathcal{H}_2$ and $\mathcal{H}_{10}$ respectively, with respective out-of-sample errors $E_{\text{out}}(g_2)$ and $E_{\text{out}}(g_{10})$.

(a) Why do we normalize f? [Hint: how would you interpret σ?]

(b) How can we obtain g_2, g_{10}? [Hint: pose the problem as linear regression and use the technology from Chapter 3.]

(c) How can we compute E_{out} analytically for a given g_{10}?

(d) Vary Q_f, N, σ and for each combination of parameters, run a large number of experiments, each time computing $E_{\text{out}}(g_2)$ and $E_{\text{out}}(g_{10})$. Averaging these out-of-sample errors gives estimates of the expected out-of-sample error for the given learning scenario (Q_f, N, σ) using $\mathcal{H}_2$ and $\mathcal{H}_{10}$. Let

$$E_{\text{out}}(\mathcal{H}_2) = \text{average over experiments}(E_{\text{out}}(g_2)),$$
$$E_{\text{out}}(\mathcal{H}_{10}) = \text{average over experiments}(E_{\text{out}}(g_{10})).$$

Define the overfit measure $E_{\text{out}}(\mathcal{H}_{10}) - E_{\text{out}}(\mathcal{H}_2)$. When is the overfit measure significantly positive (i.e., overfitting is serious) as opposed to significantly negative? Try the choices $Q_f \in \{1, 2, \ldots, 100\}$, $N \in \{20, 25, \ldots, 120\}$, $\sigma^2 \in \{0, 0.05, 0.1, \ldots, 2\}$.
Explain your observations.

(e) Why do we take the average over many experiments? Use the variance to select an acceptable number of experiments to average over.

(f) Repeat this experiment for classification, where the target function is a noisy perceptron, $f = \text{sign}\left(\sum_{q=1}^{Q_f} a_q L_q(x) + \epsilon\right)$. Notice that $a_0 = 0$, and the a_q's should be normalized so that $\mathbb{E}_{a,x}\left[(\sum_{q=1}^{Q_f} a_q L_q(x))^2\right] = 1$. For classification, the models $\mathcal{H}_2, \mathcal{H}_{10}$ contain the sign of the 2nd and 10th order polynomials respectively. You may use a learning algorithm for non-separable data from Chapter 3.

Problem 4.5   If $\lambda < 0$ in the augmented error $E_{\text{aug}}(\mathbf{w}) = E_{\text{in}}(\mathbf{w}) + \lambda \mathbf{w}^{\text{T}} \mathbf{w}$, what soft order constraint does this correspond to? *[Hint: $\lambda < 0$ encourages large weights.]*

Problem 4.6   In the augmented error minimization with $\Gamma = I$ and $\lambda > 0$:

(a) Show that $\|\mathbf{w}_{\text{reg}}\| \leq \|\mathbf{w}_{\text{lin}}\|$, justifying the term weight decay. *[Hint: start by assuming that $\|\mathbf{w}_{\text{reg}}\| > \|\mathbf{w}_{\text{lin}}\|$ and derive a contradiction.]*
In fact a stronger statement holds: $\|\mathbf{w}_{\text{reg}}\|$ is decreasing in λ.

(b) Explicitly verify this for linear models. *[Hint:*

$$\mathbf{w}_{\text{reg}}^{\text{T}} \mathbf{w}_{\text{reg}} = \mathbf{u}^{\text{T}} (\mathbf{Z}^{\text{T}} \mathbf{Z} + \lambda I)^{-2} \mathbf{u},$$

where $\mathbf{u} = \mathbf{Z}^{\text{T}} \mathbf{y}$ and Z is the transformed data matrix. Show that $\mathbf{Z}^{\text{T}} \mathbf{Z} + \lambda I$ has the same eigenvectors with correspondingly larger eigenvalues as $\mathbf{Z}^{\text{T}} \mathbf{Z}$. Expand $\mathbf{u}$ in the eigenbasis of $\mathbf{Z}^{\text{T}} \mathbf{Z}$. For a matrix A, how are the eigenvectors and eigenvalues of A^{-2} related to those of A?]

Problem 4.7   Show that the in-sample error

$$E_{\text{in}}(\mathbf{w}_{\text{reg}}) = \frac{1}{N} \mathbf{y}^{\text{T}} (I - H(\lambda))^2 \mathbf{y}$$

from Example 4.2 is an increasing function of λ, where $H(\lambda) = Z(Z^{\text{T}}Z + \lambda I)^{-1} Z^{\text{T}}$ and Z is the transformed data matrix.

To do so, let the SVD of $Z = U\Gamma V^{\text{T}}$ and let $Z^{\text{T}} Z$ have eigenvalues $\sigma_1^2, \ldots, \sigma_d^2$. Define the vector $\mathbf{a} = U^{\text{T}} \mathbf{y}$. Show that

$$E_{\text{in}}(\mathbf{w}_{\text{reg}}) = E_{\text{in}}(\mathbf{w}_{\text{lin}}) + \frac{1}{N} \sum_{i=1}^{d} a_i^2 \left(1 - \frac{\sigma_i^2}{\sigma_i^2 + \lambda} \right)^2,$$

and proceed from there.

Problem 4.8   In the augmented error minimization with $\Gamma = I$ and $\lambda > 0$, assume that E_{in} is differentiable and use gradient descent to minimize E_{aug}:

$$\mathbf{w}(t+1) \leftarrow \mathbf{w}(t) - \eta \nabla E_{\text{aug}}(\mathbf{w}(t)).$$

Show that the update rule above is the same as

$$\mathbf{w}(t+1) \leftarrow (1 - 2\eta\lambda)\mathbf{w}(t) - \eta \nabla E_{\text{in}}(\mathbf{w}(t)).$$

Note: This is the origin of the name 'weight decay': $\mathbf{w}(t)$ decays before being updated by the gradient of E_{in}.

Problem 4.9   In Tikhonov regularization, the regularized weights are given by $\mathbf{w}_{\text{reg}} = (Z^{\text{T}}Z + \lambda\Gamma^{\text{T}}\Gamma)^{-1}Z^{\text{T}}\mathbf{y}$. The Tikhonov regularizer Γ is a $k \times (d+1)$ matrix, each row corresponding to a $d+1$ dimensional vector. Each row of Z corresponds to a $d+1$ dimensional vector (the first component is 1). For each row of Γ, construct a *virtual example* $(\mathbf{z}_i, 0)$ for $i = 1, \ldots, k$, where $\mathbf{z}_i$ is the vector obtained from the ith row of Γ after scaling it by $\sqrt{\lambda}$, and the target value is 0. Add these k virtual examples to the data, to construct an augmented data set, and consider non-regularized regression with this augmented data.

(a) Show that, for the augmented data, $Z_{\text{aug}} = \begin{bmatrix} Z \\ \sqrt{\lambda} \cdot \Gamma \end{bmatrix}$ and $\mathbf{y}_{\text{aug}} = \begin{bmatrix} \mathbf{y} \\ \mathbf{0} \end{bmatrix}$.

(b) Show that solving the least squares problem with Z_{aug} and $\mathbf{y}_{\text{aug}}$ results in the same regularized weight $\mathbf{w}_{\text{reg}}$, i.e. $\mathbf{w}_{\text{reg}} = (Z_{\text{aug}}^{\text{T}}Z_{\text{aug}})^{-1}Z_{\text{aug}}^{\text{T}}\mathbf{y}_{\text{aug}}$.

This result may be interpreted as follows: an equivalent way to accomplish weight-decay-type regularization with linear models is to create a bunch of *virtual examples* all of whose target values are zero.

Problem 4.10   In this problem, you will investigate the relationship between the soft order constraint and the augmented error. The regularized weight $\mathbf{w}_{\text{reg}}$ is a solution to

$$\min E_{\text{in}}(\mathbf{w}) \text{ subject to } \mathbf{w}^{\text{T}}\Gamma^{\text{T}}\Gamma\mathbf{w} \leq C.$$

(a) If $\mathbf{w}_{\text{lin}}^{\text{T}}\Gamma^{\text{T}}\Gamma\mathbf{w}_{\text{lin}} \leq C$, then what is $\mathbf{w}_{\text{reg}}$?

(b) If $\mathbf{w}_{\text{lin}}^{\text{T}}\Gamma^{\text{T}}\Gamma\mathbf{w}_{\text{lin}} > C$, the situation is illustrated below,

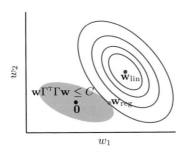

The constraint is satisfied in the shaded region and the contours of constant E_{in} are the ellipsoids (why ellipsoids?). What is $\mathbf{w}_{\text{reg}}^{\text{T}}\Gamma^{\text{T}}\Gamma\mathbf{w}_{\text{reg}}$?

(c) Show that with

$$\lambda_C = -\frac{1}{2C}\mathbf{w}_{\text{reg}}^{\text{T}}\nabla E_{\text{in}}(\mathbf{w}_{\text{reg}}),$$

$\mathbf{w}_{\text{reg}}$ minimizes $E_{\text{in}}(\mathbf{w}) + \lambda_C\mathbf{w}^{\text{T}}\Gamma^{\text{T}}\Gamma\mathbf{w}$. *[Hint: use the previous part to solve for $\mathbf{w}_{\text{reg}}$ as an equality constrained optimization problem using the method of Lagrange multipliers.]*

(continued on next page)

(d) Show that the following hold for λ_C:

    (i) If $\mathbf{w}_{\text{lin}}^{\text{T}}\Gamma^{\text{T}}\Gamma\mathbf{w}_{\text{lin}} \leq C$ then $\lambda_C = 0$ ($\mathbf{w}_{\text{lin}}$ itself satisfies the constraint).

    (ii) If $\mathbf{w}_{\text{lin}}^{\text{T}}\Gamma^{\text{T}}\Gamma\mathbf{w}_{\text{lin}} > C$, then $\lambda_C > 0$ (the penalty term is positive).

    (iii) If $\mathbf{w}_{\text{lin}}^{\text{T}}\Gamma^{\text{T}}\Gamma\mathbf{w}_{\text{lin}} > C$, then λ_C is a strictly decreasing function of C.
[Hint: show that $\frac{d\lambda_C}{dC} < 0$ for $C \in [0, \mathbf{w}_{\text{lin}}^{\text{T}}\Gamma^{\text{T}}\Gamma\mathbf{w}_{\text{lin}}]$.]

Problem 4.11   For the linear model in Exercise 4.2, the target function is a polynomial of degree Q_f; the model is $\mathcal{H}_Q$, with polynomials up to order Q. Assume $Q \geq Q_f$. $\mathbf{w}_{\text{lin}} = (\mathbf{Z}^{\text{T}}\mathbf{Z})^{-1}\mathbf{Z}^{\text{T}}\mathbf{y}$, and $\mathbf{y} = \mathbf{Z}\mathbf{w}_{\text{f}} + \boldsymbol{\epsilon}$, where $\mathbf{w}_{\text{f}}$ is the target function and $\mathbf{Z}$ is the matrix containing the transformed data.

(a) Show that $\mathbf{w}_{\text{lin}} = \mathbf{w}_{\text{f}} + (\mathbf{Z}^{\text{T}}\mathbf{Z})^{-1}\mathbf{Z}^{\text{T}}\boldsymbol{\epsilon}$. What is the average function $\bar{g}$? Show that bias $= 0$ (recall that: $\text{bias}(\mathbf{x}) = (\bar{g}(\mathbf{x}) - f(\mathbf{x}))^2$).

(b) Show that

$$\text{var} = \frac{\sigma^2}{N}\text{trace}\left(\Sigma_\Phi \, \mathbb{E}_{\mathbf{Z}}\left[\left(\tfrac{1}{N}\mathbf{Z}^{\text{T}}\mathbf{Z}\right)^{-1}\right]\right),$$

where $\Sigma_\Phi = \mathbb{E}[\Phi(x)\Phi^{\text{T}}(x)]$. [Hints: $\text{var} = \mathbb{E}[(g^{(\mathcal{D})} - \bar{g})^2]$; first take the expectation with respect to $\boldsymbol{\epsilon}$, then with respect to $\Phi(x)$, the test point, and the last remaining expectation will be with respect to $\mathbf{Z}$. You will need the cyclic property of the trace.]

(c) Argue that to first order in $\frac{1}{N}$, $\text{var} \approx \dfrac{\sigma^2(Q+1)}{N}$.
[Hint: $\frac{1}{N}\mathbf{Z}^{\text{T}}\mathbf{Z} = \frac{1}{N}\sum_{n=1}^{N}\Phi(x_n)\Phi^{\text{T}}(x_n)$ is the in-sample estimate of Σ_Φ. By the law of large numbers, $\frac{1}{N}\mathbf{Z}^{\text{T}}\mathbf{Z} = \Sigma_\Phi + o(1)$.]

For the well specified linear model, the bias is zero and the variance is increasing as the model gets larger (Q increases), but decreasing in N.

Problem 4.12   Use the setup in Problem 4.11 with $Q \geq Q_f$. Consider regression with weight decay using a linear model $\mathcal{H}$ in the transformed space with input probability distribution such that $\mathbb{E}[\mathbf{z}\mathbf{z}^{\text{T}}] = \mathbf{I}$. The regularized weights are given by $\mathbf{w}_{\text{reg}} = (\mathbf{Z}^{\text{T}}\mathbf{Z} + \lambda\mathbf{I})^{-1}\mathbf{Z}^{\text{T}}\mathbf{y}$, where $\mathbf{y} = \mathbf{Z}\mathbf{w}_{\text{f}} + \boldsymbol{\epsilon}$.

(a) Show that $\mathbf{w}_{\text{reg}} = \mathbf{w}_{\text{f}} - \lambda(\mathbf{Z}^{\text{T}}\mathbf{Z} + \lambda\mathbf{I})^{-1}\mathbf{w}_{\text{f}} + (\mathbf{Z}^{\text{T}}\mathbf{Z} + \lambda\mathbf{I})^{-1}\mathbf{Z}^{\text{T}}\boldsymbol{\epsilon}$.

(b) Argue that, to first order in $\frac{1}{N}$,

$$\text{bias} \approx \frac{\lambda^2}{(\lambda+N)^2}\|\mathbf{w}_{\text{f}}\|^2,$$

$$\text{var} \approx \frac{\sigma^2}{N}\,\mathbb{E}\left[\text{trace}(\mathbf{H}^2(\lambda))\right],$$

where $\mathbf{H}(\lambda) = \mathbf{Z}(\mathbf{Z}^{\text{T}}\mathbf{Z} + \lambda\mathbf{I})^{-1}\mathbf{Z}^{\text{T}}$.

If we plot the bias and var, we get a figure that is very similar to Figure 2.3, where the tradeoff was based on fit and complexity rather than bias and var. Here, the bias is increasing in λ (as expected) and in $\|\mathbf{w}_f\|$; the variance is decreasing in λ. When $\lambda = 0$, $\mathrm{trace}(\mathrm{H}^2(\lambda)) = Q + 1$ and so $\mathrm{trace}(\mathrm{H}^2(\lambda))$ appears to be playing the role of an effective number of parameters.

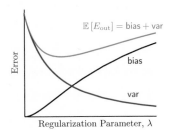

Problem 4.13   Within the linear regression setting, many attempts have been made to quantify the effective number of parameters in a model. Three possibilities are:

(i) $d_{\mathrm{eff}}(\lambda) = 2\mathrm{trace}(\mathrm{H}(\lambda)) - \mathrm{trace}(\mathrm{H}^2(\lambda))$

(ii) $d_{\mathrm{eff}}(\lambda) = \mathrm{trace}(\mathrm{H}(\lambda))$

(iii) $d_{\mathrm{eff}}(\lambda) = \mathrm{trace}(\mathrm{H}^2(\lambda))$

where $\mathrm{H}(\lambda) = \mathrm{Z}(\mathrm{Z}^\mathsf{T}\mathrm{Z} + \lambda\mathrm{I})^{-1}\mathrm{Z}^\mathsf{T}$ and Z is the transformed data matrix. To obtain d_{eff}, one must first compute $\mathrm{H}(\lambda)$ as though you are doing regression. One can then heuristically use d_{eff} in place of d_{vc} in the VC-bound.

(a) When $\lambda = 0$, show that for all three choices, $d_{\mathrm{eff}} = \tilde{d} + 1$, where $\tilde{d}$ is the dimension in the $\mathcal{Z}$ space.

(b) When $\lambda > 0$, show that $0 \le d_{\mathrm{eff}} \le \tilde{d} + 1$ and d_{eff} is decreasing in λ for all three choices. *[Hint: Use the singular value decomposition.]*

Problem 4.14   The observed target values $\mathbf{y}$ can be separated into the true target values $\mathbf{f}$ and the noise ϵ, $\mathbf{y} = \mathbf{f} + \epsilon$. The components of ϵ are iid with variance σ^2 and expectation 0. For linear regression with weight decay regularization, by taking the expected value of the in-sample error in (4.2), show that

$$
\begin{aligned}
\mathbb{E}_\epsilon[E_{\mathrm{in}}] &= \frac{1}{N}\mathbf{f}^\mathsf{T}(\mathrm{I} - \mathrm{H}(\lambda))^2\mathbf{f} + \frac{\sigma^2}{N}\mathrm{trace}\left((\mathrm{I} - \mathrm{H}(\lambda))^2\right), \\
&= \frac{1}{N}\mathbf{f}^\mathsf{T}(\mathrm{I} - \mathrm{H}(\lambda))^2\mathbf{f} + \sigma^2\left(1 - \frac{d_{\mathrm{eff}}}{N}\right),
\end{aligned}
$$

where $d_{\mathrm{eff}} = 2\mathrm{trace}(\mathrm{H}(\lambda)) - \mathrm{trace}(\mathrm{H}^2(\lambda))$, as defined in Problem 4.13(i), $\mathrm{H}(\lambda) = \mathrm{Z}(\mathrm{Z}^\mathsf{T}\mathrm{Z} + \lambda\mathrm{I})^{-1}\mathrm{Z}^\mathsf{T}$ and Z is the transformed data matrix.

(continued on next page)

(a) If the noise was not overfit, what should the term involving σ^2 be, and why?

(b) Hence, argue that the degree to which the noise has been overfit is $\sigma^2 d_{\text{eff}}/N$. Interpret the dependence of this result on the parameters d_{eff} and N, to justify the use of d_{eff} as an effective number of parameters.

Problem 4.15   We further investigate d_{eff} of Problems 4.13 and 4.14. We know that $H(\lambda) = Z(Z^\mathsf{T}Z + \lambda\Gamma^\mathsf{T}\Gamma)^{-1}Z^\mathsf{T}$. When Γ is square and invertible, as is usually the case (for example with weight decay, $\Gamma = I$), denote $\tilde{Z} = Z\Gamma^{-1}$. Let $s_0^2, \ldots, s_d^2$ be the eigenvalues of $\tilde{Z}^\mathsf{T}\tilde{Z}$ ($s_i^2 > 0$ when Z has full column rank).

(a) For $d_{\text{eff}}(\lambda) = \text{trace}(2H(\lambda) - H^2(\lambda))$, show that

$$d_{\text{eff}}(\lambda) = d + 1 - \sum_{i=0}^{d} \frac{\lambda^2}{(s_i^2 + \lambda)^2}.$$

(b) For $d_{\text{eff}}(\lambda) = \text{trace}(H(\lambda))$, show that $d_{\text{eff}}(\lambda) = d + 1 - \sum_{i=0}^{d} \frac{\lambda}{s_i^2 + \lambda}$.

(c) For $d_{\text{eff}}(\lambda) = \text{trace}(H^2(\lambda))$, show that $d_{\text{eff}}(\lambda) = \sum_{i=0}^{d} \frac{s_i^4}{(s_i^2 + \lambda)^2}$.

In all cases, for $\lambda \geq 0$, $0 \leq d_{\text{eff}}(\lambda) \leq d+1$, $d_{\text{eff}}(0) = d+1$ and d_{eff} is decreasing in λ. [*Hint: use the singular value decomposition $\tilde{Z} = USV^\mathsf{T}$, where U, V are orthogonal and S is diagonal with entries s_i.*]

Problem 4.16   For linear models and the general Tikhonov regularizer Γ with penalty term $\frac{\lambda}{N}\mathbf{w}^\mathsf{T}\Gamma^\mathsf{T}\Gamma\mathbf{w}$ in the augmented error, show that

$$\mathbf{w}_{\text{reg}} = (Z^\mathsf{T}Z + \lambda\Gamma^\mathsf{T}\Gamma)^{-1}Z^\mathsf{T}\mathbf{y},$$

where Z is the feature matrix.

(a) Show that the in-sample predictions are

$$\hat{\mathbf{y}} = H(\lambda)\mathbf{y},$$

where $H(\lambda) = Z(Z^\mathsf{T}Z + \lambda\Gamma^\mathsf{T}\Gamma)^{-1}Z^\mathsf{T}$.

(b) Simplify this in the case $\Gamma = Z$ and obtain $\mathbf{w}_{\text{reg}}$ in terms of $\mathbf{w}_{\text{lin}}$. This is called uniform weight decay.

Problem 4.17   To model uncertainty in the measurement of the inputs, assume that the true inputs $\hat{\mathbf{x}}_n$ are the observed inputs $\mathbf{x}_n$ perturbed by some noise ϵ_n: the true inputs are given by $\hat{\mathbf{x}}_n = \mathbf{x}_n + \epsilon_n$. Assume that the ϵ_n are independent of $(\mathbf{x}_n, y_n)$ with covariance matrix $\mathbb{E}[\epsilon_n\epsilon_n^\mathsf{T}] = \sigma_x^2 I$ and mean

$\mathbb{E}[\epsilon_n] = \mathbf{0}$. The learning algorithm minimizes the *expected in-sample error* $\hat{E}_{\text{in}}$, where the expectation is with respect to the uncertainty in the true $\hat{\mathbf{x}}_n$.

$$\hat{E}_{\text{in}}(\mathbf{w}) = \mathbb{E}_{\epsilon_1 \dots \epsilon_N}\left[\frac{1}{N}\sum_{n=1}^{N}(\mathbf{w}^{\mathsf{T}}\hat{\mathbf{x}}_n - y_n)^2\right].$$

Show that the weights $\hat{\mathbf{w}}_{\text{lin}}$ which result from minimizing $\hat{E}_{\text{in}}$ are equivalent to the weights which would have been obtained by minimizing $E_{\text{in}} = \frac{1}{N}\sum_{n=1}^{N}(\mathbf{w}^{\mathsf{T}}\mathbf{x}_n - y_n)^2$ for the observed data, with Tikhonov regularization. What are Γ and λ (see Problem 4.16 for the general Tikhonov regularizer)?

One can interpret this result as follows: regularization enforces a robustness to potential measurement errors (noise) in the observed inputs.

Problem 4.18   In a regression setting, assume the target function is linear, so $f(\mathbf{x}) = \mathbf{w}_f^{\mathsf{T}}\mathbf{x}$, and $\mathbf{y} = Z\mathbf{w}_f + \boldsymbol{\epsilon}$, where the entries in $\boldsymbol{\epsilon}$ are iid with zero mean and variance σ^2. Assume a regularization term $\frac{\lambda}{N}\mathbf{w}^{\mathsf{T}}Z^{\mathsf{T}}Z\mathbf{w}$ and that $\mathbb{E}[\mathbf{x}\mathbf{x}^{\mathsf{T}}] = I$. In this problem derive the optimal value for λ as follows.

(a) Show that the average function is $\bar{g}(\mathbf{x}) = \frac{1}{1+\lambda}f(\mathbf{x})$. What is the bias?

(b) Show that var is asymptotically $\frac{\sigma^2(d+1)}{N(1+\lambda)^2}$. [Hint: Problem 4.12.]

(c) Use the bias and asymptotic variance to obtain an expression for $\mathbb{E}[E_{\text{out}}]$. Optimize this with respect to λ to obtain the optimal regularization parameter. [Answer: $\lambda^* = \frac{\sigma^2(d+1)}{N\|\mathbf{w}_f\|^2}$.]

(d) Explain the dependence of the optimal regularization parameter on the parameters of the learning problem. [Hint: write $\lambda^* = \frac{(d+1)/N}{\|\mathbf{w}_f\|^2/\sigma^2}$.]

Problem 4.19   [The Lasso algorithm] Rather than a soft order constraint on the squares of the weights, one could use the absolute values of the weights:

$$\min E_{\text{in}}(\mathbf{w}) \text{ subject to } \sum_{i=0}^{d}|w_i| \leq C.$$

The model is called the lasso algorithm.

(a) Formulate and implement this as a quadratic program. Use the experimental design in Problem 4.4 to compare the lasso algorithm with the quadratic penalty by giving plots of E_{out} versus regularization parameter.

(b) What is the augmented error? Is it more convenient to optimize?

(c) With $d = 5$ and $N = 3$, compare the weights from the lasso versus the quadratic penalty. [Hint: Look at the number of non-zero weights.]

Problem 4.20   In this problem, you will explore a consistency condition for weight decay. Suppose that we make an invertible linear transform of the data,

$$\mathbf{z}_n = \mathrm{A}\mathbf{x}_n, \qquad \tilde{y}_n = \alpha y_n.$$

Intuitively, linear regression should not be affected by a linear transform. This means that the new optimal weights should be given by a corresponding linear transform of the old optimal weights.

(a) Suppose $\mathbf{w}$ minimizes the in-sample error for the original problem. Show that for the transformed problem, the optimal weights are

$$\tilde{\mathbf{w}} = \alpha(\mathrm{A}^\mathsf{T})^{-1}\mathbf{w}.$$

(b) Suppose the regularization penalty term in the augmented error is $\mathbf{w}^\mathsf{T}\mathrm{X}^\mathsf{T}\mathrm{X}\mathbf{w}$ for the original data and $\mathbf{w}^\mathsf{T}\mathrm{Z}^\mathsf{T}\mathrm{Z}\mathbf{w}$ for the transformed data. On the original data, the regularized solution is $\mathbf{w}_{\mathrm{reg}}(\lambda)$. Show that for the transformed problem, the same linear transform of $\mathbf{w}_{\mathrm{reg}}(\lambda)$ gives the corresponding regularized weights for the transformed problem:

$$\tilde{\mathbf{w}}_{\mathbf{reg}}(\lambda) = \alpha(\mathrm{A}^\mathsf{T})^{-1}\mathbf{w}_{\mathrm{reg}}(\lambda).$$

Problem 4.21   The Tikhonov smoothness penalty which penalizes derivatives of h is $\Omega(h) = \int dx \, \left(\frac{\partial^2 h(x)}{\partial x^2}\right)^2$. Show that, for linear models, this reduces to a penalty of the form $\mathbf{w}^\mathsf{T}\Gamma^\mathsf{T}\Gamma\mathbf{w}$. What is Γ?

Problem 4.22   You have a data set with 100 data points. You have 100 models each with VC-dimension 10. You set aside 25 points for validation. You select the model which produced minimum validation error of 0.25. Give a bound on the out-of-sample error for this selected function.

Suppose you instead trained each model on all the data and selected the function with minimum in-sample error. The resulting in-sample error is 0.15. Give a bound on the out-of-sample error in this case. *[Hint: Use the bound in Problem 2.14 to bound the VC-dimension of the union of all the models.]*

Problem 4.23   This problem investigates the covariance of the leave-one-out cross validation errors, $\mathrm{Cov}_\mathcal{D}[e_n, e_m]$. Assume that for well behaved models, the learning process is 'stable', and so the change in the learned hypothesis should be small, '$O\left(\frac{1}{N}\right)$', if a new data point is added to a data set of size N. Write $g_n^- = g^{(N-2)} + \delta_n$ and $g_m^- = g^{(N-2)} + \delta_m$, where $g^{(N-2)}$ is the learned hypothesis on $\mathcal{D}^{(N-2)}$, the data minus the nth and mth data points, and δ_n, δ_m are the corrections after addition of the nth and mth data points respectively.

(a) Show that $\mathrm{Var}_{\mathcal{D}}[E_{\mathrm{cv}}] = \frac{1}{N^2}\sum_{n=1}^{N}\mathrm{Var}_{\mathcal{D}}[e_n] + \frac{1}{N^2}\sum_{n \neq m}\mathrm{Cov}_{\mathcal{D}}[e_n, e_m]$.

(b) Show $\mathrm{Cov}_{\mathcal{D}}[e_n, e_m] = \mathrm{Var}_{\mathcal{D}^{(N-2)}}[E_{\mathrm{out}}(g^{(N-2)})] +$ higher order in δ_n, δ_m.

(c) Assume that any terms involving δ_n, δ_m are $O(\frac{1}{N})$. Argue that

$$\mathrm{Var}_{\mathcal{D}}[E_{\mathrm{cv}}] = \frac{1}{N}\mathrm{Var}_{\mathcal{D}}[e_1] + \mathrm{Var}_{\mathcal{D}}[E_{\mathrm{out}}(g)] + O\left(\frac{1}{N}\right).$$

Does $\mathrm{Var}_{\mathcal{D}}[e_1]$ decay to zero with N? What about $\mathrm{Var}_{\mathcal{D}}[E_{\mathrm{out}}(g)]$?

(d) Use the experimental design in Problem 4.4 to study $\mathrm{Var}_{\mathcal{D}}[E_{\mathrm{cv}}]$ and give a log-log-plot of $\mathrm{Var}_{\mathcal{D}}[E_{\mathrm{cv}}]/\mathrm{Var}_{\mathcal{D}}[e_1]$ versus N. What is the decay rate?

Problem 4.24   For $d = 3$, generate a random data set with N points as follows. For each point, each dimension of $\mathbf{x}$ has a standard Normal distribution. Similarly, generate a $(d+1)$-dimensional target weight vector $\mathbf{w}_{\mathrm{f}}$, and set $y_n = \mathbf{w}_{\mathrm{f}}^{\mathsf{T}}\mathbf{x}_n + \sigma\epsilon_n$ where ϵ_n is noise (also from a standard Normal distribution) and σ is the noise variance; set σ to 0.5.

Use linear regression with weight decay regularization to estimate $\mathbf{w}_{\mathrm{f}}$ with $\mathbf{w}_{\mathrm{reg}}$. Set the regularization parameter to $0.05/N$.

(a) For $N \in \{d+15, d+25, \ldots, d+115\}$, compute the cross validation errors $e_1, \ldots, e_N$ and E_{cv}. Repeat the experiment (say) 10^5 times, maintaining the average and variance over the experiments of e_1, e_2 and E_{cv}.

(b) How should your average of the e_1's relate to the average of the E_{cv}'s; how about to the average of the e_2's? Support your claim using results from your experiment.

(c) What are the contributors to the variance of the e_1's?

(d) If the cross validation errors were truly independent, how should the variance of the e_1's relate to the variance of the E_{cv}'s?

(e) One measure of the effective number of fresh examples used in computing E_{cv} is the ratio of the variance of the e_1's to that of the E_{cv}'s. Explain why, and plot, versus N, the effective number of fresh examples (N_{eff}) as a percentage of N. You should find that N_{eff} is close to N.

(f) If you increase the amount of regularization, will N_{eff} go up or down? Explain your reasoning. Run the same experiment with $\lambda = 2.5/N$ and compare your results from part (e) to verify your conjecture.

Problem 4.25   When using a validation set for model selection, all models were learned on the *same* $\mathcal{D}_{\mathrm{train}}$ of size $N - K$, and validated on the *same* $\mathcal{D}_{\mathrm{val}}$ of size K. We have the VC-bound (see Equation (4.12)):

$$E_{\mathrm{out}}(g_{m^*}^-) \leq E_{\mathrm{val}}(g_{m^*}^-) + O\left(\sqrt{\frac{\ln M}{2K}}\right)$$

(continued on next page)

Suppose that instead, you had no control over the validation process. So M learners, each with their own models present you with the results of their validation processes on *different* validation sets. Here is what you know about each learner:

> Each learner m reports to you the size of their validation set K_m, and the validation error $E_{\text{val}}(m)$. The learners may have used different data sets, except that they faithfully learned on a training set and validated on a held out validation set which was *only* used for validation purposes.

As the model selector, you have to decide which learner to go with.

(a) Should you select the learner with minimum validation error? If yes, why? If no, why not? *[Hint: think VC-bound.]*

(b) If all models are validated on the same validation set as described in the text, why is it okay to select the learner with the lowest validation error?

(c) After selecting learner m^* (say), show that

$$\mathbb{P}[E_{\text{out}}(m^*) > E_{\text{val}}(m^*) + \epsilon] \le M e^{-2\epsilon^2 \kappa(\epsilon)},$$

where $\kappa(\epsilon) = -\frac{1}{2\epsilon^2} \ln\left(\frac{1}{M} \sum_{m=1}^{M} e^{-2\epsilon^2 K_m} \right)$ is an "average" validation set size.

(d) Show that with probability at least $1 - \delta$, $E_{\text{out}} \le E_{\text{val}} + \epsilon^*$, for any ϵ^* which satisfies $\epsilon^* \ge \sqrt{\frac{\ln(M/\delta)}{2\kappa(\epsilon^*)}}$.

(e) Show that $\min_m K_m \le \kappa(\epsilon) \le \frac{1}{M} \sum_{m=1}^{M} K_m$. Is this bound better or worse than the bound when all models use the same validation set size (equal to the average validation set size $\frac{1}{M} \sum_{m=1}^{M} K_m$)?

Problem 4.26   In this problem, derive the formula for the exact expression for the leave-one-out cross validation error for linear regression. Let Z be the data matrix whose rows correspond to the transformed data points $\mathbf{z}_n = \Phi(\mathbf{x}_n)$.

(a) Show that:

$$Z^\mathsf{T} Z = \sum_{n=1}^{N} \mathbf{z}_n \mathbf{z}_n^\mathsf{T}; \qquad Z^\mathsf{T} \mathbf{y} = \sum_{n=1}^{N} \mathbf{z}_n y_n; \qquad \mathrm{H}_{nm}(\lambda) = \mathbf{z}_n^\mathsf{T} \mathrm{A}^{-1}(\lambda) \mathbf{z}_m,$$

where $\mathrm{A} = \mathrm{A}(\lambda) = Z^\mathsf{T} Z + \lambda \Gamma^\mathsf{T} \Gamma$ and $\mathrm{H}(\lambda) = Z \mathrm{A}(\lambda)^{-1} Z^\mathsf{T}$. Hence, show that when $(\mathbf{z}_n, y_n)$ is left out, $Z^\mathsf{T} Z \to Z^\mathsf{T} Z - \mathbf{z}_n \mathbf{z}_n^\mathsf{T}$, and $Z^\mathsf{T} \mathbf{y} \to Z^\mathsf{T} \mathbf{y} - \mathbf{z}_n y_n$.

(b) Compute $\mathbf{w}_n^-$, the weight vector learned when the nth data point is left out, and show that:

$$\mathbf{w}_n^- = \left(\mathrm{A}^{-1} + \frac{\mathrm{A}^{-1} \mathbf{z}_n \mathbf{z}_n^\mathsf{T} \mathrm{A}^{-1}}{1 - \mathbf{z}_n^\mathsf{T} \mathrm{A}^{-1} \mathbf{z}_n} \right) (Z^\mathsf{T} \mathbf{y} - \mathbf{z}_n y_n).$$

[Hint: use the identity $(\mathrm{A} - \mathbf{x}\mathbf{x}^{\mathsf{T}})^{-1} = \mathrm{A}^{-1} + \frac{\mathrm{A}^{-1}\mathbf{x}\mathbf{x}^{\mathsf{T}}\mathrm{A}^{-1}}{1 - \mathbf{x}^{\mathsf{T}}\mathrm{A}^{-1}\mathbf{x}} \cdot]

(c) Using (a) and (b), show that $\mathbf{w}_n^- = \mathbf{w} + \frac{\hat{y}_n - y_n}{1 - \mathrm{H}_{nn}}\mathrm{A}^{-1}\mathbf{z}_n$, where $\mathbf{w}$ is the regression weight vector using all the data.

(d) The prediction on the validation point is given by $\mathbf{z}_n^{\mathsf{T}}\mathbf{w}_n^-$. Show that

$$\mathbf{z}_n^{\mathsf{T}}\mathbf{w}_n^- = \frac{\hat{y}_n - \mathrm{H}_{nn}y_n}{1 - \mathrm{H}_{nn}}.$$

(e) Show that $e_n = \left(\frac{\hat{y}_n - y_n}{1 - \mathrm{H}_{nn}}\right)^2$, and hence prove Equation (4.13).

Problem 4.27 Cross validation gives an accurate estimate of $\bar{E}_{\text{out}}(N-1)$, but it can be quite sensitive, leading to problems in model selection. A common heuristic for 'regularizing' cross validation is to use a measure of error $\sigma_{\text{cv}}(\mathcal{H})$ for the cross validation estimate in model selection.

(a) One choice for σ_{cv} is the standard deviation of the leave-one-out errors divided by $\sqrt{N}$, $\sigma_{\text{cv}} \approx \frac{1}{\sqrt{N}}\sqrt{\text{var}(e_1, \ldots, e_n)}$. Why divide by $\sqrt{N}$?

(b) For linear models, show that $\sqrt{N}\sigma_{\text{cv}} = \frac{1}{N}\sum_{n=1}^{N}\left(\frac{\hat{y}_n - y_n}{1 - \mathrm{H}_{nn}}\right)^4 - E_{\text{cv}}^2$.

(c) (i) Given the best model $\mathcal{H}^*$, the conservative one-sigma approach selects the simplest model within $\sigma_{\text{cv}}(\mathcal{H}^*)$ of the best.

(ii) The bound minimizing approach selects the model which minimizes $E_{\text{cv}}(\mathcal{H}) + \sigma_{\text{cv}}(\mathcal{H})$.

Use the experimental design in Problem 4.4 to compare these approaches with the 'unregularized' cross validation estimate as follows. Fix $Q_f = 15$, $Q = 20$, and $\sigma = 1$. Use each of the two methods proposed here as well as traditional cross validation to select the optimal value of the regularization parameter λ in the range $\{0.05, 0.10, 0.15, \ldots, 5\}$ using weight decay regularization, $\Omega(\mathbf{w}) = \frac{\lambda}{N}\mathbf{w}^{\mathsf{T}}\mathbf{w}$. Plot the resulting out-of-sample error for the model selected using each method as a function of N, with N in the range $\{2 \times Q, 3 \times Q, \ldots, 10 \times Q\}$.

What are your conclusions?

Chapter 5

Three Learning Principles

The study of learning from data highlights some general principles that are fascinating concepts in their own right. Having gone through the mathematical analysis and empirical illustrations of the first few chapters, we have a good foundation from which to articulate some of these principles and explain them in concrete terms.

In this chapter, we will discuss three principles. The first one is related to the choice of model and is called Occam's razor. The other two are related to data; sampling bias establishes an important principle about obtaining the data, and data snooping establishes an important principle about handling the data. A genuine understanding of these principles will protect you from the most common pitfalls in learning from data, and allow you to interpret generalization performance properly.

5.1 Occam's Razor

Although it is not an exact quote of Einstein's, it is often attributed to him that "An explanation of the data should be made *as simple as possible, but no simpler.*" A similar principle, *Occam's Razor*, dates from the 14th century and is attributed to William of Occam, where the 'razor' is meant to trim down the explanation to the bare minimum that is consistent with the data.

In the context of learning, the penalty for model complexity which was introduced in Section 2.2 is a manifestation of Occam's razor. If $E_{in}(g) = 0$, then the explanation (hypothesis) is consistent with the data. In this case, the most plausible explanation, with the lowest estimate of E_{out} given in the VC bound (2.14), happens when the complexity of the explanation (measured by $d_{vc}(\mathcal{H})$) is as small as possible. Here is a statement of the underlying principle.

> **The simplest model that fits the data is also the most plausible.**

Applying this principle, we should choose as simple a model as we think we can get away with. Although the principle that simpler is better may be intuitive, it is neither precise nor self-evident. When we apply the principle to learning from data, there are two basic questions to be asked.

1. What does it mean for a model to be simple?

2. How do we know that simpler is better?

Let's start with the first question. There are two distinct approaches to defining the notion of complexity, one based on a family of objects and the other based on an individual object. We have already seen both approaches in our analysis. The VC dimension in Chapter 2 is a measure of complexity, and it is based on the hypothesis set $\mathcal{H}$ as a whole, i.e., based on a family of objects. The regularization term of the augmented error in Chapter 4 is also a measure of complexity, but in this case it is the complexity of an individual object, namely the hypothesis h.

The two approaches to defining complexity are not encountered only in learning from data; they are a recurring theme whenever complexity is discussed. For instance, in information theory, *entropy* is a measure of complexity based on a family of objects, while *minimum description length* is a related measure based on individual objects. There is a reason why this is a recurring theme. The two approaches to defining complexity are in fact related.

When we say a family of objects is complex, we mean that the family is 'big'. That is, it contains a large variety of objects. Therefore, each individual object in the family is *one of many*. By contrast, a simple family of objects is 'small'; it has relatively few objects, and each individual object is *one of few*.

Why is the sheer number of objects an indication of the level of complexity? The reason is that both the number of objects in a family and the complexity of an object are related to how many parameters are needed to specify the object. When you increase the number of parameters in a learning model, you simultaneously increase how diverse $\mathcal{H}$ is and how complex the individual h is. For example, consider 17th order polynomials versus 3rd order polynomials. There is more variety in 17th order polynomials, and at the same time the individual 17th order polynomial is more complex than a 3rd order polynomial.

The most common definitions of object complexity are based on the number of bits needed to describe an object. Under such definitions, an object is simple if it has a short description. Therefore, a simple object is not only intrinsically simple (as it can be described succinctly), but it also has to be one of few, since there are fewer objects that have short descriptions than there are that have long descriptions, as a matter of simple counting.

Exercise 5.1

Consider hypothesis sets $\mathcal{H}_1$ and $\mathcal{H}_{100}$ that contain Boolean functions on 10 Boolean variables, so $\mathcal{X} = \{-1, +1\}^{10}$. $\mathcal{H}_1$ contains all Boolean functions which evaluate to $+1$ on exactly one input point, and to -1 elsewhere; $\mathcal{H}_{100}$ contains all Boolean functions which evaluate to $+1$ on exactly 100 input points, and to -1 elsewhere.

(a) How big (number of hypotheses) are $\mathcal{H}_1$ and $\mathcal{H}_{100}$?

(b) How many bits are needed to specify one of the hypotheses in $\mathcal{H}_1$?

(c) How many bits are needed to specify one of the hypotheses in $\mathcal{H}_{100}$?

We now address the second question. When Occam's razor says that simpler is better, it doesn't mean simpler is more elegant. It means simpler has a better chance of being right. Occam's razor is about performance, not about aesthetics. If a complex explanation of the data performs better, we will take it.

The argument that simpler has a better chance of being right goes as follows. We are trying to fit a hypothesis to our data $\mathcal{D} = \{(\mathbf{x}_1, y_1), \cdots, (\mathbf{x}_N, y_N)\}$ (assume y_n's are binary). There are fewer simple hypotheses than there are complex ones. With complex hypotheses, there would be enough of them to shatter $\mathbf{x}_1, \cdots, \mathbf{x}_N$, so it is certain that we can fit the data set regardless of what the labels $y_1, \cdots, y_N$ are, even if these are completely random. Therefore, fitting the data does not mean much. If, instead, we have a simple model with few hypotheses and we still found one that perfectly fits the dichotomy $\mathcal{D} = \{(\mathbf{x}_1, y_1), \cdots, (\mathbf{x}_N, y_N)\}$, this is surprising, and therefore it means something.

Occam's Razor has been formally proved under different sets of idealized conditions. The above argument captures the essence of these proofs; if something is less likely to happen, then when it does happen it is more significant. Let us look at an example.

Example 5.1. Suppose that one constructs a physical theory about the resistivity of a metal under various temperatures. In this theory, aside from some constants that need to be determined, the resistivity ρ has a linear dependence on the temperature T. In order to verify that the theory is correct and to obtain the unknown constants, 3 scientists conduct the following three experiments and present their data to you.

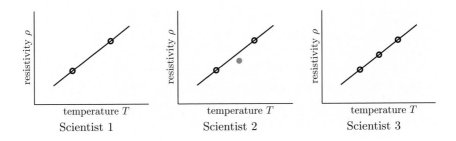

It is clear that Scientist 3 has produced the most convincing evidence for the theory. If the measurements are exact, then, Scientist 2 has managed to falsify the theory and we are back to the drawing board. What about Scientist 1? While he has not falsified the theory, has he provided any evidence for it? The answer is no, for we can reverse the question. Suppose that the theory was not correct, what could the data have done to prove him wrong? Nothing, since any two points can be joined by a line. Therefore, the model is not just likely to fit the data in this case, it is certain to do so. This renders the fit totally insignificant when it does happen.   □

This example illustrates a concept related to Occam's Razor, which is the *axiom of non-falsifiability*. The axiom asserts that the data should have some chance of falsifying a hypothesis, if we are to conclude that it can provide evidence for the hypothesis. One way to guarantee that every data set has some chance at falsification is for the VC dimension of the hypothesis set to be less than N, the number of data points. This is discussed further in Problem 5.1. Here is another example of the same concept.

Example 5.2. Financial firms try to pick good traders (predictors of whether the market will go up or not). Suppose that each trader is tested on their prediction (up or down) over the next 5 days and those who perform well will be hired. One might think that this process should produce better and better traders on Wall Street. Viewed as a learning problem, consider each trader to be a prediction hypothesis. Suppose that the hiring pool is 'complex'; we are interviewing 2^5 traders who happen to be a diverse set of people such that their predictions over the next 5 days are all different. Necessarily one of these traders gets it all correct, and will be hired. Hiring the trader through this process may or may not be a good thing, since the process will pick someone even if the traders are just flipping coins to make their predictions. A perfect predictor always exists in this group, so finding one doesn't mean much. If we were interviewing only two traders, and one of them made perfect predictions, that would mean something.   □

Exercise 5.2

Suppose that for 5 weeks in a row, a letter arrives in the mail that predicts the outcome of the upcoming Monday night football game. You keenly watch each Monday and to your surprise, the prediction is correct each time. On the day after the fifth game, a letter arrives, stating that if you wish to see next week's prediction, a payment of $50.00 is required. Should you pay?

(a) How many possible predictions of win-lose are there for 5 games?

(b) If the sender wants to make sure that at least one person receives correct predictions on all 5 games from him, how many people should he target to begin with?

(c) After the first letter 'predicting' the outcome of the first game, how many of the original recipients does he target with the second letter?

(d) How many letters altogether will have been sent at the end of the 5 weeks?

(e) If the cost of printing and mailing out each letter is $0.50, how much would the sender make if the recipient of 5 correct predictions sent in the $50.00?

(f) Can you relate this situation to the growth function and the credibility of fitting the data?

Learning from data takes Occam's Razor to another level, going beyond "as simple as possible, but no simpler." Indeed, we may opt for 'a simpler fit than possible', namely an imperfect fit of the data using a simple model over a perfect fit using a more complex one. The reason is that the price we pay for a perfect fit in terms of the penalty for model complexity in (2.14) may be too much in comparison to the benefit of the better fit. This idea was illustrated in Figure 3.7, and is a manifestation of overfitting. The idea is also the rationale behind the recommended policy in Chapter 3: *first* try a linear model – one of the simplest models in the arena of learning from data.

5.2 Sampling Bias

A vivid example of sampling bias happened in the 1948 US presidential election between Truman and Dewey. On election night, a major newspaper carried out a telephone poll to ask people how they voted. The poll indicated that Dewey won, and the paper was so confident about the small error bar in its poll that it declared Dewey the winner in its headline. When the actual votes were counted, Dewey lost – to the delight of a smiling Truman.

©Associated Press

This was not a case of statistical anomaly, where the newspaper was just incredibly unlucky (remember the δ in the VC bound?). It was a case where the sample was doomed from the get-go, regardless of its size. Even if the experiment were repeated, the result would be the same. In 1948, telephones were expensive and those who had them tended to be in an elite group that favored Dewey much more than the average voter did. Since the newspaper did its poll by telephone, it inadvertently used an in-sample distribution that was different from the out-of-sample distribution. That is what sampling bias is.

> **If the data is sampled in a biased way, learning will produce a similarly biased outcome.**

Applying this principle, we should make sure that the training and testing distributions are the same; if not, our results may be invalid, or, at the very least, require careful interpretation.

If you recall, the VC analysis made very few assumptions, but one assumption it did make was that the data set $\mathcal{D}$ is generated from the same distribution that the final hypothesis g is tested on. In practice, we may encounter data sets that were not generated under those ideal conditions. There are some techniques in statistics and in learning to compensate for the 'mismatch' between training and testing, but not in cases where $\mathcal{D}$ was generated with the exclusion of certain parts of the input space, such as the exclusion of households with no telephones in the above example. There is nothing that can be done when this happens, other than to admit that the result will not be reliable – statistical bounds like Hoeffding and VC require a match between the training and testing distributions.

There are many examples of how sampling bias can be introduced in data collection. In some cases it is inadvertently introduced by an oversight, as in the case of Dewey and Truman. In other cases, it is introduced because certain types of data are not available. For instance, in our credit example of Chapter 1, the bank created the training set from the database of previous customers and how they performed for the bank. Such a set necessarily excludes those who applied to the bank for credit cards and were rejected, because the bank does not have data on how they *would have performed* if they were accepted. Since future applicants will come from a mixed population including some who would have been rejected in the past, the 'test set' comes from a different distribution than the training set, and we have a case of sampling bias. In this particular case, if no data on the applicants that were rejected is available, nothing much can be done other than to acknowledge that there is a bias in the final predictor that learning will produce, since a representative training set is just not available.

Exercise 5.3

In an experiment to determine the distribution of sizes of fish in a lake, a net might be used to catch a representative sample of fish. The sample is then analyzed to find out the fractions of fish of different sizes. If the sample is big enough, statistical conclusions may be drawn about the actual distribution in the entire lake. Can you smell ☺ sampling bias?

There are other cases, arguably more common, where sampling bias is introduced by human intervention. It is not that uncommon for someone to throw away training examples they don't like! A Wall Street firm who wants to develop an automated trading system might choose data sets when the market was 'behaving well' to train the system, with the semi-legitimate justification that they don't want the noise to complicate the training process. They will surely achieve that if they get rid of the 'bad' examples, but they will create a system that can be trusted only in the periods when the market does behave well! What happens when the market is not behaving well is anybody's guess. In general, throwing away training examples based on their values, e.g., examples that look like outliers or don't conform to our preconceived ideas, is a fairly common sampling bias trap.

Other biases. Sampling bias has also been called selection bias in the statistics community. We will stick with the more descriptive term sampling bias for two reasons. First, the bias arises in how the data was *sampled*; second, it is less ambiguous because in the learning context, there is another notion of selection bias drifting around – *selection* of a final hypothesis from the learning model based on the data. The performance of the selected hypothesis on the data is optimistically biased, and this could be denoted as a selection bias. We have referred to this type of bias simply as bad generalization.

There are various other biases that have similar flavor. There is even a special type of bias for the research community, called publication bias! This refers to the bias in published scientific results because negative results are often not published in the literature, whereas positive results are. The common theme of all of these biases is that they render the standard statistical conclusions invalid because the basic premise for such conclusions, that the sampling distribution is the same as the overall distribution, does not hold any more. In the field of learning from data, it is sampling bias in the training set that we need to worry about.

5.3   Data Snooping

Data snooping is the most common trap for practitioners in learning from data. The principle involved is simple enough,

> **If a data set has affected any step in the learning process, its ability to assess the outcome has been compromised.**

Applying this principle, if you want an unbiased assessment of your learning performance, you should keep a test set in a vault and never use it for learning in any way. This is basically what we have been talking about all along in training versus testing, but it goes beyond that. Even if a data set has not been 'physically' used for training, it can still affect the learning process, sometimes in subtle ways.

> **Exercise 5.4**
>
> Consider the following approach to learning. By looking at the data, it appears that the data is linearly separable, so we go ahead and use a simple perceptron, and get a training error of zero after determining the optimal set of weights. We now wish to make some generalization conclusions, so we look up the d_{vc} for our learning model and see that it is $d+1$. Therefore, we use this value of d_{vc} to get a bound on the test error.
>
> (a) What is the problem with this bound - is it correct?
>
> (b) Do we know the d_{vc} for the learning model that we actually used? It is this d_{vc} that we need to use in the bound.

To avoid the pitfall in the above exercise, it is extremely important that you choose your learning model *before* seeing any of the data. The choice can be based on general information about the learning problem, such as the number of data points and prior knowledge regarding the input space and target function, but not on the actual data set $\mathcal{D}$. Failure to observe this rule will invalidate the VC bounds, and any generalization conclusions will be up in the air. Even a careful person can fall into the traps of data snooping. Consider the following example.

Example 5.3. An investment bank wants to develop a system for forecasting currency exchange rates. It has 8 years worth of historical data on the US Dollar (USD) versus the British Pound (GBP), so it tries to use the data to see if there is any pattern that can be exploited. The bank takes the series of daily changes in the USD/GBP rate, normalizes it to zero mean and unit variance, and starts to develop a system for forecasting the direction of the change. For each day, it tries to predict that direction based on the fluctuations in the previous 20 days. 75% of the data is used for training, and the remaining 25% is set aside for testing the final hypothesis.

The test shows great success. The final hypothesis has a hit rate (percentage of time getting the direction right) of 52.1%. This may seem modest, but in the world of finance you can make a lot of money if you get that hit rate consistently. Indeed, over the 500 test days (2 years worth, as each year has about 250 trading days), the cumulative profit of the system is a respectable 22%.

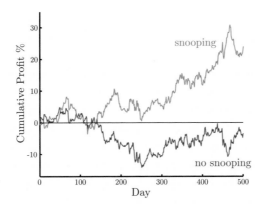

When the system is used in live trading, the performance deteriorates significantly. In fact, it loses money. Why didn't the good test performance continue on the new data? In this case, there is a simple explanation and it has to do with data snooping. Although the bank was careful to set aside test points that were not used for training in order to properly evaluate the final hypothesis, the test data had in fact affected the training process in a subtle way. When the original series of daily changes was normalized to zero mean and unit variance, *all of the data* was involved in this step. Therefore, the test data that was extracted had already contributed to the choices made by the learning algorithm by contributing to the values of the mean and the variance that were used in normalization. Although this seems like a minor effect, it *is* data snooping. When you plot the cumulative profit on the test set with or without that snooping step, you see how snooping resulted in an over-optimistic expectation compared to the realistic expectation that avoids snooping.

It is not the normalization that was a bad idea. It is the involvement of test data in that normalization, which contaminated this data and rendered its estimate of the final performance inaccurate.   □

One of the most common occurrences of data snooping is the reuse of the same data set. If you try learning using first one model and then another and then another on the same data set, you will eventually 'succeed'. As the saying goes, if you torture the data long enough, it will confess ☺. If you try all possible dichotomies, you will eventually fit any data set; this is true whether we try the dichotomies directly (using a single model) or indirectly (using a sequence of models). The effective VC dimension for the series of trials will not be that of the last model that succeeded, but of the entire union of models that could have been used depending on the outcomes of different trials.

Sometimes the reuse of the same data set is carried out by different people. Let's say that there is a public data set that you would like to work on. Before you download the data, you read about how other people did with this data set using different techniques. You naturally pick the most promising techniques as a baseline, then try to improve on them and introduce your own ideas. Although you haven't even seen the data set yet, you are already guilty of data snooping. Your choice of baseline techniques was affected by the data set, through the actions of others. You may find that your estimates of the performance will turn out to be too optimistic, since the techniques you are using have already proven well-suited to *this particular* data set.

To quantify the damage done by data snooping, one has to assess the penalty for model complexity in (2.14) taking the snooping into consideration. In the public data set case, the effective VC dimension corresponds to a much bigger hypothesis set than the $\mathcal{H}$ that your learning algorithm uses. It covers all hypotheses that were considered (and mostly rejected) by everybody else in the process of coming up with the solutions that they published and that you used as your baseline. This is a potentially huge set with very high VC dimension, hence the generalization guarantees in (2.14) will be much worse than without data snooping.

Not all data sets subjected to data snooping are equally 'contaminated'. The bounds in (1.6) in the case of a choice between a finite number of hypotheses, and in (2.12) in the case of an infinite number, provide guidelines for the level of contamination. The more elaborate the choice made based on a data set, the more contaminated the set becomes and the less reliable it will be in gauging the performance of the final hypothesis.

> **Exercise 5.5**
>
> Assume we set aside 100 examples from $\mathcal{D}$ that will not be used in training, but will be used to select one of three final hypotheses g_1, g_2, g_3 produced by three different learning algorithms that train on the rest on the data. Each algorithm works with a different $\mathcal{H}$ of size 500. We would like to characterize the accuracy of estimating $E_{\text{out}}(g)$ on the selected final hypothesis if we use the same 100 examples to make that estimate.
>
> (a) What is the value of M that should be used in (1.6) in this situation?
>
> (b) How does the level of contamination of these 100 examples compare to the case where they would be used in training rather than in the final selection?

In order to deal with data snooping, there are basically two approaches.

1. Avoid data snooping: A strict discipline in handling the data is required. Data that is going to be used to evaluate the final performance should be 'locked in a safe' and only brought out after the final hypothesis has been decided. If intermediate tests are needed, separate data sets should be used for that. Once a data set has been used, it should be treated as contaminated as far as testing the performance is concerned.

2. Account for data snooping: If you have to use a data set more than once, keep track of the level of contamination and treat the reliability of

your performance estimates in light of this contamination. The bounds (1.6) and (2.12) can provide guidelines for the relative reliability of different data sets that have been used in different roles within the learning process.

Data snooping versus sampling bias.   Sampling bias was defined based on how the data was obtained before any learning; data snooping was defined based on how the data affected the learning, in particular how the learning model is selected. These are obviously different concepts. However, there are cases where sampling bias occurs as a consequence of 'snooping' – looking at data that you are not supposed to look at. Here is an example.

Consider predicting the performance of different stocks based on historical data. In order to see if a prediction rule is any good, you take all currently traded companies and test the rule on their stock data over the past 50 years. Let us say that you are testing the "buy and hold" strategy, where you would have bought the stock 50 years ago and kept it until now. If you test this 'hypothesis', you will get excellent performance in terms of profit. Well, don't get too excited! You inadvertently biased the results in your favor by picking only *currently traded companies*, which means that the companies that did not make it are not part of your evaluation. When you put your prediction rule to work, it will be used on all companies whether they will survive or not, since you cannot identify which companies today will be the 'currently traded' companies 50 years from now. This is a typical case of sampling bias, since the problem is that the training data is not representative of the test data. However, if we trace the origin of the bias, we did 'snoop' in this case by looking at future data of companies to determine which of these companies to use in our training. Since we are using information in training that we would not have access to in real trading, this is viewed as a form of data snooping.

5.4 Problems

Problem 5.1   The idea of *falsifiability* – that a claim can be rendered false by observed data – is an important principle in experimental science.

> **Axiom of Non-Falsifiability.** *If the outcome of an experiment has no chance of falsifying a particular proposition, then the result of that experiment does not provide evidence one way or another toward the truth of the proposition.*

Consider the proposition "There is $h \in \mathcal{H}$ that approximates f as would be evidenced by finding such an h with in-sample error zero on $\mathbf{x}_1, \cdots, \mathbf{x}_N$." We say that the proposition is falsified if no hypothesis in $\mathcal{H}$ can fit the data perfectly.

(a) Suppose that $\mathcal{H}$ shatters $\mathbf{x}_1, \cdots, \mathbf{x}_N$. Show that this proposition is not falsifiable *for any* f.

(b) Suppose that f is random ($f(\mathbf{x}) = \pm 1$ with probability $\frac{1}{2}$, independently on every $\mathbf{x}$), so $E_{\text{out}}(h) = \frac{1}{2}$ for every $h \in \mathcal{H}$. Show that

$$\mathbb{P}[\text{falsification}] \geq 1 - \frac{m_{\mathcal{H}}(N)}{2^N} \ .$$

(c) Suppose $d_{\text{vc}} = 10$ and $N = 100$. If you obtain a hypothesis h with zero E_{in} on your data, what can you 'conclude' from the result in part (b)?

Problem 5.2   Structural Risk Minimization (SRM) is a useful framework for model selection that is related to Occam's Razor. Define a *structure* – a nested sequence of hypothesis sets:

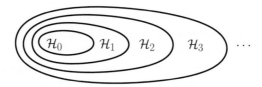

The SRM framework picks a hypothesis from each $\mathcal{H}_i$ by minimizing E_{in}. That is, $g_i = \underset{h \in \mathcal{H}_i}{\text{argmin}}\, E_{\text{in}}(h)$. Then, the framework selects the final hypothesis by minimizing E_{in} *and* the model complexity penalty Ω. That is, $g^* = \underset{i=1,2,\cdots}{\text{argmin}}(E_{\text{in}}(g_i) + \Omega(\mathcal{H}_i))$. Note that $\Omega(\mathcal{H}_i)$ should be non-decreasing in i because of the nested structure.

(a) Show that the in-sample error $E_{\text{in}}(g_i)$ is non-increasing in i.

(b) Assume that the framework finds $g^* \in \mathcal{H}_i$ with probability p_i. How does p_i relate to the complexity of the target function?

(c) Argue that the p_i's are unknown but $p_0 \leq p_1 \leq p_2 \leq \cdots \leq 1$.

(d) Suppose $g^* = g_i$. Show that

$$\mathbb{P}\left[|E_{\text{in}}(g_i) - E_{\text{out}}(g_i)| > \epsilon \mid g^* = g_i\right] \leq \frac{1}{p_i} \cdot 4m_{\mathcal{H}_i}(2N)e^{-\epsilon^2 N/8}.$$

Here, the conditioning is on selecting g_i as the final hypothesis by SRM. [Hint: Use the Bayes theorem to decompose the probability and then apply the VC bound on one of the terms]

You may interpret this result as follows: if you use SRM and end up with g_i, then the generalization bound is a factor $\frac{1}{p_i}$ worse than the bound you would have gotten had you simply started with $\mathcal{H}_i$.

Problem 5.3   In our credit card example, the bank starts with some vague idea of what constitutes a good credit risk. So, as customers $\mathbf{x}_1, \mathbf{x}_2, \ldots, \mathbf{x}_N$ arrive, the bank applies its vague idea to approve credit cards for some of these customers. Then, only those who got credit cards are monitored to see if they default or not.

For simplicity, suppose that the first N customers were given credit cards. Now that the bank knows the behavior of these customers, it comes to you to improve their algorithm for approving credit. The bank gives you the data $(\mathbf{x}_1, y_1), \ldots, (\mathbf{x}_N, y_N)$.

Before you look at the data, you do mathematical derivations and come up with a credit approval function. You now test it on the data and, to your delight, obtain perfect prediction.

(a) What is M, the size of your hypothesis set?

(b) With such an M, what does the Hoeffding bound say about the probability that the true performance is worse than 2% error for $N = 10000$?

(c) You give your g to the bank and assure them that the performance will be better than 2% error and your confidence is given by your answer to part (b). The bank is thrilled and uses your g to approve credit for new clients. To their dismay, more than half their credit cards are being defaulted on. Explain the possible reason(s) behind this outcome.

(d) Is there a way in which the bank could use your credit approval function to have your probabilistic guarantee? How? [Hint: The answer is yes!]

Problem 5.4   The S&P 500 is a set of the largest 500 companies currently trading. Suppose there are $10,000$ stocks currently trading, and there have been $50,000$ stocks which have ever traded over the last 50 years (some of these have gone bankrupt and stopped trading). We wish to evaluate the profitability of various 'buy and hold' strategies using these 50 years of data (roughly $12,500$ trading days).

Since it is not easy to get stock data, we will confine our analysis to today's S&P 500 stocks, for which the data is readily available.

(a) A stock is profitable if it went up on more than 50% of the days. Of your S&P stocks, the most profitable went up on 52% of the days ($E_{in} = 0.48$).

(i) Since we picked the best among 500, using the Hoeffding bound,

$$\mathbb{P}[|E_{in} - E_{out}| > 0.02] \leq 2 \times 500 \times e^{-2 \times 12500 \times 0.02^2} \approx 0.045.$$

There is a greater than 95% chance this stock is profitable. Where did we go wrong?

(ii) Give a better estimate for the probability that this stock is profitable. *[Hint: What should the correct M be in the Hoeffding bound?]*

(b) We wish to evaluate the profitability of 'buy and hold' for general stock trading. We notice that all of our 500 S&P stocks went up on at least 51% of the days.

(i) We conclude that buying and holding a stocks is a good strategy for general stock trading. Where did we go wrong?

(ii) Can we say *anything* about the performance of buy and hold trading?

Problem 5.5   You think that the stock market exhibits reversal, so if the price of a stock sharply drops you expect it to rise shortly thereafter. If it sharply rises, you expect it to drop shortly thereafter.

To test this hypothesis, you build a trading strategy that buys when the stocks go down and sells in the opposite case. You collect historical data on the current S&P 500 stocks, and your hypothesis gave a good annual return of 12%.

(a) When you trade using this system, do you expect it to perform at this level? Why or why not?

(b) How can you test your strategy so that its performance in sample is more reflective of what you should expect in reality?

Problem 5.6   One often hears "Extrapolation is harder than interpolation." Give a possible explanation for this phenomenon using the principles in this chapter. *[Hint: training distribution versus testing distribution.]*

Epilogue

This book set the stage for a deeper exploration into Learning From Data by developing the foundations. It *is* possible to learn from data, and you have all the basic tools to do so. The linear model coupled with the right features and an appropriate nonlinear transform, together with the right amount of regularization, pretty much puts you into the thick of the game, and you will be in good stead as long as you keep in mind the three basic principles: simple is better (Occam's razor), avoid data snooping and beware of sampling bias.

Where to go from here? There are two main directions. One is to learn more sophisticated learning techniques, and the other is to explore different learning paradigms. Let us preview these two directions to give the reader a better understanding of the 'map' of learning from data.

The linear model can be used as a building block for other popular techniques. A cascade of linear models, mostly with soft thresholds, creates a neural network. A robust algorithm for linear models, based on quadratic programming, creates support vector machines. An efficient approach to nonlinear transformation in support vector machines creates kernel methods. A combination of different models in a principled way creates boosting and ensemble learning. There are other successful models and techniques, and more to come for sure.

In terms of other paradigms, we have briefly mentioned unsupervised learning and reinforcement learning. There is a wealth of techniques for these learning paradigms, including methods that mix labeled and unlabeled data. Active learning and online learning, which we also mentioned briefly, have their own techniques and theories. In addition, there is a school of thought that treats learning as a completely probabilistic paradigm using a Bayesian approach, and there are useful probabilistic techniques such as Gaussian processes. Last but not least, there is a school that treats learning as a branch of the theory of computational complexity, with emphasis on asymptotic results.

Of course, the ultimate test of any engineering discipline is its impact in real life. There is no shortage of successful applications of learning from data. Some of the application domains have specialized techniques that are worth exploring, e.g., computational finance and recommender systems.

Learning from data is a very dynamic field. Some of the hot techniques and theories at times become just fads, and others gain traction and become part of the field. What we have emphasized in this book are the necessary fundamentals that give any student of learning from data a solid foundation, and enable him or her to venture out and explore further techniques and theories, or perhaps to contribute their own.

Further Reading

Learning From Data **book forum** (at AMLBook.com).

Y. S. Abu-Mostafa. The Vapnik-Chervonenkis dimension: Information versus complexity in learning. *Neural Computation*, 1(3):312–317, 1989.

Y. S. Abu-Mostafa, X. Song, A. Nicholson, and M. Magdon-Ismail. The bin model. Technical Report CaltechCSTR:2004.002, California Institute of Technology, 2004.

R. Ariew. *Ockham's Razor: A Historical and Philosophical Analysis of Ockham's Principle of Parsimony.* University of Illinois Press, 1976.

R. Bell, J. Bennett, Y. Koren, and C. Volinsky. The million dollar programming prize. *IEEE Spectrum*, 46(5):29–33, 2009.

A. Blumer, A. Ehrenfeucht, D. Haussler, and M. K. Warmuth. Occam's razor. *Information Processing Letters*, 24(6):377–380, 1987.

A. Blumer, A. Ehrenfeucht, D. Haussler, and M. K. Warmuth. Learnability and the Vapnik-Chervonenkis dimension. *Journal of the Association for Computing Machinery*, 36(4):929–965, 1989.

S. Boyd and L. Vandenberghe. *Convex Optimization.* Cambridge University Press, 2004.

P. Burman. A comparative study of ordinary cross-validation, v-fold cross-validation and the repeated learning-testing methods. *Biometrika*, 76(3): 503–514, 1989.

T. M. Cover. Geometrical and statistical properties of systems of linear inequalities with applications in pattern recognition. *IEEE Transactions on Electronic Computers*, 14(3):326–334, 1965.

M. H. DeGroot and M. J. Schervish. *Probability and Statistics.* Addison Wesley, fourth edition, 2011.

V. Fabian. Stochastic approximation methods. *Czechoslovak Mathematical Journal*, 10(1):123–159, 1960.

W. Feller. *An Introduction to Probability Theory and Its Applications*. Wiley, third edition, 1968.

A. Frank and A. Asuncion. UCI machine learning repository, 2010. URL http://archive.ics.uci.edu/ml.

J. H. Friedman. On bias, variance, 0/1 loss, and the curse-of-dimensionality. *Data Mining and Knowledge Discovery*, 1(1):55–77, 1997.

S. I. Gallant. Perceptron-based learning algorithms. *IEEE Transactions on Neural Networks*, 1(2):179–191, 1990.

Z. Ghahramani. Unsupervised learning. In *Advanced Lectures in Machine Learning (MLSS '03)*, pages 72–112, 2004.

G. H. Golub and C. F. van Loan. *Matrix computations*. Johns Hopkins University Press, 1996.

D. C. Hoaglin and R. E. Welsch. The hat matrix in regression and ANOVA. *American Statistician*, 32:17–22, 1978.

W. Hoeffding. Probability inequalities for sums of bounded random variables. *Journal of the American Statistical Association*, 58(301):13–30, 1963.

R. C. Holte. Very simple classification rules perform well on most commonly used datasets. *Machine Learning*, 11(1):63–91, 1993.

R. A. Horn and C. R. Johnson. *Matrix Analysis*. Cambridge University Press, 1990.

L. P. Kaelbling, M. L. Littman, and A. W. Moore. Reinforcement learning: A survey. *Journal of Artificial Intelligence Research*, 4:237–285, 1996.

A. I. Khuri. *Advanced calculus with applications in statistics*. Wiley-Interscience, 2003.

R. Kohavi. A study of cross-validation and bootstrap for accuracy estimation and model selection. In *Proceedings of the 14th International Joint Conference on Artificial intelligence (IJCAI '95)*, volume 2, pages 1137–1143, 1995.

J. Langford. Tutorial on practical prediction theory for classification. *Journal of Machine Learning Research*, 6:273–306, 2005.

L. Li and H.-T. Lin. Optimizing 0/1 loss for perceptrons by random coordinate descent. In *Proceedings of the 2007 International Joint Conference on Neural Networks (IJCNN '07)*, pages 749–754, 2007.

H.-T. Lin and L. Li. Support vector machinery for infinite ensemble learning. *Journal of Machine Learning Research*, 9(2):285–312, 2008.

M. Magdon-Ismail and K. Mertsalov. A permutation approach to validation. *Statistical Analysis and Data Mining*, 3(6):361–380, 2010.

M. Magdon-Ismail, A. Nicholson, and Y. S. Abu-Mostafa. Learning in the presence of noise. In S. Haykin and B. Kosko, editors, *Intelligent Signal Processing*. IEEE Press, 2001.

M. Markatou, H. Tian, S. Biswas, and G. Hripcsak. Analysis of variance of cross-validation estimators of the generalization error. *Journal of Machine Learning Research*, 6:1127–1168, 2005.

M. L. Minsky and S. Papert. *Perceptrons: An Introduction to Computational Geometry*. MIT Press, expanded edition, 1988.

T. Poggio and S. Smale. The mathematics of learning: Dealing with data. *Notices of the American Mathematical Society*, 50(5):537–544, 2003.

K. Popper. *The logic of scientific discovery*. Routledge, 2002.

F. Rosenblatt. The perceptron: A probabilistic model for information storage and organization in the brain. *Psychological Review*, 65(6):386–408, 1958.

F. Rosenblatt. *Principles of Neurodynamics: Perceptrons and the Theory of Brain Mechanisms*. Spartan, 1962.

B. Settles. Active learning literature survey. Technical Report 1648, University of Wisconsin-Madison, 2010.

J. Shawe-Taylor, P. L. Bartlett, R. C. Williamson, and M. Anthony. A framework for structural risk minimisation. In *Learning Theory: 9th Annual Conference on Learning Theory (COLT '96)*, pages 68–76, 1996.

L. G. Valiant. A theory of the learnable. *Communications of the ACM*, 27 (11):1134–1142, 1984.

V. N. Vapnik and A. Y. Chervonenkis. On the uniform convergence of relative frequencies of events to their probabilities. *Theory of Probability and Its Applications*, 16:264–280, 1971.

V. N. Vapnik, E. Levin, and Y. L. Cun. Measuring the VC-dimension of a learning machine. *Neural Computation*, 6(5):851–876, 1994.

G.-X. Yuan, C.-H. Ho, and C.-J. Lin. Recent advances of large-scale linear classification. *Proceedings of IEEE*, 2012.

T. Zhang. Solving large scale linear prediction problems using stochastic gradient descent algorithms. In *Machine Learning: Proceedings of the 21th International Conference (ICML '04)*, pages 919–926, 2004.

Appendix

Proof of the VC Bound

In this Appendix, we present the formal proof of Theorem 2.5. It is a fairly elaborate proof, and you may skip it altogether and just take the theorem for granted, but you won't know what you are missing ☺ !

Theorem A.1 (Vapnik, Chervonenkis, 1971).

$$\mathbb{P}\left[\sup_{h \in \mathcal{H}} |E_{\text{in}}(h) - E_{\text{out}}(h)| > \epsilon\right] \leq 4m_{\mathcal{H}}(2N)e^{-\frac{1}{8}\epsilon^2 N}.$$

This inequality is called the VC Inequality, and it implies the VC bound of Theorem 2.5. The inequality is valid for any target function (deterministic or probabilistic) and any input distribution. The probability is over data sets of size N. Each data set is generated *iid* (independent and identically distributed), with each data point generated independently according to the joint distribution $P(\mathbf{x}, y)$. The event $\sup_{h \in \mathcal{H}} |E_{\text{in}}(h) - E_{\text{out}}(h)| > \epsilon$ is equivalent to the union over all $h \in \mathcal{H}$ of the events $|E_{\text{in}}(h) - E_{\text{out}}(h)| > \epsilon$; this union contains the event that involves g in Theorem 2.5. The use of the supremum (a technical version of the maximum) is necessary since $\mathcal{H}$ can have a continuum of hypotheses.

The main challenge to proving this theorem is that $E_{\text{out}}(h)$ is difficult to manipulate compared to $E_{\text{in}}(h)$, because $E_{\text{out}}(h)$ depends on the entire input space rather than just a finite set of points. The main insight needed to overcome this difficulty is the observation that we can get rid of $E_{\text{out}}(h)$ altogether because the deviations between E_{in} and E_{out} can be essentially captured by deviations between two in-sample errors: E_{in} (the original in-sample error) and the in-sample error on a *second* independent data set (Lemma A.2). We have seen this idea many times before when we use a test or validation set to estimate E_{out}. This insight results in two main simplifications:

1. The supremum of the deviations over infinitely many $h \in \mathcal{H}$ can be reduced to considering only the dichotomies implementable by $\mathcal{H}$ on the

two independent data sets. That is where the growth function $m_{\mathcal{H}}(2N)$ enters the picture (Lemma A.3).

2. The deviation between two *independent* in-sample errors is 'easy' to analyze compared to the deviation between E_{in} and E_{out} (Lemma A.4).

The combination of Lemmas A.2, A.3 and A.4 proves Theorem A.1.

A.1 Relating Generalization Error to In-Sample Deviations

Let's introduce a second data set $\mathcal{D}'$, which is independent of $\mathcal{D}$, but sampled according to the same distribution $P(\mathbf{x}, y)$. This second data set is called a *ghost* data set because it doesn't really exist; it is a just a tool used in the analysis. We hope to bound the term $\mathbb{P}[|E_{\text{in}} - E_{\text{out}}|$ is large] by another term $\mathbb{P}[|E_{\text{in}} - E'_{\text{in}}|$ is large], which is easier to analyze.

The intuition behind the formal proof is as follows. For any single hypothesis h, because $\mathcal{D}'$ is fresh, sampled independently from $P(\mathbf{x}, y)$, the Hoeffding Inequality guarantees that $E'_{\text{in}}(h) \approx E_{\text{out}}(h)$ with a high probability. That is, when $|E_{\text{in}}(h) - E_{\text{out}}(h)|$ is large, with a high probability $|E_{\text{in}}(h) - E'_{\text{in}}(h)|$ is also large. Therefore, $\mathbb{P}[|E_{\text{in}}(h) - E_{\text{out}}(h)|$ is large] can be approximately bounded by $\mathbb{P}[|E_{\text{in}}(h) - E'_{\text{in}}(h)|$ is large].

We are trying to bound the probability that E_{in} is far from E_{out}. Let $E'_{\text{in}}(h)$ be the 'in-sample' error for hypothesis h on $\mathcal{D}'$. Suppose that E_{in} is far from E_{out} with some probability (and similarly E'_{in} is far from E_{out}, with that same probability, since E_{in} and E'_{in} are identically distributed). When N is large, the probability is roughly Gaussian around E_{out}, as illustrated in the figure to the right. The red region represents the cases when E_{in} is far from E_{out}. In those cases, E'_{in} is far from E_{in} about half the time, as illustrated by the green region. That is, $\mathbb{P}[|E_{\text{in}} - E_{\text{out}}|$ is large] can be approximately bounded by $2\,\mathbb{P}\,[|E_{\text{in}} - E'_{\text{in}}|$ is large].

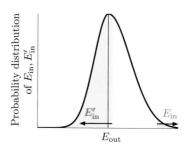

This argument provides some intuition that the deviations between E_{in} and E_{out} can be captured by the deviations between E_{in} and E'_{in}. The argument can be carefully extended to multiple hypotheses.

Lemma A.2.

$$\left(1 - 2e^{-\frac{1}{2}\epsilon^2 N}\right)\mathbb{P}\left[\sup_{h \in \mathcal{H}} |E_{\text{in}}(h) - E_{\text{out}}(h)| > \epsilon\right] \leq \mathbb{P}\left[\sup_{h \in \mathcal{H}} |E_{\text{in}}(h) - E'_{\text{in}}(h)| > \tfrac{\epsilon}{2}\right],$$

where the probability on the RHS is over $\mathcal{D}$ and $\mathcal{D}'$ jointly.

188

Proof. We can assume that $\mathbb{P}\left[\sup_{h\in\mathcal{H}}|E_{\text{in}}(h) - E_{\text{out}}(h)| > \epsilon\right] > 0$, otherwise there is nothing to prove.

$$\mathbb{P}\left[\sup_{h\in\mathcal{H}}|E_{\text{in}}(h) - E'_{\text{in}}(h)| > \tfrac{\epsilon}{2}\right]$$

$$\geq \mathbb{P}\left[\sup_{h\in\mathcal{H}}|E_{\text{in}}(h) - E'_{\text{in}}(h)| > \tfrac{\epsilon}{2} \text{ and } \sup_{h\in\mathcal{H}}|E_{\text{in}}(h) - E_{\text{out}}(h)| > \epsilon\right] \quad (\text{A.1})$$

$$= \mathbb{P}\left[\sup_{h\in\mathcal{H}}|E_{\text{in}}(h) - E_{\text{out}}(h)| > \epsilon\right] \times$$

$$\mathbb{P}\left[\sup_{h\in\mathcal{H}}|E_{\text{in}}(h) - E'_{\text{in}}(h)| > \tfrac{\epsilon}{2} \,\middle|\, \sup_{h\in\mathcal{H}}|E_{\text{in}}(h) - E_{\text{out}}(h)| > \epsilon\right].$$

Inequality (A.1) follows because $\mathbb{P}[\mathcal{B}_1] \geq \mathbb{P}[\mathcal{B}_1 \text{ and } \mathcal{B}_2]$ for any two events $\mathcal{B}_1, \mathcal{B}_2$. Now, let's consider the last term:

$$\mathbb{P}\left[\sup_{h\in\mathcal{H}}|E_{\text{in}}(h) - E'_{\text{in}}(h)| > \tfrac{\epsilon}{2} \,\middle|\, \sup_{h\in\mathcal{H}}|E_{\text{in}}(h) - E_{\text{out}}(h)| > \epsilon\right].$$

The event on which we are conditioning is a set of data sets with non-zero probability. Fix a data set $\mathcal{D}$ in this event. Let h^* be any hypothesis for which $|E_{\text{in}}(h^*) - E_{\text{out}}(h^*)| > \epsilon$. One such hypothesis must exist given that $\mathcal{D}$ is in the event on which we are conditioning. The hypothesis h^* does not depend on $\mathcal{D}'$, but it does depend on $\mathcal{D}$.

$$\mathbb{P}\left[\sup_{h\in\mathcal{H}}|E_{\text{in}}(h) - E'_{\text{in}}(h)| > \tfrac{\epsilon}{2} \,\middle|\, \sup_{h\in\mathcal{H}}|E_{\text{in}}(h) - E_{\text{out}}(h)| > \epsilon\right]$$

$$\geq \mathbb{P}\left[|E_{\text{in}}(h^*) - E'_{\text{in}}(h^*)| > \tfrac{\epsilon}{2} \,\middle|\, \sup_{h\in\mathcal{H}}|E_{\text{in}}(h) - E_{\text{out}}(h)| > \epsilon\right] \quad (\text{A.2})$$

$$\geq \mathbb{P}\left[|E'_{\text{in}}(h^*) - E_{\text{out}}(h^*)| \leq \tfrac{\epsilon}{2} \,\middle|\, \sup_{h\in\mathcal{H}}|E_{\text{in}}(h) - E_{\text{out}}(h)| > \epsilon\right] \quad (\text{A.3})$$

$$\geq 1 - 2e^{-\frac{1}{2}\epsilon^2 N}. \quad (\text{A.4})$$

1. Inequality (A.2) follows because the event "$|E_{\text{in}}(h^*) - E'_{\text{in}}(h^*)| > \tfrac{\epsilon}{2}$" implies "$\sup_{h\in\mathcal{H}}|E_{\text{in}}(h) - E'_{\text{in}}(h)| > \tfrac{\epsilon}{2}$".

2. Inequality (A.3) follows because the events "$|E'_{\text{in}}(h^*) - E_{\text{out}}(h^*)| \leq \tfrac{\epsilon}{2}$" and "$|E_{\text{in}}(h^*) - E_{\text{out}}(h^*)| > \epsilon$" (which is given) imply "$|E_{\text{in}}(h) - E'_{\text{in}}(h)| > \tfrac{\epsilon}{2}$".

3. Inequality (A.4) follows because h^* is fixed with respect to $\mathcal{D}'$ and so we can apply the Hoeffding Inequality to $\mathbb{P}[|E'_{\text{in}}(h^*) - E_{\text{out}}(h^*)| \leq \tfrac{\epsilon}{2}]$.

Notice that the Hoeffding Inequality applies to $\mathbb{P}[|E'_{\text{in}}(h^*) - E_{\text{out}}(h^*)| \leq \tfrac{\epsilon}{2}]$ for any h^*, as long as h^* is fixed with respect to $\mathcal{D}'$. Therefore, it also applies to any weighted average of $\mathbb{P}[|E'_{\text{in}}(h^*) - E_{\text{out}}(h^*)| \leq \frac{\epsilon}{2}]$ based on h^*. Finally, since h^* depends on a particular $\mathcal{D}$, we take the weighted average over all $\mathcal{D}$ in the event

$$\text{“} \sup_{h \in \mathcal{H}} |E_{\text{in}}(h) - E_{\text{out}}(h)| > \epsilon \text{”}$$

on which we are conditioning, where the weight comes from the probability of the particular $\mathcal{D}$. Since the bound holds for every $\mathcal{D}$ in this event, it holds for the weighted average. ∎

Note that we can assume $e^{-\frac{1}{2}\epsilon^2 N} < \frac{1}{4}$, because otherwise the bound in Theorem A.1 is trivially true. In this case, $1 - 2e^{-\frac{1}{2}\epsilon^2 N} > \frac{1}{2}$, so the lemma implies

$$\mathbb{P}\left[\sup_{h \in \mathcal{H}} |E_{\text{in}}(h) - E_{\text{out}}(h)| > \epsilon\right] \leq 2\,\mathbb{P}\left[\sup_{h \in \mathcal{H}} |E_{\text{in}}(h) - E'_{\text{in}}(h)| > \frac{\epsilon}{2}\right].$$

A.2 Bounding Worst Case Deviation Using the Growth Function

Now that we have related the generalization error to the deviations between in-sample errors, we can actually work with $\mathcal{H}$ restricted to two data sets of size N each, rather than the infinite $\mathcal{H}$. Specifically, we want to bound

$$\mathbb{P}\left[\sup_{h \in \mathcal{H}} |E_{\text{in}}(h) - E'_{\text{in}}(h)| > \frac{\epsilon}{2}\right],$$

where the probability is over the joint distribution of the data sets $\mathcal{D}$ and $\mathcal{D}'$. One equivalent way of sampling two data sets $\mathcal{D}$ and $\mathcal{D}'$ is to first sample a data set S of size $2N$, then randomly partition S into $\mathcal{D}$ and $\mathcal{D}'$. This amounts to randomly sampling, *without replacement*, N examples from S for $\mathcal{D}$, leaving the remaining for $\mathcal{D}'$. Given the joint data set S, let

$$\mathbb{P}\left[\sup_{h \in \mathcal{H}} |E_{\text{in}}(h) - E'_{\text{in}}(h)| > \frac{\epsilon}{2} \,\middle|\, S\right]$$

be the probability of deviation between the two in-sample errors, where the probability is taken over the random partitions of S into $\mathcal{D}$ and $\mathcal{D}'$. By the law of total probability (with $\sum$ denoting sum or integral as the case may be),

$$\mathbb{P}\left[\sup_{h \in \mathcal{H}} |E_{\text{in}}(h) - E'_{\text{in}}(h)| > \frac{\epsilon}{2}\right]$$

$$= \sum_{S} \mathbb{P}[S] \times \mathbb{P}\left[\sup_{h \in \mathcal{H}} |E_{\text{in}}(h) - E'_{\text{in}}(h)| > \frac{\epsilon}{2} \,\middle|\, S\right]$$

$$\leq \sup_{S} \mathbb{P}\left[\sup_{h \in \mathcal{H}} |E_{\text{in}}(h) - E'_{\text{in}}(h)| > \frac{\epsilon}{2} \,\middle|\, S\right].$$

Let $\mathcal{H}(S)$ be the dichotomies that $\mathcal{H}$ can implement on the points in S. By definition of the growth function, $\mathcal{H}(S)$ cannot have more than $m_{\mathcal{H}}(2N)$ dichotomies. Suppose it has $M \leq m_{\mathcal{H}}(2N)$ dichotomies, realized by $h_1, \ldots, h_M$. Thus,

$$\sup_{h \in \mathcal{H}} |E_{\text{in}}(h) - E'_{\text{in}}(h)| = \sup_{h \in \{h_1, \ldots, h_M\}} |E_{\text{in}}(h) - E'_{\text{in}}(h)| .$$

Then,

$$\mathbb{P}\left[\sup_{h \in \mathcal{H}} |E_{\text{in}}(h) - E'_{\text{in}}(h)| > \tfrac{\epsilon}{2} \,\middle|\, S\right]$$

$$= \mathbb{P}\left[\sup_{h \in \{h_1, \ldots, h_M\}} |E_{\text{in}}(h) - E'_{\text{in}}(h)| > \tfrac{\epsilon}{2} \,\middle|\, S\right]$$

$$\leq \sum_{m=1}^{M} \mathbb{P}\left[|E_{\text{in}}(h_m) - E'_{\text{in}}(h_m)| > \tfrac{\epsilon}{2} \,\middle|\, S\right] \tag{A.5}$$

$$\leq M \times \sup_{h \in \mathcal{H}} \mathbb{P}\left[|E_{\text{in}}(h) - E'_{\text{in}}(h)| > \tfrac{\epsilon}{2} \,\middle|\, S\right], \tag{A.6}$$

where we use the union bound in (A.5), and overestimate each term by the supremum over all possible hypotheses to get (A.6). After using $M \leq m_{\mathcal{H}}(2N)$ and taking the sup operation over S, we have proved:

Lemma A.3.

$$\mathbb{P}\left[\sup_{h \in \mathcal{H}} |E_{\text{in}}(h) - E'_{\text{in}}(h)| > \tfrac{\epsilon}{2}\right]$$

$$\leq m_{\mathcal{H}}(2N) \times \sup_{S} \sup_{h \in \mathcal{H}} \mathbb{P}\left[|E_{\text{in}}(h) - E'_{\text{in}}(h)| > \tfrac{\epsilon}{2} \,\middle|\, S\right],$$

where the probability on the LHS is over $\mathcal{D}$ and $\mathcal{D}'$ jointly, and the probability on the RHS is over random partitions of S into two sets $\mathcal{D}$ and $\mathcal{D}'$.

The main achievement of Lemma A.3 is that we have pulled the supremum over $h \in \mathcal{H}$ outside the probability, at the expense of the extra factor of $m_{\mathcal{H}}(2N)$.

A.3 Bounding the Deviation between In-Sample Errors

We now address the purely combinatorial problem of bounding

$$\sup_{S} \sup_{h \in \mathcal{H}} \mathbb{P}\left[|E_{\text{in}}(h) - E'_{\text{in}}(h)| > \tfrac{\epsilon}{2} \,\middle|\, S\right],$$

which appears in Lemma A.3. We will prove the following lemma. Then, Theorem A.1 can be proved by combining Lemmas A.2, A.3 and A.4 taking $1 - 2e^{-\frac{1}{2}\epsilon^2 N} \geq \frac{1}{2}$ (the only case we need to consider).

Lemma A.4. For *any h* and *any S*,

$$\mathbb{P}\left[|E_{\text{in}}(h) - E'_{\text{in}}(h)| > \tfrac{\epsilon}{2} \,\big|\, S\right] \le 2e^{-\frac{1}{8}\epsilon^2 N},$$

where the probability is over random partitions of S into two sets $\mathcal{D}$ and $\mathcal{D}'$.

Proof. To prove the result, we will use a result, which is also due to Hoeffding, for sampling *without replacement*:

Lemma A.5 (Hoeffding, 1963)**.** Let $\mathcal{A} = \{a_1, \ldots, a_{2N}\}$ be a set of values with $a_n \in [0,1]$, and let $\mu = \frac{1}{2N}\sum_{n=1}^{2N} a_n$ be their mean. Let $\mathcal{D} = \{z_1, \ldots, z_N\}$ be a sample of size N, sampled from $\mathcal{A}$ uniformly *without* replacement. Then

$$\mathbb{P}\left[\left|\frac{1}{N}\sum_{n=1}^{N} z_n - \mu\right| > \epsilon\right] \le 2e^{-2\epsilon^2 N}.$$

We apply Lemma A.5 as follows. For the $2N$ examples in S, let $a_n = 1$ if $h(\mathbf{x}_n) \ne y_n$ and $a_n = 0$ otherwise. The $\{a_n\}$ are the errors made by h on S. Now randomly partition S into $\mathcal{D}$ and $\mathcal{D}'$, i.e., sample N examples from S without replacement to get $\mathcal{D}$, leaving the remaining N examples for $\mathcal{D}'$. This results in a sample of size N of the $\{a_n\}$ for $\mathcal{D}$, sampled uniformly without replacement. Note that

$$E_{\text{in}}(h) = \frac{1}{N}\sum_{a_n \in \mathcal{D}} a_n, \quad \text{and} \quad E'_{\text{in}}(h) = \frac{1}{N}\sum_{a'_n \in \mathcal{D}'} a'_n.$$

Since we are sampling without replacement, $S = \mathcal{D} \cup \mathcal{D}'$ and $\mathcal{D} \cap \mathcal{D}' = \emptyset$, and so

$$\mu = \frac{1}{2N}\sum_{n=1}^{2N} a_n = \frac{E_{\text{in}}(h) + E'_{\text{in}}(h)}{2}.$$

It follows that $|E_{\text{in}} - \mu| > t \iff |E_{\text{in}} - E'_{\text{in}}| > 2t$. By Lemma A.5,

$$\mathbb{P}\left[|E_{\text{in}}(h) - E'_{\text{in}}(h)| > 2t\right] \le 2e^{-2t^2 N}.$$

Substituting $t = \frac{\epsilon}{4}$ gives the result. ∎

Notation

" · "	event (in probability)
$\{\cdots\}$	set
$\|\cdot\|$	absolute value of a number, or cardinality (number of elements) of a set, or determinant of a matrix
$\|\cdot\|^2$	square of the norm; sum of the squared components of a vector
$\lfloor\cdot\rfloor$	floor; largest integer which is not larger than the argument
$[a,b]$	the interval of real numbers from a to b
$\llbracket\cdot\rrbracket$	evaluates to 1 if argument is true, and to 0 if it is false
∇	gradient operator, e.g., ∇E_{in} (gradient of $E_{\text{in}}(\mathbf{w})$ with respect to $\mathbf{w}$)
$(\cdot)^{-1}$	inverse
$(\cdot)^{\dagger}$	pseudo-inverse
$(\cdot)^{\text{T}}$	transpose (columns become rows and vice versa)
$\binom{N}{k}$	number of ways to choose k objects from N distinct objects (equals $\frac{N!}{(N-k)!k!}$ where '!' is the factorial)
$A \setminus B$	the set A with the elements from set B removed
$\mathbf{0}$	zero vector; a column vector whose components are all zeros
$\{1\} \times \mathbb{R}^d$	d-dimensional Euclidean space with an added 'zeroth coordinate' fixed to 1
ϵ	tolerance in approximating a target
δ	bound on the probability of exceeding ϵ (the approximation tolerance)
η	learning rate (step size in iterative learning, e.g., in stochastic gradient descent)
λ	regularization parameter
λ_C	regularization parameter corresponding to weight budget C
Ω	penalty for model complexity; either a bound on generalization error, or a regularization term
θ	logistic function $\theta(s) = e^s/(1+e^s)$
Φ	feature transform, $\mathbf{z} = \Phi(\mathbf{x})$
Φ_{Q}	Qth-order polynomial transform

ϕ	a coordinate in the feature transform Φ, $z_i = \phi_i(\mathbf{x})$
μ	probability of a binary outcome
ν	fraction of a binary outcome in a sample
σ^2	variance of noise
$\mathcal{A}$	learning algorithm
$\mathrm{argmin}_a(\cdot)$	the value of a at which the minimum of the argument is achieved
$\mathcal{B}$	an event (in probability), usually 'bad' event
b	the bias term in a linear combination of inputs, also called w_0
bias	the bias term in bias-variance decomposition
$B(N, k)$	maximum number of dichotomies on N points with a break point k
C	bound on the size of weights in the soft order constraint
d	dimensionality of the input space $\mathcal{X} = \mathbb{R}^d$ or $\mathcal{X} = \{1\} \times \mathbb{R}^d$
$\tilde{d}$	dimensionality of the transformed space $\mathcal{Z}$
$d_{\mathrm{vc}}, d_{\mathrm{vc}}(\mathcal{H})$	VC dimension of hypothesis set $\mathcal{H}$
$\mathcal{D}$	data set $\mathcal{D} = (\mathbf{x}_1, y_1), \cdots, (\mathbf{x}_N, y_N)$; technically not a set, but a vector of elements $(\mathbf{x}_n, y_n)$. $\mathcal{D}$ is often the training set, but sometimes split into training and validation/test sets.
$\mathcal{D}_{\mathrm{train}}$	subset of $\mathcal{D}$ used for training when a validation or test set is used.
$\mathcal{D}_{\mathrm{val}}$	validation set; subset of $\mathcal{D}$ used for validation.
$E(h, f)$	error measure between hypothesis h and target function f
e^x	exponent of x in the natural base $e = 2.71828\cdots$
$\mathrm{e}(h(\mathbf{x}), f(\mathbf{x}))$	pointwise version of $E(h, f)$, e.g., $(h(\mathbf{x}) - f(\mathbf{x}))^2$
e_n	leave-one-out error on example n when this nth example is excluded in training [cross validation]
$\mathbb{E}[\cdot]$	expected value of argument
$\mathbb{E}_{\mathbf{x}}[\cdot]$	expected value with respect to $\mathbf{x}$
$\mathbb{E}[y\|\mathbf{x}]$	expected value of y given $\mathbf{x}$
E_{aug}	augmented error (in-sample error plus regularization term)
E_{in}, $E_{\mathrm{in}}(h)$	in-sample error (training error) for hypothesis h
E_{cv}	cross validation error
E_{out}, $E_{\mathrm{out}}(h)$	out-of-sample error for hypothesis h
$E_{\mathrm{out}}^{\mathcal{D}}$	out-of-sample error when $\mathcal{D}$ is used for training
$\bar{E}_{\mathrm{out}}$	expected out-of-sample error
E_{val}	validation error
E_{test}	test error
f	target function, $f\colon \mathcal{X} \to \mathcal{Y}$
g	final hypothesis $g \in \mathcal{H}$ selected by the learning algorithm; $g\colon \mathcal{X} \to \mathcal{Y}$
$g^{(\mathcal{D})}$	final hypothesis when the training set is $\mathcal{D}$
$\bar{g}$	average final hypothesis [bias-variance analysis]

g^-	final hypothesis when trained using $\mathcal{D}$ *minus* some points
$\mathbf{g}$	gradient, e.g., $\mathbf{g} = \nabla E_{\text{in}}$
h	a hypothesis $h \in \mathcal{H}$; $h: \mathcal{X} \to \mathcal{Y}$
$\tilde{h}$	a hypothesis in transformed space $\mathcal{Z}$
$\mathcal{H}$	hypothesis set
$\mathcal{H}_\Phi$	hypothesis set that corresponds to perceptrons in Φ-transformed space
$\mathcal{H}(C)$	restricted hypothesis set by weight budget C [soft order constraint]
$\mathcal{H}(\mathbf{x}_1, \ldots, \mathbf{x}_N)$	dichotomies (patterns of ± 1) generated by $\mathcal{H}$ on the points $\mathbf{x}_1, \cdots, \mathbf{x}_N$
H	The hat matrix [linear regression]
I	identity matrix; square matrix whose diagonal elements are 1 and off-diagonal elements are 0
K	size of validation set
L_q	qth-order Legendre polynomial
ln	logarithm in base e
$\log_2$	logarithm in base 2
M	number of hypotheses
$m_\mathcal{H}(N)$	the growth function; maximum number of dichotomies generated by $\mathcal{H}$ on any N points
$\max(\cdot, \cdot)$	maximum of the two arguments
N	number of examples (size of $\mathcal{D}$)
$o(\cdot)$	absolute value of this term is asymptotically negligible compared to the argument
$O(\cdot)$	absolute value of this term is asymptotically smaller than a constant multiple of the argument
$P(\mathbf{x})$	(marginal) probability or probability density of $\mathbf{x}$
$P(y \mid \mathbf{x})$	conditional probability or probability density of y given $\mathbf{x}$
$P(\mathbf{x}, y)$	joint probability or probability density of $\mathbf{x}$ and y
$\mathbb{P}[\cdot]$	probability of an event
Q	order of polynomial transform
Q_f	complexity of f (order of polynomial defining f)
$\mathbb{R}$	the set of real numbers
$\mathbb{R}^d$	d-dimensional Euclidean space
s	signal $s = \mathbf{w}^{\mathsf{T}}\mathbf{x} = \sum_i w_i x_i$ (i goes from 0 to d or 1 to d depending on whether $\mathbf{x}$ has the $x_0 = 1$ coordinate or not)
$\text{sign}(\cdot)$	sign function, returning $+1$ for positive and -1 for negative
$\sup_a(.)$	supremum; smallest value that is $\geq$ the argument for all a
T	number of iterations, number of epochs
t	iteration number or epoch number
$\tanh(\cdot)$	hyperbolic tangent function; $\tanh(s) = (e^s - e^{-s})/(e^s + e^{-s})$
$\text{trace}(\cdot)$	trace of square matrix (sum of diagonal elements)
V	number of subsets in V-fold cross validation ($V \times K = N$)
$\mathbf{v}$	direction in gradient descent (not necessarily a unit vector)

$\hat{\mathbf{v}}$	unit vector version of $\mathbf{v}$ [gradient descent]
var	the variance term in bias-variance decomposition
$\mathbf{w}$	weight vector (column vector)
$\tilde{\mathbf{w}}$	weight vector in transformed space $\mathcal{Z}$
$\hat{\mathbf{w}}$	selected weight vector [pocket algorithm]
$\mathbf{w}^*$	weight vector that separates the data
$\mathbf{w}_{\text{lin}}$	solution weight vector to linear regression
$\mathbf{w}_{\text{reg}}$	regularized solution to linear regression with weight decay
$\mathbf{w}_{\text{PLA}}$	solution weight vector of perceptron learning algorithm
w_0	added coordinate in weight vector $\mathbf{w}$ to represent bias b
$\mathbf{x}$	the input $\mathbf{x} \in \mathcal{X}$. Often a column vector $\mathbf{x} \in \mathbb{R}^d$ or $\mathbf{x} \in \{1\} \times \mathbb{R}^d$. x is used if input is scalar.
x_0	added coordinate to $\mathbf{x}$, fixed at $x_0 = 1$ to absorb the bias term in linear expressions
$\mathcal{X}$	input space whose elements are $\mathbf{x} \in \mathcal{X}$
X	matrix whose rows are the data inputs $\mathbf{x}_n$ [linear regression]
XOR	exclusive OR function (returns 1 if the number of 1's in its input is odd)
y	the output $y \in \mathcal{Y}$
$\mathbf{y}$	column vector whose components are the data set outputs y_n [linear regression]
$\hat{\mathbf{y}}$	estimate of $\mathbf{y}$ [linear regression]
$\mathcal{Y}$	output space whose elements are $y \in \mathcal{Y}$
$\mathcal{Z}$	transformed input space whose elements are $\mathbf{z} = \Phi(\mathbf{x})$
Z	matrix whose rows are the transformed inputs $\mathbf{z}_n = \Phi(\mathbf{x}_n)$ [linear regression]

Index